THE JOURNEY OF
MARTIN NADAUD

THE JOURNEY
OF
MARTIN NADAUD

A Life and Turbulent Times

Gillian Tindall

Chatto & Windus
LONDON

Published by Chatto & Windus 1999

2 4 6 8 10 9 7 5 3 1

Copyright © Gillian Tindall 1999

Gillian Tindall has asserted her right under the
Copyright, Designs and Patents Act 1988 to be identified
as the author of this work

First published in Great Britain in 1999 by Chatto & Windus
Random House, 20 Vauxhall Bridge Road, London SW1V 2SA

Random House Australia (Pty) Limited
20 Alfred Street, Milsons Point, Sydney,
New South Wales 2061, Australia

Random House New Zealand Limited
18 Poland Road, Glenfield,
Auckland 10, New Zealand

Random House South Africa (Pty) Limited
Endulini, 5A Jubilee Road, Parktown 2193, South Africa

Random House UK Limited Reg. No. 954009

A CIP catalogue record for this book
is available from the British Library

ISBN 0–7011–6867–6

Papers used by Random House UK Limited are natural,
recyclable products made from wood grown in sustainable forests.
The manufacturing processes conform to the environmental
regulations of the country of origin.

Printed and bound in Great Britain by
Butler & Tanner, Frome and London

Contents

List of Illustrations

A Note on Nomenclature

The French word *maçon* includes a wider swathe of workers, from skilled master-craftsmen to humble hod-carriers, than does its more specialised English derivative 'mason'. Over most of France, all buildings until the twentieth century were constructed of stone, rough or finely worked, rendered over or left on display: that is what *maçonnerie* – masonry – implies. The *maçons* were, and are, distinct from the cruder road and rail builders (*terrassiers*) and therefore cannot readily be compared with the British navvies or with the Irish building labourers of more recent times. Nor did they really equate with the British 'tramping artisans' of the nineteenth century, for the latter were more truly itinerant: the *maçons de la Creuse* only tramped with a particular destination in view. Needing one ordinary English word to translate the French one, 'mason' is therefore the word I shall use, as being more nearly appropriate than any other.

· I ·

Departure in the Dark

The journey starts with a line of men, and a few boys not quite grown, in the dark before the sun begins to rise in a watery sky, making their way down a muddy track in central France.

They move quickly, stealing a march before the day proper begins: they have a long way to go, that day and for several days ahead. Many of them wear stiff Sunday jackets and trousers, made tight after the fashion of that time, and broad-brimmed felt hats or even top-hats; but some travel in their loose working clothes that glimmer light through the darkness, bleached by the dust of plaster and stone. Over their shoulders they carry small packs or bundles on sticks. They are joined along the way by other men, emerging from isolated farm hamlets and lanes. I do not think they talk much yet. Each has just said goodbye to a household where the children clung to them, the old people loaded them with recommendations and warnings, and the women cried as if they would never see them again. In some cases, this would turn out to be true.

Then the dawn is breaking, and at the first big village they reach there are others again, waiting for them at the inn. The troop has swollen to forty or fifty and it is time to make a brief stop for the first reviving glass of cheap white wine and a general loosening of tongues. The year's adventure has once again begun.

It is 26 March 1830, and Martin Nadaud, who is fourteen years old, is joining his father and uncle for the first time on the long walk to Paris. The celebrated *maçons de la Creuse*,

the itinerant builders out of the fastnesses of central France,
are on the move to their building sites in far-off cities.

A great many French people today, living in towns, with no
particular interest in how or when those towns were built up
and often with only a vague idea that the Creuse is 'somewhere down there in the mountains' will nevertheless react
animatedly to the phrase *maçons de la Creuse*. They may
even begin to hum an air or recite a line or two of verse.
Tucked away somewhere in their cultural baggage is the
builders' song, which was written down in the 1870s, when a
general literacy had set in, but which seems to be based on a
much older original. It exists in various versions, but a
number of the verses are more or less constant:

> *Les voilà donc partis*
> *Pour faire leur campagne;*
> *Ils s'en vont à Paris,*
> *En Bourgogne, en Champagne.*
> *Ils sont fiers, et d'ailleurs*
> *S'ils ont la main calleuse,*
> *Ce sont des travailleurs*
> *Les maçons de la Creuse.*
>
> *Voyez le Panthéon,*
> *Voyez les Tuileries,*
> *Le Louvre et l'Odéon,*
> *Le Palais de l'Industrie –*
> *De tous ces monuments*
> *La France est orgueilleuse;*
> *Soyez reconnaissants*
> *Aux maçons de la Creuse.*

(There, off they go again,
Off on their campaign,
On their way to Paris,
Burgundy and Champagne.
They are proud of what they do

And if their hands are rough
It's because they're building workers,
These Creusois strong and tough.

There is the Panthéon
And there the Tuileries,
The Louvre and the Odéon,
The Palace of Industry;
Of all these monuments
France is proud enough,
So let us be grateful to
These Creusois strong and tough.)

Panthéon, Louvre, Palace of Industry and the rest, indeed much of the Paris of the late eighteenth and early to mid-nineteenth centuries, which is what we mostly see today, was built by men from the Creuse. Another more variable verse attributes to them 'ancient fortifications' and 'old castles with towers'. It doesn't mention the great cathedrals of the Middle Ages, for by the time the *maçons* had become a cohesive presence in Paris and other large cities they were also well known for their left-wing republicanism – which is to say, in French terms, their lack of enthusiasm for the Catholic Church. But there is nevertheless a persistent story that the glories of French perpendicular architecture, including Notre Dame herself, owe much to the skills of the men from central France.

Most of the modern Département of the Creuse forms, along with the Corèze and the Haute-Vienne, the area traditionally known as the Limousin after the dominant town of Limoges. For centuries men migrated from this region to work and earn money by building far from home. Certainly by the early seventeenth century the phenomenon of the trained band, ready to travel to where their skills were needed, seems to have been well established. When Louis XIII and Richelieu were laying siege in 1627 to the Huguenot stronghold of La Rochelle on the Atlantic coast, a body of Limousin masons was recruited to construct a stone cause-way. Later in the century, when Louis XIV was erecting his

great palace at Versailles, this provided work over the years
for more than three thousand Limousins, and some of them
died there, mainly in falls from scaffolding. The eighteenth
century saw more great buildings in stone and a steady, if
unspectacular, increase in workmen moving about the country. This was the era when the concept of the Tour de la
France was established as a tradition by which members of
trade guilds (*compagnons*) would go on their travels to
perfect their skills, part of a complex system of apprenticeship.

The juggernaut of the French Revolution abolished *com-
pagnonage* – or rather, drove it underground. The fractured
years that followed dislocated building plans everywhere and
kept the masons at home on their small-holdings. But when
Napoleon came to power there were new projects: in spite of
the competing demands of army service, the masons' own
seasonal rhythms were re-established. In the first years of the
new century eight or ten thousand men were leaving the
Limousin annually for Paris, Lyon and a few other major
towns. Once Napoleonic re-organisation had split the traditional regions into their present *départements*, and also
demanded that all carry passes and identity papers, it
becomes possible to see more exactly how many were literal
maçons de la Creuse.

In 1808, eleven thousand men left the Creuse to work, and
nearly three quarters of them were in the building trade. By
1820 the number had risen to fifteen thousand and was more
than twenty thousand five years later. About twenty-four
thousand left in 1830, the year that young Martin Nadaud
first took to the road. Slump and boom, those constants of
the building trade, made the figures vary over the next
decade, but by 1846, when the graph begins to level out for
good, thirty-four thousand were leaving the Creuse annually,
or 12 per cent of the total Creusois population. The great
majority of them were masons, or workers in related trades
such as roofers and carpenters.

Leaving – but also returning. For the Creusois masons had
a characteristic which distinguishes their story from that of

the one-way drift to the towns which is the tale of all developing societies. Their story is different again from the odyssey of the uprooted British navvy moving on wherever the next canal, railway line, housing development or motor-way promises a decent wage. The Creusois masons left their deeply rural homes for a quite other life in Paris or Lyon: by the mid-nineteenth century one man of active working age out of every two, and sometimes two out of three, were doing so, relinquishing their farms to the women and the old. But it was only a temporary abandonment, for the regular mass-departure in March once the snows had retreated was balanced by a mass-return in the late autumn. They were like migrant birds, swallows in habit and also in nickname. Towards 1 November, All Saints Day, when building sites were becoming inhospitable and the daylight hours too short for employers, who then paid a standard daily rate, the masons became restive and homesick. The braziers of the chestnut sellers in the Paris streets recalled to their nostrils the staple winter food of central France – '*Ça sent la châtaigne*'. So, they would set off back again down the long roads; with any luck their packs were heavier with bags of hoarded coins. By the 1830s it was reckoned that some four to five million francs annually were finding their way home with the men. Twenty years later, the figure had nearly doubled. With this money the entire rural economy of the Creuse and adjacent regions was sustained.

One of the paradoxes that surrounded the lives of these men becomes apparent. Paris and the other big cities represented adventure, risks and also chances unknown in the homeland: this might seem to offer a whole potential change of identity. But all the evidence is that typically the mason stayed as he was. He had the French peasant's rooted attachment not just to his own particular few hectares of earth but to his *pays*, the patch of France with its own dialect, customs and food from which his family had sprung. More than anything else he wanted money to bring home in triumph each winter at the end of what was always referred to as 'the campaign'. At home there would be repairs needed to the old buildings and a new plough, cow or field to buy. There would be the loan from an uncle or a neighbour to service, the sisters' dowries to be provided, not to mention paying off the wife's expenses from the birth of the new baby, as yet unseen ... So, although these men spent the prime years of their lives mostly far from home, subject to all sorts of alien influences, strong counter-ties bound them to their roots. Superficially adapting to city streets, most of them in their social contacts and in their emotions remained Limousin peasants, though rather well-informed ones. It was not so much a matter of leaving the Creuse as of taking it to Paris with them.

But why did the Creuse develop such a monopoly of providing the labour that built France?

The answer lies in the nature of the land itself. I possess a little blue-and-gold-bound Hachette Guide to the Creuse, published in 1882; by this time the persistent nineteenth-century French governmental drive towards national conformity and away from regional distinctiveness was steaming ahead. The tone of the Guide is therefore somewhat patronising, though it does admit to the *pays* having a certain rugged beauty, and includes engravings to prove it.

'The Département of the Creuse is almost wholly formed of a primordial landmass covered with a thin layer of earth ... This schistic and granite rock, situated at quite a high altitude, is intercut with narrow valleys usually only three or four hundred metres in depth: such territory can hardly be favourable to a developed agriculture ... A relatively poor soil, whether in the mountains or on the more gentle slopes of the plateaux: chestnut groves, rough grazing, uncultivated heaths and meagre fields of rye still cover large areas. More modern methods of land use have so far made little progress.'

Views differ as to whether it was the poverty of the land that made it necessary for the most able-bodied men to seek other sources of income, or whether the farms remained backward and unproductive because the owners were devoting their energies to building cities elsewhere. But all agreed that the schist and granite that did not grow much wheat, and the stony fields that had to be cleared by hand, had produced over the centuries a race of accomplished stone-workers. Even in the days when their own houses were quite small – low, thatched shelters where humans and cattle shared the same barely partitioned space – the masons built fine walls, piecing the selected stones together according to their individual shapes. Their painstaking work survives, solid and weatherproof, if rather sombre, to this day.

Their names do not. With a very few exceptions, the individual men who travelled so far with such hardship, and left their mark on so much of the grandiose architecture that has come to represent France's history, have themselves disappeared from history. Léonce de Lavergne, a nineteenth-century economist and member of the Académie des Sciences, wrote: 'Numberless generations of obscure peasant farmers have lived there without taking any part in our national uprisings. The passing centuries have not touched them. When the Revolution came it swept away the tithe-system and the clergy lands were sold, but the ordinary inhabitants do not seem to be much better off for this.' The more sympathetic observer Daniel Halévy, who compiled his *Visites aux Paysans du Centre* between 1907 and 1934, noted: 'The written history of these regions is very odd. It opens extremely late: there is very little, it seems, till the nineteenth century. The country people who lived there, far from towns and main roads, remained for a long time without a voice of their own or anyone to speak for them. They were nevertheless there; they did things, cared about things, and thus had their effect, without anyone realising it, on the heart and soul of the nation.'

So it was too with the ones who went to the cities. A few, more intelligent or ambitious than their fellows, settled there, starting building firms of their own, but these were the exceptions: most did not want to. Even fewer brought back to their *pays* such a harvest of urban experience that it transformed their later lives. One who did was François Michaud (1810–90), an accomplished mason and self-taught sculptor. In his long retirement he ornamented the tiny

Creusois hamlet where his family had their origins with a galaxy of stone people and animals, including Napoleon, the republican President Jules Grévy, a bosomy mermaid, a badger, a pig and other creatures. His belief system, an eclectic mixture of pantheistic anti-clericalism and radical republicanism, was formed during his time as a mason in Paris, and it was not untypical. A handful of other self-taught masons similarly acquired left-wing ideals on the building scaffolds of Paris, and eventually occupied positions of power in the world of politics and government. But these were all men of the later nineteenth and early twentieth centuries, the time when literacy was becoming general, education was far more available, and the questionable civilisation of roads, railways and newspapers had spread even into France's most mountainous recesses.

Martin Nadaud was, like Michaud, of an earlier generation: he made his way in harder times. Born into a Creusois peasant family in 1815, the year of Waterloo, he presents a unique case. He is the one mason with a remembered name who stands now for all the others.

I do not think that this was how Nadaud saw himself. By the end of his long and fortune-tossed life he had amassed, by his own standards, other claims to distinction. Yet the Nadaud that survives in memory a hundred years after his death is a slim silhouette, flitting through respectful footnotes in the pages of social histories or occasionally figuring, plaster-trough and trowel in hand, in local Creusois pageants. He is not the elder statesman of the later years. He is not even the vociferous *Quarante-huitard* ('Forty-eighter') on the Paris barricades of the revolution that brought down France's last king. He is a boy born into a peasant world where most things were still done as they had been four hundred years previously, a boy who set off for Paris in the dawn because he had no choice.

Les Mémoires de Léonard, un Garçon Maçon: when, late in life, Nadaud chose this lightly fictionalised title as a starting-point for his official Memoirs, he seems to have envisaged that younger generations might be encouraged by his example, comparing his origins with his present state. But today the historian, and the occasional French novelist, who treat the Memoirs as a useful quarry for documentary detail of life long ago on the farms or in the garrets of Paris, do not see the frock-coated old gentleman who put it all down on paper. They see a bright-eyed boy mixing mortar for his father.

When I first came across this boy, while I was researching the far more obscure life of a nineteenth-century French country-woman, I was not aware that the old gentleman in the frock-coat had ever existed. It was only after I had got hold of the Memoirs themselves, in a worn-edged, red-bound incomplete edition of 1912, that I began to realise I was dealing not just with an interesting peasant-turned-mason but with someone who was, or had been, a French national monument.

There were, I discovered, schools named after Martin Nadaud. And an irregular square in Paris, near Père Lachaise cemetery, with plane trees and a café called by his name. He had even had, for much of this century, his own Métro station: I came across one of the name-boards from it, a replacement board in the acidic yellow and chocolate of the 1950s, in the small museum in Bourganeuf (Creuse). And indeed Bourganeuf, the miniature town that Nadaud represented between 1876 and 1889 as a Member of Parliament, erected a statue to him in 1902. It is not there any more. The Germans took it when they occupied France during the Second World War, but there is a modest bust in its place outside the Mairie.

There is also, in a semi-abandoned hamlet called La Martinèche some 10 kilometres from Bourganeuf, the house that the local guide refers to as his *maison natale*, his birthplace. In fact, this is misleading. Certainly Nadaud was born at La Martinèche, spent his childhood there and returned in old age eventually to die there. But when you make your way to it from the little local centre of Pontarion, up a winding road that is much more heavily forested than in Nadaud's day, what you find is a four-square house in good quality machine-cut stone. It has two clear storeys, plus a run of small attic windows under the eaves: it must have seven or eight good rooms. It is the kind of *maison bourgeoise* that successful returned masons built for themselves or for their relatives in the towns of the Creuse; it looks rather out of place here in the depths of the country. It was certainly not built before the 1860s, and the evidence I have gleaned suggests that it may date, rather, from the '70s. Today it is firmly shuttered. No one lives there any more. Recent attempts to be allowed to see inside, whether made by me or by local French citizens, have met with bureaucratic rebuffs.

Behind and rather to the side, butting against this uncompromising house like an old cow-shed, is an older and more modest building in the beautiful patchworked stone of peasant origin. Its roof has been retiled in the last forty years or so; it has been lived in and cared for till relatively recently, but now a couple of the windows are broken; the house is beginning to die. This, surely, is Nadaud's actual birthplace, the one that figures in his account as having been built by his father and grandfather some seven years before his entry into the world. It represented, then, progress and modernity, in comparison with the windowless, earth-floored hovel that had preceded it as the family home. A date is proudly cut into the door-lintel – '8081'. The man who carved it was presumably literate, but the father and son who heaved it into place were not. They cemented it in upside-down. One may imagine the comments of the carver on his subsequent return from Paris or Lyon.

On the four-square house is an official plaque, dating from the 1920s:

Dans cette maison est vécu et mort Martin Nadaud, réprésentative du peuple en 1848, exilé en 1852, professeur au collège de Wimbledon (Angleterre), Préfet de la Creuse, Conseiller Municipal à Paris, Député et Quaestor.

('In this house lived and died Martin Nadaud, people's

representative in 1848, exiled in 1852, professor at Wimbledon College (England), Préfet of the Creuse, Municipal Councillor in Paris, Member of Parliament and Quaestor.')

There is no mention of his fundamental profession as mason that shaped his life and his ideas. You might also think that here, in La Martinèche of all places, *Les Mémoires de Léonard*, the child who played here and minded the cattle, would be relevant. But of this book, Nadaud's most individual and enduring stake in immortality, there is no mention either.

Clearly, in La Martinèche, we are in the presence of the national monument, the latter-day *éminence grise*. We might, for a few minutes only, walk round this statue and look at it.

The man whom local obituaries referred to as 'the venerable doyen of democracy' was born when the trauma of the French Revolution was twenty years past but still very much present in memory. The heroic Napoleonic efforts to weld France into a great power had only just ended in Napoleon's military defeat and his imprisonment on St Helena. Nadaud grew up, therefore, under the Restoration, first Louis XVIII, then Charles X. The return of these monarchs, which was accompanied by the discreet rehabilitation of the landed gentry, did not please his father (whose own name, confusingly, *was* Léonard). Nor did it please his uncle, who had been wounded on the field of Waterloo and loved to sing impassioned battle songs. The family was Bonapartist, which at that time meant anti-royalist and anti-clerical. A generation later, the father's Bonapartism was translated, by natural progression, into the son's republicanism: for Martin Nadaud, it was Louis-Napoleon, Napoleon's nephew and France's second and last Emperor, who became the *bête noire*. In spite of Léonard's nostalgic attachment to the Bonaparte succession, he eventually came round to his son's way of thinking. Martin Nadaud was to claim in his Memoirs that his father had been buried wearing the 'Phrygian bonnet' (actually a prosaic red woollen cap) that was traditionally associated with the Revolution and with France's subsequent popular uprisings. I suspect this was not literally true but the essential point is that the Nadaud family always espoused what they saw as the cause of the oppressed. French politics run down the generations like messages in seaside rock. Had Léonard and Martin been living a hundred years later, they would have been stalwarts of the home-grown French Communist Party and probably valiant *résistants* under the German Occupation.

So the statue is of a People's hero. It is of the archetypal working man made good, risen by his own efforts to a position of power and esteem from which he might hope to lead his fellow workers out of slavery and into freedom in the approved fashion.

'To read his writings is to sense there the beating of a heart that has been touched. The trials that he recalls, he has undergone himself. The tribulations that he describes, he has himself suffered. The aspirations of the classes whose history he writes are also his own' (Louis Blanc, in his preface to Nadaud's *Histoire des Classes Ouvrières en Angleterre*).

'One may say that his political life was based upon two main qualities: enthusiasm and compassion' (Victor Schoelcher, in his preface to Nadaud's published speeches).

'Reading Nadaud, one becomes better oneself, because one is in the presence of a working man who has pushed to the limit a love of his own people, his country and his profession' (Henri Germouty, Nadaud's first editor, in his biographical preface to the Memoirs).

'This Creusois mason, one of the first working-class Members of Parliament, has written in crude ink and with an elementary school pen a naïve masterpiece that breathes out the unchanged air of the Revolution of 1848' (Gaston Bonheur, the pseudonym of Gaston Tesseyre, a twentieth-century journalist).

In these terms, the outlines of the statue may readily be sketched. Nadaud arrived in Paris to start work on building sites in the spring of 1830. In July came the uprising that toppled Charles X. He was replaced by Louis-Philippe, of the moderate, Orléanist branch of the Bourbons. Through the '30s, during the long campaigns that were punctuated by brief periods back home, Nadaud worked his way up in his profession. He progressed from being a 'boy', mixing mortar and hod-carrying for an older man, to being a *limousin* with his own boy under him – the origin of so many of the building workers had, over the course of time, come to designate the trade itself. Eventually he rose to become a *maître-compagnon*, a skilled general mason. After a while he also worked in the evenings to better himself, for his idea at that point was to become an entrepreneur with his own team of men. Speaking the Creusois *patois* when he first arrived in Paris and able to read and write only in a rudimentary manner, he set himself to improve his mastery of French, his literacy and his mathematical skills. By and by, he was in turn giving lessons in these things to some of his fellow masons.

Gradually he became drawn into republican circles, met men of better education than himself and expanded his ideas. When the Revolution of '48 swept Louis-Philippe from the throne, and a brief honeymoon of universal franchise followed, Nadaud was an obvious symbolic choice as a Member of the new Parliament: he was elected in 1849. A picturesque target for the attention of journalists and cartoonists, he made impassioned speeches on town-planning, drainage and the need to allow workers to form trade unions. It was even proposed, in those heady days when Louis-Napoleon still seemed an enlightened figure, that Nadaud might do very well as President of the Republic.

However, by half-way through 1851, Louis-Napoleon had transformed himself into a more oppressive force, and in December he staged a *coup d'état*. As a result, Nadaud spent the entire Second Empire in exile in England. He did not return to France – or at least, that is the official version – till September 1870, when the collapse of the Empire in the wake of the Franco-Prussian war turned French society upside-down one more time. As a returning 'Forty-eighter', he was welcomed back with open arms by the new Minister of the Interior, Léon Gambetta. He was at once sent off to the

Creuse, the land he had left forty years earlier as a semi-literate builder's lad, to fulfil the key administrative post of Préfet. It is hard to imagine a greater triumph.

His later life followed a predictable if less spectacular path. He was out of a job by the following February, but one was found for him, after the upsets of the Paris Commune, as a municipal councillor in Paris. Five years later he was elected Member of Parliament for Bourganeuf, Creuse, just as he had been twenty-seven years before. He continued to make speeches on town improvements, the need for more railways both over and under ground, and the rights and needs of workers, prisoners and the old and sick. In 1887 he was made a *quaestor de la Chambre* (a paid post corresponding vaguely to that of parliamentary whip). Two years later, in his mid-seventies, he retired to La Martinèche to write his Memoirs. He died at the end of 1898, esteemed and loved by many. The writer and republican George Sand, long dead herself by then, was much quoted by his obituarists. He was, she had said, 'exempt from all base passions, good in the true sense of the word'.

This, then, is the statue.

But the actual statue, as we know, has been gone these fifty years and more. And, in any case, what connection did it ever really have with the talkative adolescent whose feet bled in new boots on the road to Paris? Or with the one who refused to eat butcher's meat during his first years there because it seemed to him exotic, vaguely disgusting food fit only for townspeople? Or with the young man who drank and fought and bought new tight trousers, and who once, visiting his wife-to-be back home in the winter Creuse, lost his way and risked death in the snows of that wild, roadless land?

When I had learnt a little more about Nadaud's long and changeful life, I began trying out his name on other people to see what the reaction was.

I found that he had a small band of enthusiastic supporters in the Creuse itself, along with a modest outpost in Paris in the Mairie of the Twentieth Arrondissement, where he was Councillor at a key period in the city's evolution. But otherwise, although with some well-read French citizens his name evoked a general image of a mason and of the peasantry of deepest France, the socialist Great Man seemed to have passed from the collective memory. When I happened to encounter, at an official Anglo-French function, a senior socialist Great Man of today, I mentioned the name of Nadaud to him, thinking that he at least might be well informed – might even say '*Ah, en effet!* One of my boyhood heroes.' The Minister listened politely as I rattled through the outline of Nadaud's life, and asked an intelligent question or two. He had, he said, never heard of this interesting person before. Was it perhaps the case that he was better known in England?

I could only tell him that the eighteen years during which Nadaud had lived and worked in London and its suburbs appeared to have left absolutely no trace upon the ground. During that time he also visited Glasgow, Dublin and the Manchester area and observed how strikes and workers' solidarity were managed English-style. However, the British annals of Labour history have nothing listed under his name. Even the archivist of the Wimbledon boys' comprehensive school that today occupies the building where Nadaud taught had no idea that, 130 years before, the place had harboured an illustrious political exile. He was, he said, glad to have been told: the only Famous Old Master he had known about till then was a German composer.

I began to feel obscurely haunted by a true story that a French friend more cynical than the Minister had recounted to me. At some point in the 1930s, the French right-wing monarchist association Action Française decided to play an April Fool's joke. It caused a letter to be sent to some fifty Ministers, left-wing Members of Parliament, Academicians and the like, saying that a committee was being formed to honour the life and work of the deceased republican statesman Hippolyte Perigois – in fact, I am not quite sure of the name, but it was some carefully concocted appellation of that kind. 'Hippolyte' is associated with nineteenth-century *petit bourgeois* aspirations to culture, while 'Perigois' is redolent of regionalism and basic peasant stock. Each of the recipients of the letter was asked if he would like to 'participate' in the coming celebration of the Great Man's centenary and perhaps even chair the steering committee?

Out of all those who received the letter, only three, more suspicious perhaps than the others or simply more honest, wrote back to say they were sorry but they'd never heard of Hippolyte Perigois. All the rest answered the letter in terms of vague enthusiasm, many accepted the honour of chairing the proceedings. One actually responded by saying that he had recently been re-reading the Great Man's writings (one appreciates the 're') and held him in profound admiration.

I began to fear at moments that people to whom I talked about Nadaud might think I was subversively nurturing an Hippolyte Perigois. I even found myself waking once or twice in the night and wondering wildly if Martin Nadaud *was* Hippolyte Perigois and I had somehow invented him.

My feeling was compounded when I went back to the library from which I had obtained the red-bound 1912 edition of Nadaud's Memoirs several years previously. I found that, in the interval, a wind of modernisation had blown up; the old, serviceable, dog-eared index cards with their useful librarians' notes had been destroyed, and the catalogue was now on computer – or allegedly so. In the change, the Memoirs had simply disappeared, leaving neither physical nor technological trace.

Fortunately the Département of the Creuse is less technologically advanced than the large centres of culture, even as it was a hundred and fifty years ago. In the Bibliothèque Municipale in the county town of Guéret, the smallest *Préfecture* in France, the librarian produced the Memoirs in a better and more copiously annotated edition. When I told her my plans, she allowed me to carry the book away with me to England for a much longer stretch of time than a normal library loan. I owe that librarian much.

Reunited with the Memoirs, and thus with the young

Nadaud as well as the elder one, I was able to take further stock of his remarkably successful career.

I came to the conclusion that his life had been rather sad. One might even use the word tragic.

There are two published likenesses of Nadaud, besides various political cartoons. The first, a lithograph, was made when he was a Member of the brief Parliament that preceded the Second Empire. It shows a stocky young man who seems if anything younger than his actual age, which was mid-thirties. He has dark hair and a neat frill of beard round an otherwise hairless face, after the fashion of the time. It is an unremarkable, peasant face, slightly pudgy, but the mouth is gentle and finely formed. Only the dark eyes, looking out on the world with a bright, wary intensity, indicate the quality of the man within. The photocopy of this that I have is from a print dedicated to his father and mother in the rapid, but only semi-joined, handwriting that he had by then developed. It is dated 16 January 1852.

Léonard Nadaud had by that time retired to the Creuse. He and his wife must have been glad to receive this likeness of their only son, for at that time in France photographs were something rare, found only among the upper bourgeoisie. In January 1852 they could not have known whether they would ever see their boy again, for Nadaud's fate, following the *coup d'état* the month before, had not yet been decided.

The second picture of Nadaud, taken in the 1880s, is the one that formed the basis of all subsequent likenesses including the Bourganeuf statue. It shows the elder statesman, a patriarch with a copious white beard. A constituent recalled him electioneering at this period: '. . . with the broad shoulders and neck of an old fighter and with his thick white hair he was an imposing figure.' But the eyes and mouth in the photograph again belie the immediate comfortable impression. They are pained, almost agonised. There is grief in that face, one would say.

His achievements were undoubted and, as if to reassure himself as well as others, he did not hesitate, late in life, to bring them to public attention. The question is, why should he have such an emotional need to do so?

He was a widower while still young. He spent eighteen years – years that should have been his prime – in a foreign land under an assumed name. For much of that period he never saw his only child. In turn, that child died before her time and he found himself in old age with three grandchildren under his emotional and financial charge. His ultimate retirement from politics was forced on him because he was not re-elected by his constituents, and he failed in his alternative bid for election to the Senate, the upper house.

Of all these adult griefs, his Memoirs make only fleeting and uninformative mention, or no mention at all.

The traditional, linear way of assessing a life, by the status and achievements visible in its final years, does not necessarily represent what that life has really been. We will return to the young future mason, growing up in a remote valley with all his life ahead.

A Child of the Creuse

Martin Nadaud's homeland might be rock covered with thin soil, but it was also a land of rivers. 'Creuse' literally means a hollow; the image is of water running deep at the bottom of a steep valley, and this is the reality found in variations all over this old segment of the Limousin. A local surgeon, Dr F. Villard, a generation younger than Nadaud, wrote: 'All these waters criss-crossing the Département in all directions, winding round the mountains ... give the countryside a picturesque, dour and wild aspect during the winter months, but in the summer ensure abundant and beautiful vegetation ... Because of the general altitude, the climate all over is fairly severe. Autumn is the best season; spring and summer tend to be short and rainy; winters set in early and last long.' He allowed, however, that the dairy herds grazing on these well-watered slopes produced creamy milk, that the lambs fed on aromatic mountain herbs made good meat and that game and fish were plentiful: 'One can catch salmon, and a range of trout whose flesh is exquisite.'

The same note is struck by Nadaud at the beginning of his Memoirs. From the vantage point of old age this was his essential childhood image: 'A few hundred metres from our hamlet runs the Taurion, a sizeable stream full of fish that winds its way to Pontarion where it waters the great meadow beside the feudal tower there, one-time scene of bloody battles between Protestants and Catholics ... During the sixty years that I have lived in Paris or London, on short visits to my native land I have often seen again the places where I watched flocks and the streams where I caught chub and even trout in the hand. But the place I liked best of all was the summit of one of the three crags that surround our village, the one known as the Puy Maria. There are stones standing up there which were shaped, according to legend, by the old labourers of Gaul.'

These smooth rocks, with dew-ponds on their summits and a heart-lifting view for many miles around, are now thought to owe their shapes to glacial forces. Probably only some steps cut into one face are the work of men, but it is typical of Nadaud's comprehensive and personal view that he liked the idea of the rocks having been shaped in the distant past by stone-cutters like himself. Similarly, his notion of the Gauls as both his direct forebears and the rightful occupants of the lands (*nos ancêtres les gallois*) is not good history but is typical of both the man and his time. Several nineteenth-century historians, especially Henri Martin, whom Nadaud read when he was in the long process of educating himself, believed that the ordinary country people of France were the descendants of the Celtic Gauls while the upper classes were Germanic Franks, outsiders by origin. Today, this seems a race-burdened fantasy, but it drew on the age-old peasant wariness of strangers and townsfolk, and also on the nineteenth-century reformer's ideological objections to the aristocracy – 'The Gauls', Nadaud claimed, 'always wanted a Republic but only managed to found local ones, anticipating the greater Republic that presides today over the destiny of our dear country.'

However childish Gaullism now seems – its chief modern currency is in the beloved comic personage of Astérix – in figurative form it did express a truth. France, in the first half of the nineteenth century, was far from being the monolithic, consciously egalitarian nation-state it was to become under the Third Republic. There is a good case for saying that up to the 1860s or even the 1880s, large parts of France functioned like subject states only partially colonised by a distant power in Paris. From the provinces, this power was perceived as alien, almost foreign, and of course the distrust was mutual. In 1830 the novelist Stendhal famously characterised south-west France as the part where 'people believe in witches and don't know how to read and don't speak French'. This description could be applied equally to the entire Massif Central, including the Creuse.

Journeys were slow, both actually on the ground and in terms of the cultural transmission of news and ideas. Roads and railways reached rural areas in France significantly later than they did in England. Physical distances created and enhanced social ones, and it is not always immediately obvious to someone looking through English eyes how great these spaces were. France consists of more than twice the landmass of Great Britain, and her inaccessible mountain terrain is not confined (as is the case in the UK) to the extreme north and west but occupies a huge central area. Even today, when France is among the world's most prosperous and modern nations, its heart is profoundly rural and conservative; two hundred years ago it was wrapped in a state of primitive self-sufficiency that had hardly altered in the preceding four centuries.

Less than half the land in the Creuse was in agricultural use and nearly all of this was split up into holdings of a few hectares per family. The rest consisted of untouched heaths, moors and dense forests out of which small fields had been laboriously hacked. Wolves roamed the country; on winter nights their howls could sometimes be heard by the nervous country people as they crept out together ('safety in numbers') to answer calls of nature under the stars before turning in. Complex patterns of local paths joined one hamlet or village to the next, but many of these were only wide enough to take a walker, a pack-horse, or a man carrying a load on his own back: it is hard now to imagine this world in which the mere construction of a track that could accommodate a cart or a carriage constituted a substantial modern improvement – and even where these were created they were often in such a churned and pot-holed state that any vehicle travelling above walking pace risked overturning. Such spills, sometimes accompanied by a broken axle, were regarded as commonplace on a long journey by those forced to undertake anything so perilous. Even *diligences*, those ramshackle and lumbering versions of the British stage-coach, often came off the road. They were also, in the early part of the nineteenth century, still vulnerable to attacks from highway thieves just as they had been under the *Ancien Régime*. It is true that two eighteenth-century 'royal' routes crossed parts of the Creuse, but these, like the Napoleonic roads elsewhere in France, had been constructed for through-travel rather than for the benefit of local inhabitants; there were no adequate secondary routes linking the smaller towns till well into the nineteenth century. Occasional enthusiastic travellers' reports about France's 'splendid road revolution' should not be taken at face value. It entirely depended where you were coming from and where you wanted to go to. Similarly, the French railway system evolved late; again it was based on concepts of long-distance and often military travel rather than local use, and there was an extended delay in many areas between the establishment of the major line and the addition of branch lines to serve country market towns.

French society in the nineteenth century was developing at a different rate from British society and by different means: its significant historical markers do not occur in the same places. By 1800 Britain's political revolutions, including regicide, had more or less receded into history. Its industrial revolution was well under way, transforming tracts of countryside, turning villages into smoky cities. All over England there was a good network of gravel roads and express coach services between the main towns – which were in any case larger and more numerous than the tiny towns scattered over the face of France, many of them still within their medieval walls. In the world of Jane Austen both the wolves and the witches had been gone for some time; even villages had shops, even cottagers bought manufactured goods. In contrast, as late as 1840, the French Finance Minister, Jacques Laffitte, was lamenting that, though French industry was at last beginning to produce goods for a mass market, half the population of France 'seemed lost in the fourteenth century and content to remain there'. In Martin

Nadaud's childhood and for some time afterwards, peasant farming families like his had little use for money except for large transactions concerning land, stock and loans. They grew or made for themselves or bartered with their neighbours everything they needed for day-to-day living, just as their ancestors had always done before them.

Like their ancestors, too, they spoke a language full of o's and final s's and c's, which, while it was related to French in the way that Spanish or Italian are, was not comprehensible to a standard French speaker. A fundamental reason for the split between the developed society north of the Loire, towards Paris, and the rest of France was this linguistic difference. Essentially, through the ages we now call 'dark', two main tongues had evolved from soldiers' Latin over the area that now constitutes a large part of France: the *langue d'oeil* in the north and the *langue d'oc* further south – hence 'Languedoc' as the name of the region. Each of these two tongues had scores of local variants; language need be fully comprehensible only to the people you are likely to meet. In the centuries when few people moved far from their place of birth and seldom met a face to which they could not put a name, languages could be truly local. It has been estimated that in central France, where the mountainous territory cut off one valley from another, real differences in *patois* occurred every twenty miles or so. But *patois* is in itself a pejorative term, indicating that the speaker thinks he is in possession of the true language and the other speech is just a degraded variant of it. Such, indeed, was the attitude of the northern French to the *langue d'oc*, for the version of the *langue d'oeil* current in the Ile de France – the region round Paris – had been gradually taking over as 'correct' speech since the Middle Ages. As the commercial and administrative power of Paris grew, so the other *langue d'oeil* variants wilted before the dominance of the Parisian dialect.

But the *langue d'oc* was too different from the Parisian speech just to disintegrate under its influence. Rather, it remained for hundreds of years as a separate tongue – or, as ever, many separate tongues. Since it ceased to be used by the well-educated and was rarely written down, there was no cohesive force to weld it into one version. Of course, when people did begin to move around more this was not particularly convenient. The public markets and cattle fairs, which became such a feature of life in the nineteenth century when at last some road improvements were under way, showed up the problem. It was noticed, for instance, that pig-slaughterers from the Lower Creuse could not make themselves understood when they travelled to fairs in the north of the *département*. And as for the problems of those who ventured further, into the unknown territory of the Indre . . .

In 1835 the first Minister of Public Instruction, who had been appointed to try to get localities to set up schools with the hope of turning rural savages into French citizens, undertook a language survey. His inspectors found that in the Indre, immediately north of the Creuse, something that could pass as French was generally spoken, or at any rate understood, but that from the Creuse southwards *patois* ruled. Unsurprisingly, much of the teaching in the early schools had to be in *patois*, in spite of governmental disapproval, and in spite of the fact that the written word was in French.

It was no accident that a linguistic fissure appeared between the Indre and the Creuse, for there is a real frontier here that is far older than that traced by Napoleon's bureaucrats. The old name for what is now the northern Creuse was La Marche – the step – which indicates its status as border country. It marked the boundary between lowland France and highland, between the province of the Dukes of Berry and the mountain fiefs. Different lords, different history, different landscape, different crops, building materials, architecture, eating-habits – and, naturally, different speech. Even today, driving north along the D.940 from Guéret to La Châtre, you pass a point at which, within a very few kilometres, you are aware of the change. The road descends off the plateau, winding gradually downwards till it reaches the little hill town of Genouillac (once a centre of power, now struggling to find an economic justification). It

descends again and continues on to the aptly named hamlet
of Bordessoule; immediately after that you become aware of
being in a softer, more fertile region. The road becomes
straight with wide fields and modern cereal crops on each
side. A poster appears saying you are entering the Land of
George Sand. The Creuse has been left behind. Each time I
have made this journey, going and coming from Guéret while
researching this book, I have been aware of this vestigial
frontier, and have thought of the travelling masons for whom
Bordessoule marked the last outpost of their own *pays* before
their assault on foreign parts.

Yet the masons themselves became part of the mechanisms of
change. By 1863 the school inspectors found that a quarter of
the population of France still spoke no French – an estimate
which leaves aside the fact that, to many more, even if they
spoke French it remained a foreign, Sunday-best language
reserved for conversations with inquisitive officials and the
like. But in the Creuse over the previous thirty years French
had made considerable headway. The large numbers of men
going to work in Paris and elsewhere evidently had an effect.
To speak French was an advantage for them; it led to better
jobs, and anyway, in the city, the language was readily
acquired.

   Literacy in the Creuse was also higher by the 1860s than in
most remote regions. Many men by then had learnt to read
and write in the new schools and, although it was not then
the custom to educate women, quite a few men encouraged
their wives into literacy too, so as to keep properly in touch
during the long separations. Till then, any communication
from a husband had had to pass via some literate acquaintance or public letter-writer in Paris, and was usually
addressed to the Mayor or secretary of the home Commune.
This functionary would go and read it to the wife –
presumably turning it back into the *patois* in which the
couple would normally have spoken. Such messages tended
to be mainly about money and of a brief and summary kind.

For example, in 1826 a mason who hailed from a village near la Souterraine took advantage of a home-going work-mate to send 238 francs, 10 centimes to the Mayor of his village. The accompanying note said that the Mayor should use the money to settle the mason's debt on a land-purchase and that the remainder, 66 francs, should be passed on to his wife for household expenses for which she should account – 'I hear she wants to sell her cow and its calf. Tell her that she's not to sell any animal whatsoever and that she ought to buy a pig with the money she's got now.'

Present-day thinking might dismiss this as a typical example of the high-handed male attitude of the period. It is true that the Creusois masons, like poor men the world over, tended to show authoritarian attitudes towards their women-folk and children – but it is equally true that only by such a public gesture of authority could the exiled mason feel he had any hand in what was happening at home in the years he was away. In practice, wives seem to have enjoyed a higher status in Creusois society than they did in many parts of France, because of all the responsibilities and decisions they had to take on their own. It was also largely their own labour – even when they were pregnant or nursing, even if they had young children or very old people to care for – that replaced that of the absent man.

The few letters from later in the century that have escaped destruction through time and chance and make their appearance, here and there, on loan in rural exhibitions, are more intimate in tone. A degree of painstaking literacy must have come as a lifeline, emotional as well as practical, to many couples: it allowed them to communicate in greater privacy, even though a letter was not then the exclusively personal message that it has since become. A mason writing from Paris to his father-in-law in 1842 raised the possibility of his young wife's going to school in the local market town – 'as we said when I was leaving . . . For my part, I wouldn't grudge the few hundred francs it would cost for this little skill that she'll have for ever and which will always be useful to her.' Evidently the wife did attend school, for nine years later we find the same man writing directly to her: 'Send me your news often, for my most recent leaving was the most painful so far. Let me know if our little boy's eye trouble is really better, and if my father-in-law has got his shot-gun back . . .'

Nadaud would teach his own young wife to read during a winter holiday, as he had taught his sisters and a couple of other girls living in the same hamlet. His parents, however, remained illiterate. His mother 'never knew a single word of French . . . She never wore shoes on her feet either [her son means that she wore clogs or went barefoot in summer] and she never had any other cloak to put on her back but the one she had been given on her wedding day.' She probably never had coffee or sugar either, shop-bought delicacies that did not enter peasant life till after the mid-century. Even when on a long journey on foot in company with her son and with something to celebrate, she would not enter an inn. 'In her conception of things, these luxuries were only for the upper classes.' She sought out a spring and used her apron, folded up tight, to contain water for them to drink.

Nadaud was twenty and home for a visit on the occasion he is recalling here. Already, he and his mother inhabited different worlds. Fifty years later, when he came to set the memory down, she appeared to him as antique as a figure from a fairy-story – one of those stories told round the fire in his youth in those all-night *veillées* that had themselves, by the end of the century, become a thing of the past. Indeed, this whole section of his Memoirs reads today like one of those French regional novels, by which the twentieth-century urban French reassure themselves as to both the nearness of their rural roots and the distance they have moved from them:

'Our *veillées* always took place in the same house, presided over by one particular old woman . . . Old Fouéssine was the midwife of the hamlet; she had attended to our mothers when each of us was born, and knew how to make use of plants. No doctor then had ever come near us.

'No one ever contradicted her; she used to state quite calmly that Peter or Paul, dead those several years, had been

back to revisit their neighbours and that they had passed on
the names of those who were in paradise or in hell. She also
knew who had kept company with werewolves . . .

'We would emerge from these gatherings so scared that we
needed to hold hands to get back to our own house . . . I
remember that my mother used to come and sit by my bed
and talk to me till sleep overcame me.'

Nadaud's mother was born in 1790, just as the Revolution
far away in Paris was beginning to set in motion events and
ideas that would, in the long run, sweep away the static,
medieval life-style for ever, even in the remote Creuse. She
died in 1852, four years before the first railway station
anywhere in the area opened at la Souterraine, on the main
line that was then making its way down from Paris to
Limoges. She was not to see the far-reaching changes that this
line, and later ones, were to bring: she remained all her life a
woman of the old world that was to pass away. But Nadaud,
born in the year of Napoleon's downfall, lived a life that
spanned an extraordinary era of change.

His family were poor, even by the standards of a society in
which most working people were poor. On his father's side,
his grandmother had been an orphan, taken in as an infant
by cousins who were themselves poverty-stricken, and she
was sent out to go begging casual work from village to village
as soon as she was big enough. 'So she grew up, not even
knowing her proper name or where she had been born.' One
guesses that she was illegitimate. But she was apparently
pretty and pleasant. '*Ah oui, mon petit,*' she told her young
grandson, 'when I was in a barn [the dances were always held
in barns] I wasn't the last one to be asked.' A voice out of a
distant, dateless time. 'One day someone told her she had a
girl cousin who was to be found selling chestnuts in the
market at Bourganeuf . . . This cousin took a liking to the
girl, and so introduced her to her brother, Jean Nadaud . . . A
solid, handsome fellow, good-hearted but almost to the point
of being simple . . . Hard-working and thrifty [my grand-
mother] was the making of our family.'

There was a family legend that the Nadauds had made a

little money in the fifteenth century collecting rags to be pressed into paper (a new-fangled commodity then much in demand) but the family fortunes had stagnated since. The old rag-picker's house, the one where people and animals lived under the same roof and 'bits of hay and seed fell from the loft above onto the table where they all ate', had only been rebuilt a few years before Martin Nadaud's birth – presumably on the proceeds of itinerant masonry. This was the house with the date reversed in the lintel, and it was regarded as a considerable improvement on the old one. Tales of starvation winters, of serfdom and of oppressive lords were told as matters of recent date: Nadaud's childhood was well populated with people whose assumptions about life had been formed under the *Ancien Régime*.

He was to live on into a time when the younger generation did not even speak the *patois*, when telegrams went back and forth from Paris in a matter of minutes, when railways and tramways had penetrated every part of France, when the Paris Métro was being constructed – and when every village in France contained a school, which the future soldiers of the First World War were even then attending.

Nadaud does not describe his childhood home in detail. The descriptions we have of hamlets like La Martinèche in their well-populated days date from much later in the century. By that time the bourgeoisie of the towns was taking a real interest for the first time in how the peasantry of France was living, and there is a note of reformist disapproval for the primitive conditions they found. The fact that country people had lived in these settlements perhaps since prehistory, before the larger villages and towns even existed, was ignored in the drive towards modernity. Also overlooked was the fact that those travelling from a home like La Martinèche to dwell in a large town were apt to find the latter place crowded, unhealthy, dirty and – with its incomprehensible indoor lavatories right next to living quarters – downright disgusting.

'The small-holdings are grouped in hamlets of ten or eleven houses, with a territory of about 100 hectares in all and a population of fifty or so ... Seen from afar, these little Republics half-hidden among cherry and chestnut trees look so cheerful and peaceful as to evoke the Golden Age ... When you get nearer this illusion vanishes. Muddy paths, thatched roofs almost touching one another so that the smallest fire instantly spreads and devours all, low, heavy walls, windowless bedrooms where whole families sleep, cattle sheds up against living quarters, manure in every corner – one has difficulty in understanding how human beings can live in such squalor. Everything else is in keeping: furniture and utensils of the most basic and primitive sort, and for clothing the wool of their own sheep and linen woven by the shepherdesses.'

– Thus the critical and anglophile Léonce de Lavergne in the Creuse in 1855. It is hard to see what he had against homespun cloth, unless it was simply that this meant the peasants were not supporting France's belated industrial revolution. Dr Villard, cited earlier, a Creusois himself, took a less fastidious view, but was equally obsessed with rural hygiene or rather the lack of it.

'Often the floor inside is of earth; when paving does exist, it is usually formed by large slabs laid down without mortar, so that household dirt and water collect in the crevices. Box beds to which little air gets in stand around the walls of this one room, which serves as dining room, bedroom and gathering place for the entire family and sometimes for the chickens too. From the beams are hung loaves of bread, hams, drying cheeses and baskets full of other provisions.'

Villard, like de Lavergne, expatiates on the manure heaps, the dirty duck ponds, the mud and snow in winter, the bad smells in summer – 'and never any latrines in the hamlets! There would be plenty of space for them, but, no, the people believe in living as their ancestors have always done.' He admits that the Creusois peasantry did drink clean water, but complains that they wouldn't wash their hands ('it *never* seems to occur to them') and that they resisted his medical advice to do so (1870s).

It might be added that Dr Villard, in another pamphlet, also characterised the habit of going away to Paris or to another big town to work as another tiresome and illogical example of 'doing what the ancestors have always done'. Evidently he had his own fixed views on the proper place of the peasantry in the scheme of things and that place was on the land.

In these descriptions, one scarcely recognises the beloved homesteads the masons laboured so hard to enlarge and improve, according to their lights, left with such pangs and returned to with such delight when winter set in. During the winter of 1829–30, the last one before Martin Nadaud joined the other men on the road, his father and uncle were at home – 'That winter was cruelly hard. Thick snow covered the land and our sheep stayed in the byre, fed on leaves and bracken.

'Our *veillées* lasted into the night. My father, who was a cheerful man when he was not being crossed, knew how to keep us happy and amused with his stories of life in Paris.

'As I could read fairly well now, he fed my interest with pamphlets and old Army Bulletins describing the heroic deeds of his great man, Napoleon' – Léonard Nadaud had worked on the property of one of Napoleon's generals: 'The General's servants had furnished his rich and powerful memory with so many facts that we listened to him in fascination, and it was midnight before we knew it. It amazes me today that a man who could not read or write had got so well into his head the main events of the Imperial era.'

But how had it happened that Léonard's son could read?

The early pages of the Memoirs show a life and a situation which was not just Martin Nadaud's own but was typical of a boy, any boy, who grew up in a family of migrant masons. It was to underline this that Nadaud called his central protagonist not by his own name but 'Léonard' – the most classic Limousin name, shared by a local saint. It is my belief that at this stage in his account he was consciously telling a story – though probably an essentially truthful one – with its own pace and sequence of events. Much later, as was inevitable, the archetypal nature of the tale falters and declines into a more individual but less interesting record of his public life, with many gaps in it.

Yet, paradoxically, an early and important theme is one that sets him already a little apart from the general run of peasant boys growing up in the 1820s: Martin Nadaud was to get an education. The Guizot Law on the setting up of local schools was not passed till 1833. Before that, any schools that existed in country regions were the private enterprise of individuals, often rather eccentric or even disreputable ones, who just happened to possess a modicum of literacy and numeracy themselves. Most parents did not think it worth while sending their sons to school. But evidently Martin Nadaud's father had some of that same foresight and determination that were later to come out so strikingly in the son. At a jolly winter reunion of masons and their families in Pontarion he encountered the local church-warden, who was known to teach the alphabet and a few notions of writing it, and said to him, 'Here's a little lad I'd like to send you if you want to take him on.'

The churchwarden agreed, but the rest of the family were scandalised. 'My mother protested energetically, saying that she needed me for the farm work' (that, one can believe, since her husband was so often away). Neighbours sitting near by were of the same opinion and so was the grandfather:

'"Ever since you came back this time you've been going on about that boy and your plans for him. You'd have done better to stay in Paris instead of coming home just to talk about schooling. Not one of my brothers, nor me, nor you have ever learnt our letters and we've earned our bread all the same.

'"I told you all those bits of printed paper [the Army Bulletins] that you would buy in the Marché Saint-Jean would end up by overheating your brain. The same thing happened to a landlord I had in the rue de la Mortellerie. He had a son as he wanted to send to school. And what did the son turn into? A little good-for-nothing who only spoke to us to make fun of us. And later he really went to the bad and became the shame of his family."'

The remarks sound entirely authentic, but the scene is being set almost as in a novel. We understand from it that the grandfather too had taken the road to Paris in his younger days (about 1780) and had lodged in the rue de la Mortellerie, the classic masons' rookery near the river and Notre Dame of which we shall hear again.

The father had his way, and Martin Nadaud went each day to be taught not a great deal by the churchwarden. Léonard Nadaud returned to Paris for nine months. When he came back he was not very pleased with the progress made so far by his 'turbulent and combative' young son. A real teacher was due to come to Pontarion: Martin should go there.

'– At this, a new family quarrel erupted. The main argument of my mother and grandfather was that I had already cost them twelve francs and that I hadn't been there when needed to mind the cows and sheep.

'These words put my father, who had only just come back from Paris, into a great state of anger, and he could be difficult if you pushed him too far. He silenced his wife by threatening to hit her, and accused his father of preferring to spend money drinking in the inn rather than on his grandson's education.'

There is a certain irony in a man so convinced of the value of education having no other argument against his wife but his fists. One sees the tension the masons must at times have been under, living as they did in two separate and physically different worlds.

Martin Nadaud goes to the new schoolmaster, staying there to eat at midday. By and by he is to be found winning a prize – an oak-wreath and two small religious books 'which must have cost nearly a franc each', bestowed on him by the local lady of the feudal castle in Pontarion. In spite of their lack of enthusiasm either for the aristocracy or the Church, 'my parents were overjoyed, and spared me neither tears, kisses nor compliments.

'Once back at the house, my father said to my mother: "Do you still begrudge the money we're spending on our boy? Poor lad, it's my hope he'll be able to do what I haven't been able to do myself. If I'd known how to read and write, you'd be better off than you are. I haven't gone short of chances to earn money, but having no learning I've had to stay as a plain mason with my nose always in the mortar."'

Soon after, Martin Nadaud fell off a wall where he was chatting to builders, and took a while to recover. Meanwhile, the teacher became sick and closed the school. The boy clearly was not at this time the natural scholar he later became; he ran wild, bird's-nesting, fishing and taking rides on one of the cows he was supposed to be minding. There was trouble, and an accident to someone else. Two more ineffective schoolmasters were tried, and there was a further eruption when Léonard Nadaud came back from Paris once more – 'excuses, tears, nothing pacified [my father] and my poor mother got a beating just as I did'. To teach him a further lesson, the father then dragged his son off to help construct a field ditch and a retaining wall. He was to work all through the day in silence and in the bitter cold 'although my hands were covered in cracks'. These would have been caused by the lime used in mortar. Then, and still today with modern cement, novices on building sites may suffer from sore and bleeding fingers till their skin toughens.

Some fifty years later, when Martin Nadaud was an elder statesman, history repeated itself. He in turn felt that he was giving his orphaned grandson the educational chances he missed himself in youth and that the boy was not grateful nor working as hard as he might. Nadaud presumably did not resort to physical violence, since the boy was at boarding school, but the tone of some of the grandfatherly letters that have survived is intemperate in the extreme.

It must have been a relief to both Léonard and Martin Nadaud when at last a better teacher was found. He was an old soldier of the Imperial Army (like the schoolmaster

Fourchon in Balzac's *Les Paysans*) who had opened a school in Saint-Hilaire, a little place on the cart track between Bourganeuf and Aubusson – 'Soon his reputation as an educated man and a good teacher spread. A well-to-do figure in Bourganeuf . . . sent three of his sons to him, which gave the newcomer the seal of approval for the whole locality.' Martin Nadaud was taken to see the man: 'It didn't take him long to tell my father that I knew almost nothing but that I seemed to him alert and intelligent.' However, Saint-Hilaire was too far away from La Martinèche, 7 or 8 kilometres along winding country paths, for the child to go and come each day. It was therefore decided that a local housewife, Jeannette, should find a bed for him and *tremper la soupe* – the standard country phrase meaning 'let him share in the family's morning and evening broth', which was the basis of the peasant diet. To save money, the rest of the fare was supplied from home: 'Every week for eighteen months my mother had to bring me a circular loaf of bread and a cheese. So, every Sunday, I kept a look out for her on the path, where she was coming along with her bundle over her shoulder on a stick. Jeannette would invite her in to sit down for a few minutes' rest: she would kiss me, urge me to work hard and then set off home again, happy to hear me praised by Jeannette and sometimes by my master as well.'

The schoolmaster, too, lodged with Jeannette, and in the evenings Nadaud thrilled to the stories of battles told by him and two military cronies, one the head of the local Gendarmerie. With some prescience, the schoolmaster wrote to Léonard Nadaud (who must have had to get someone else to read him the letter): 'If your son goes on applying himself as he's doing at present, he'll become something more than a mason.' More prosaically, but perhaps with the same implication, Nadaud adds at this point: 'If I hadn't encountered this man at that time . . . I would never have known how to multiply or divide or that there are different parts of speech.'

This teacher was a fine figure of a man whose oratory impressed his pupil, perhaps for life. His only defect was that he drank too much (this completing the resemblance to Balzac's character) and this led to minor scandals that gradually tarnished his reputation. But by that time Nadaud's elementary education had gone as far as it could.

One episode that occurred rather earlier, while Nadaud was still failing to work and risking his absent father's wrath, throws further light on what a French commentator has called *la brutalité des moeurs*: the general roughness of the times, even among members of the respectable poor like the Nadauds and their neighbours. A schoolmate, named Bayle, in one of the small schools where Nadaud did little but misbehave himself, used to bully weaker boys – 'He was three or four years older than me . . . He spoilt our games, knocked down our ninepins, stole our tops and even used to hit us.

'Alongside the school another house was being built. Bayle used to go up the ladders, hide behind the walls and make a pest of himself, wetting on us or throwing sand down.

'One day, three or four of us had our revenge; we were furious, and as we saw him come down the ladder we pulled it away. The poor devil fell so hard onto a pile of large stones that he never recovered, and several months later he died from the effects of his fall.'

This created considerable talk in the village (Pontarion), and there were murmurings about 'putting the boys in prison'. The women, in particular, spoke aloud of young Nadaud as a bad lot. In the end, nothing further happened, but – 'I was the person most affected by this accident. For a long time I did not dare look people in the face. I felt guilty, for I had been the ringleader in the trick we had played.' It seems as if this last fact was kept from Léonard Nadaud, away in Paris at the time as usual; at any rate, there is no mention of terrible recriminations within the household.

One can well imagine the policemen, social workers and psychologists who would descend today on a village where such an alarming and tragic event had taken place. But such were the times that, though people were highly disapproving, clearly no one regarded the event as exceptional or blamed the family.

Indeed, in one of the few other direct accounts we have of peasant life in that era, testimonies from that world 'without history', an analogous incident occurs. In Emile Guillaumin's *La Vie d'un Simple* (1904), a prank involving boys dressed in sheets succeeds all too well. The narrator hits out in fear, with a stick, at an apparent menacing ghost, really a boy like himself, and injures him badly. The boy subsequently dies. Guillaumin was of a later generation but was recounting the memories of his grandfather; there is no reason to suppose he lifted any themes from Nadaud's Memoirs. His overall tone is different, bleaker, less forgiving: 'It was a kind of self-defence, so I wasn't that remorseful . . . but the thought of it did trouble me.'

In the Memoirs, the Bayle incident is never referred to again. Since everyone in the countryside knew each other, one cannot help wondering how members of the Bayle and Nadaud families greeted one another for the next thirty years when they met at jollities in Soubrebost, the village Commune to which La Martinèche is an outlying hamlet.

In the later pages of his Memoirs, Nadaud is at pains to present himself in a good light, at the cost of distorting a number of events and evading other topics altogether. It therefore seemed to me at first sight remarkable, though impressive, that he should have chosen to recount this highly discreditable episode from his childhood. I even wondered if it were untrue: perhaps it was there to convey a figurative meaning about the redemptive power of a sin comprehended – or possibly to stand in for a different, unmentioned and worse episode on a building site after he had graduated to working life?

However, when I checked the worn, leather-bound Register of Deaths in Soubrebost in the 1820s – the volume is held today in the spacious new Archive building in Guéret – there in faded ink on the handmade paper I found Bayle, Antoine. He was the son of François Bayle and Jeanne Magriat, small farmers dwelling in the village of Soubrebost. He died on 20 March in the year 1825 when he was ten years old. So he was not 'three or four years older' than Nadaud: the difference in their ages was a matter of months. It was not really a case of a big boy bullying much smaller ones at all.

It would seem that, in telling of his first victory over an oppressor, Nadaud altered this detail, perhaps unconsciously, to make the tale fit better into the frame which had come to shape his whole thinking on social relations. Nadaud, shortish but stocky and pugnacious, perpetually saw himself as championing the weak and dispossessed against the powerful. This was the story he was telling himself about life. There were to be many other occasions in later years when it did not wholly accord with the facts.

· 3 ·

The Long Road to Paris

The pre-dawn departure of the masons, setting off to Paris, was an experience as repetitive for them over the years as a bad dream.

For his great entry into the world of adult male life, Martin Nadaud's mother had had a suit made for him out of the wool of their own sheep, spun, woven and then felted to resist the weather – 'jacket, trousers and waistcoat all of the same stuff. Stiff as cardboard, they impeded movement. With them, I wore heavy shoes that would soon begin to rub, and a high-crowned hat in the fashion of the times.' Thus armoured for his first campaign the fourteen-year-old said goodbye to his family: 'It was a moment of real distress and pain. I think that if my father and I had been about to be laid in earth the lamentations of the women would hardly have been louder.' Women, for the grandfather had died two years before of 'taking a cold on his chest', one night coming back from the inn at Pontarion when he strayed into a stream and fell asleep. Henceforth the mother, the elder sister Magdelaine (rising eighteen), the six-year-old sister Françoise and the grandmother must manage the farm without male help.

'My grandmother's love for me was so great that I had to be dragged from her arms.' What Nadaud does not add, but what appears in the local Death Registers, is that this grandmother had lost what was probably her youngest son, a boy of twelve, three years before Martin Nadaud's birth. One may guess that the grandson fulfilled the place of this dead boy in her emotions. 'Although I was so young at the time, the care and consideration that the good woman had for me

are still part of my perception of life; and, since then, I have
had reason to know about the generosity of spirit, the
treasures of kindness and devotion, that lie within most
women's hearts.'

As an affirmation it is striking. It was intended, no doubt,
as a valedictory word on this grandmother, whom he
probably never saw again. His subsequent account is not
quite clear, but it seems as if, for reasons connected with
family debts, he was not to return to the Creuse for three
years, by which time she was dead. But the remark contains a
hint that is repeated, with variations, throughout his Memoirs, without ever progressing to a more specific avowal. The
persistent impression is of a boy who, having passed his early
childhood largely under feminine influence, always related
well to women and found them indulgent towards him.

His fate for most of his adult life, regardless of other
vicissitudes of fortune, was to live in a largely male world, or
rather in a series of such worlds. Incidental references to
women in his Memoirs are therefore sparse, but each time
one occurs it tends to be surrounded by a particular glow of
affectionate, almost wondering gratitude that makes one
wonder, in turn, what else is not being expressly said.

The fears that the women had for the youngsters they saw off
are all too well validated by the fate of three of the four other
teenage boys who left the locality at the same time as
Nadaud. Destinations ran in families. While the Nadauds
were headed for Paris, the boys from the other families were
making their way over the mountains to the silk-weaving
town of Lyon. Before long, three of them were to die in on-
site accidents.

Not having been trained, in spite of the hardness of their
lives, in the Anglo-Saxon tradition of repressing emotion, the
boys seized a few minutes alone together in a barn at a
crossroads to bid a tearful goodbye to one another. It was
just as well that very soon after this the growing Paris
contingent reached Pontarion: the first brief stop, the first

glass of white wine, last admonitions from old codgers and the relief of knowing that you were now properly on your way.

An established track ran on to Sardent, an ancient hill village – a 'town' in medieval terms – that has its own miniature square and a monthly market to this day. But the main route north to Guéret ran further west, from Limoges via Bourganeuf; after Sardent the troop of masons had to strike across country on narrow paths that recent heavy rains had made liquid with mud. They reached a forest region: in some places branches barred their way, scattering showers of drops when pushed aside. The wet penetrated young Nadaud's new shoes, and he was feeling already that he would rather turn round and go home. Fortunately the arrival at Guéret towards 11.00 a.m., with the prospect of a meal at an inn where they were expected, cheered everyone up. 'My father introduced me to the innkeeper, saying, "A new customer for you, Gerbeau." At once, he called over his wife, who kissed me and proceeded to fill my pockets with little treats.' Nadaud, at fourteen, was apparently a 'strong boy' in the time-honoured phrase, but one can imagine that he was still the sort of round-faced child who could evoke maternal feelings. 'From that moment my relationship with this inn was established, and I never passed through Guéret again without stopping by.' Later in life the married daughter, by then in charge of the inn, rendered him various services, till 'at her death, I felt as bereft as if she had been one of my own family'.

Of such enduring networks of support were the lives of the itinerant masons made. The punishing march to Paris was divided into known and tested stages, each one in itself like a campaign. There was even a treasurer to the group, who functioned like a quartermaster-sergeant in the army, going ahead to make arrangements for food and shelter and to fix a price. This had to be someone senior and well respected, for he took charge of the substantial kitty into which each man had put 10 francs, but he also had to be fit enough to outstrip other walkers: it was Nadaud's father, then forty-three, who fulfilled this role.

From Guéret the road ran on and on, up and down the hills, with only brief stops to drink at inns. 'To encourage youngsters who were flagging, the older men hummed country songs in our ears to make us laugh.' They finally reached Genouillac, but while supper was being eaten there Léonard Nadaud pointed out to the assembled company that so many other masons were arriving from other parts of the Creuse that they themselves might do well to walk still further to get ahead of the crowd for the following morning. So, having already walked the best part of 60 kilometres (38 miles), off they set again for another 6 kilometres under a bright moon.

'I was one of those who began to lag behind. Another marcher, Chabannat, a fine, strong young man, came alongside me to encourage me, offering to carry my pack. I should have been far more relieved if he had been able to take over my new shoes, which were blistering my heels.'

It was finally at Bordessoule, just on the frontier of his native land, that Nadaud spent the first night of his new life. He and the other exhausted boys took in, wide-eyed, a train of mules loaded with casks of wine accompanied by uncouth-looking drivers with an impenetrable *patois* of their own, for at this date the medieval pack-horse system was still current in France. Then there was a huge, noisy kitchen-dining room, where whole quarters of meat such as the boys had never seen before were cooking on spits in the enormous fireplace. Except for a little home-cured pork and the occasional chicken or rabbit, they did not eat meat at home.

Today, as I travel by car so lightly and easily between Guéret, Bordessoule and the string of towns further north that the masons were to reach only with such effort, I think of that inn. There is no inn along the road at that point now: I wonder if the old building, unidentified, still stands?

Léonard Nadaud made his son swallow a few mouthfuls of mulled wine (then as now regarded in France as a sovereign remedy for depleted energies). He helped him up to bed in an attic where insect-ridden straw palliasses were covered with sheets so dirty they were black. When people making the return trip from Paris passed by about the middle of November, innkeepers put on clean sheets which then had to do till the end of March. Naturally, in these conditions, the masons did not undress any part of themselves except their long-suffering feet.

'My father was very disconcerted to find my feet rubbed raw and bleeding. He greased them for me, and wrapped them up in some strips of cloth.'

What else could he do? Fortunately exhaustion brought heavy sleep, and in the morning Nadaud and the other boys were cheerful and set off singing. But by the following night, after another forced march almost as long that brought the company to the town of Issoudun on the far side of the Indre, young Nadaud's feet were of course worse.

'Today, it seems to me the height of cruelty to subject children of thirteen and fourteen to such a harsh ordeal . . . Once arrived in Issoudun, I had it fixed in my head that there was no way I was going to do another stretch like that the day after.

'By way of comfort, all my father said was "I walked to the Vendée when I was younger than you, and I didn't snivel like you seem to be doing."'

Again, what else could he do? He had to get his son to Paris, he could not leave him now in Issoudun. Martin Nadaud had not had any choice about whether he would go to Paris, but then nor had Léonard Nadaud before him: if you came from a family of itinerant masons and were able-bodied, that was what you did.

One must suppose that some men liked this male world more than others – that some, no doubt, were glad enough to spend a large part of their lives away from the domestic hearth – but personal choice and decision hardly figured, any more than they did in the eternal routines of peasant existence for those who stayed at home. Léonard Nadaud had first left home at thirteen, and by the time he returned from Paris for the last time in 1840 he had worked on building sites there for forty-two years. Remembering him at that moment, his son wrote long afterwards: 'The life of this man was a model of honesty and responsibility. Over the years, quite a few families had entrusted him with the task of taking their sons to Paris; he'd given good advice to all of them and helped them as much as he could. A trusted workman, his reputation as a skilled mason was high.' But his working life, like that of all his kind, was a series of strokes of good and ill fortune over which he had little control: there was to be a very bad moment in 1833 when, returning home from a period of slump in the building trade, he wept in front of his son in the cemetery at Soubrebost because circumstances had forced him to borrow a small sum of money at an extortionate rate – '"I've always worked so much, I've always tried to save, but look where it's got me."' It was the son who broke out of the narrow cycle of imperatives into a wider world of choice and ambition – a world that brought him a great deal but that was perhaps, in comparison with his father's, lonely and at times bleak.

Condemned to make the best of things in Issoudun, Léonard Nadaud hushed his son when he went on about his feet, but asked him – 'implored' is the word Martin Nadaud uses – to make an effort and eat the dinner that was put before them. To please his exacting father, the boy did, and cheered up. Becoming tipsy on the unaccustomed wine, he chattered away, to the amusement of the assembled company which was now about a hundred strong – '"Ah, the little beggar's got a tongue in his head, for sure! Once he's done a few campaigns there'll be no holding him."'

Between Guéret and La Châtre, in the southern Indre, the masons had passed along an established coach-road, built in the previous decade. But north of La Châtre it petered out. The royal road from Toulouse to Paris went via Limoges and then on to Argenton, well to the west of the masons' trajectory, as the A.20 motorway does today. Amazing as it may seem, there was then no clear route between La Châtre and Châteauroux, two principal towns of the Indre. As George Sand, who lived just north of La Châtre, famously described it: 'there was no road, or rather there were a hundred . . . a labyrinth of twisting tracks, of marshy ponds and great heathlands . . . people continually got lost'. The way the masons followed, as they headed steadily for the Loire, ran from La Châtre to Issoudun and was hardly better. The situation was to change in the next decade, for many roads were built under Louis-Philippe. But when Nadaud and his troop had trudged past the garden walls of George Sand's country house (where, unimaginably, he was to be entertained to tea in the 1860s) 'we had to strike out across the plains of Saint-Chartier. We followed bad tracks that had been broken up by carts and were scattered with pools and large stones. This stage of the journey was all the more difficult in that every so often we would sink into muddy water over our ankles. Squelching water in our shoes was the most disagreeable thing of all.'

George Sand's viewpoint, as a landowner, was rather different. Although she was sympathetic to the working man, her first loyalty was to the peasant farmers. She wrote of the travelling bands of masons: 'As they always cut straight across the countryside, people complained about them.'

This was not the only cause for complaint. Even Nadaud admits that their behaviour was not always above reproach: 'As we all left together in the morning from a town or village, we would give voice to the whoops that traditionally sounded at the old Creusois round-dances in our barns . . . The noise was deafening and, needless to say, we didn't worry about waking up any local people who might be still asleep.'

In fact, these simulated battle cries were surely deliberately provoking? Many commentators of the period mention that the masons and the peasantry of the alien regions through which they passed used to square up to each other. Peasant farmers in the fields, seeing the great troop pass, many of them in white plasterers' smocks, would call out carefully chosen insults about flocks of geese and turkeys. Of course the masons responded in kind –

'There were in our group two strong-arm types . . . [one]

well known in boxing circles. At once they said to my father, who was a likely lad himself [*un fort luron*] "Léonard, let's go for it." They all put their packs down –' Responsible and senior Léonard Nadaud may have been, but evidently that did not exclude the taste for a good fight. Fortunately, seeing the masons about to come over the hedges after them, the peasantry ran off and settled for making faces at a distance. 'It was easy to see that these men didn't really hate us. They just wanted to tease us and get a rise out of us.'

Although Nadaud is indignant, in retrospect, about the way the masons were treated, these ritualised threats of violent retaliation probably helped to maintain solidarity and morale among these men as they marched, like soldiers, 'on campaign'. There is a mention, too, of messages being carried to masons in Paris, as if there was a real possibility of an army of reinforcements being raised there to descend on the foolish inhabitants of the Berry or the Sologne to teach them a lesson.

These age-old male war-games took other forms too. There was a long tradition of members of different skilled trades who encountered one another on these mass journeys automatically engaging in combat with sticks. But it must also be true that the highly local nature of *pays*, *patois*, cultures and customs then persisting meant that men of different regions seemed genuinely exotic and savage to each other. The lack of a national road network was both a symptom and a cause of this separatism: strangers who were technically fellow French citizens were perceived as foreign tribes, though the 1830s were probably the last years in which this was so. Nadaud, travelling in the footsteps of so many who had gone that way before him, was living out the end of a long tradition. By the 1840s the roads had improved and there was a greater and cheaper choice of wheeled conveyances; by 1850 the railway line from Paris was snaking its way in stages down towards the mountainous central regions. After 1856, the masons of the Creuse tramped only as far as the new stations at Saint-Sulpice

Laurière and la Souterraine. Nadaud rounds off his description of his first, epic journey with the comment 'I have gone
into all this detail . . . because the men of my generation were
to be the last to submit themselves to such an exhausting
ordeal. Indeed, with the railway in the offing, a golden age
was about to begin.'

The modern editor of the Memoirs, the historian Maurice
Agulhon, points out: 'There is no trace of irony here. For
Martin Nadaud, who had know such a hard life early on . . .
the progress represented by the rest of the century was self-
evident.' No wonder, much later in life, trains figured
prominently in his schemes for a better world. The tramp of
heavily laden men continued to resound in his consciousness.

It resounds, too, in the minds of those who today, a
century after Nadaud and his kind have been dead and more
or less forgotten, are seeking to revive their memory. In the
1990s a group of Creusois, most of them the direct
descendants of masons or other building workers, organised
several commemorative route marches between the Creuse
and Paris. Needless to say, such expeditions are eased with
vins d'honneur in the towns through which they pass,
canteens and First Aid facilities en route, and mini-buses at
strategic points to give lifts to those whose legs fail them.
Naturally the more serious participants are well equipped
with waterproof clothing and modern walking boots; over-
night stops feature, garnished not with filthy sheets but hot
showers. 'Even so,' one healthy man told me, 'we found it
hard. After 40 or 50 kilometres at the same pace, your
trousers rub your thighs and make them sore. I thought a lot
about what it was like for our great-great-grandfathers.'

From Issoudun onwards the masons had joined the main
north–south route, today's N.20, via Vierzon as far as
Salbris, another day of close on 60 kilometres. There, a
rumour of trouble with locals had run ahead of them:
gendarmes were standing about in the town square. But
Léonard Nadaud's band had their hotel ready booked and

went docilely there. The following day was to be the last –
hurrahs all round, hats thrown in the air – since, after
another 50 kilometres, they saw rising above the fields the
great cathedral of Orléans. They had reached the Loire. Here,
it was becoming the custom for the masons to load
themselves into rented *coucous*, lumbering, over-laden covered wagons whose foul-mouthed drivers bargained hard and
had to be coerced from tavern to tavern along the way.
Nadaud and three other boys made the journey in the basket-
work cradle slung under the vehicle, which was intended for
luggage. 'It was like being in a heaving ship. In this rolling
way, I first reached Paris.'

It was, however, to be another twenty-two years before
Nadaud saw the sea, and that was when he set sail for
England. Till then, France's greatest city and her deepest
rural region, plus the long road that linked them, were the
totality of his experience. Arriving in Paris with a child's
intimate awareness of his native countryside engraved on his
mind, he then, in common with others of his kind, proceeded
to transfer this sense of physical identification to the Paris
streets. The broad avenues, cobbled alleys, high buildings and
hidden corners of Paris – the hills, valleys, woods, hedgerows,
standing stones and streams of the Lower Creuse: these two
territories, apparently so different, became in the course of
years two equal kingdoms. In each, the peasants-turned-
masons dealt directly with the raw material of place, creating
with their own hands the landscapes of their own and others'
lives.

As soon as they arrived in Paris, Martin Nadaud's father
took him to the quai de la Grève, that general meeting place
that figures in all accounts of Parisian popular life. Today, it
has disappeared under the later nineteenth-century embank-
ment of the quai de l'Hôtel de Ville and the twentieth-century
urban freeway along the river. But in the 1830s much of the
quai was as it had been for centuries, an expanse of shingle
and sand sloping down to the water with an anchorage for

boats. Further up the slope the land had been levelled out into an open space. On this place de la Grève pedlars and hucksters congregated, popular demonstrations and uprisings took place. It was also a traditional site of public executions, though in fact the year 1830 was to see the last one there. This was also the last year in which the place bore its old name: after that it officially became the place de l'Hôtel de Ville, from the Town Hall on its eastern side. But its chief renown, for hundreds of years, was as an informal hiring ground for men in search of work: the masons congregated there on returning to Paris, to find one another and to exchange news. From this, the word *grève*, which literally means a shore-line or strand, has attached itself to the idea of workers' solidarity: in modern French *une grève* means a strike.

'Before taking me to our lodgings . . . my father took me to the quai de la Grève, by the Seine, to wash my face and hands. I was certainly in need of this; my hands were coal-black. By rubbing them with sand I managed to clean them up a bit. I took off my jacket and waistcoat to try to rid them of the fleas that were now devouring me.'

Then round the corner, past the rue de la Mortellerie, celebrated for masons, and on to 62 rue de la Tissanderie (Street of the Weaving), an ancient, narrow artery that led into the rue St Antoine. It was to disappear twenty years later, along with the Marché St Jean, under the extension of the rue de Rivoli.

'Arriving at the lodging-house [*garni*], we found only the two Champesne daughters there . . . both dressed entirely in black: their mother had just died. The eldest came at once to kiss me. I stared down, not daring to look her in the face. She said, "Well, well, *père* Nadaud, you told us your son was so lively. He looks quite shy to me."'

The father told her to wait and see. Indeed, a year or so later, when Martin Nadaud had a bad accident, it was this daughter who prevented him from being sent to hospital (then dreaded as a place of infection and death) and looked after him herself. For the rest of his life he was grateful to her:

'One needs to have known the state of depression into which a young man can fall after such a disaster as this, to know how much a kind female face and a gentle word can soothe one . . . When I had been freshly bandaged, she would come and sit beside my bed knitting or sewing, so I never got bored.'

To his sadness, this paragon married a man whose political views were the opposite of his own, and whom he character-ised as *un réactionnaire dénué de toute raison* – 'He was so rude to me one day when I came to call that, long before she died, it was no longer possible for me to visit that home where I had been so well treated.'

What was this Paris like, where Nadaud settled to work in what were, in many ways, the closing years of an era?

Compared with London at the same period, which was in full expansion into the first modern megalopolis, the forerun-ner of many twentieth-century ones, Paris was still a concentrated, confined city of the old world. French visitors to England in the first half of the century were struck by London's extraordinary proliferation and by the fact that this was largely unplanned. Louis Simond, an amiable and well-born traveller who visited England with apparent ease regardless that the war with Napoleon was still in process, remarked even at that early date: 'We have spent several days in the county of Hertford, twenty miles to the north of London. One travels half the distance between two rows of brick houses. New ones get themselves built every day . . . London is stretching out her great arms on all sides, as if to embrace the whole countryside. Yet her population is not growing in proportion, it is simply displacing itself from the centre to the outskirts. The centre has become a trading counter, a place of business. Instead, the people live more spaciously in the suburbs, with better air and more cheaply.'

If this development was striking to a Frenchman before 1815, it was doubly so fifteen years later after a post-war building boom had scattered the brick terraces much more widely across the fields. In Paris, too, a preoccupation with 'air' and 'spaciousness' was to become increasingly evident as the century went on, but the perceived problem was to be resolved in a very different way.

The Paris of the first half of the nineteenth century had not changed in any fundamental way from the late-medieval city. She had of course expanded over the centuries but slowly, by the gradual accretion of another concentric ring. From time to time, as the old walls encircling the city were overtaken and fell into disrepair, a new corset of masonry would be built further out to encircle the newer districts, but the object was largely containment and customs barriers rather than expansion. Paris remained, at least in conception, a walled urban fortress. Her centre neither changed nor shifted; the heart of Paris remained the Ile de la Cité, the site of the original Roman settlement in the middle of the Seine, plus the square mile or so of streets on both the right bank and the left that had been there for hundreds of years. Nadaud, living as a young mason at various addresses in the warren of right bank streets across from the Ile de la Cité, was occupying the same high houses hanging over the same dirty gullies that had been Parisian homes since the fifteenth century, in some cases since the thirteenth. Even the population of these streets had not greatly altered. The rue de la Mortellerie, initially a path through a fishing hamlet, had acquired its name by 1212 when it was settled by *morteliers*, those who worked with mortar. More than six hundred years later the Creusois masons still had their lodgings there; water-sellers still hawked their barrels from house to house as in medieval days, and the street was the site of an open drain that had become notorious. Here is Victor Hugo on it, in apocalyptic mode:

'The wide course of the sewer from the Marais [the one-time aristocratic quarter next to that of the Hôtel de Ville] . . . remained open to the sky till 1833 on the rue Saint-Louis, almost opposite the inn-sign of the Messager Galant. The drain leading to it had an opening on the rue de la Mortellerie, which was famous for its pestilent smell. With its pointed iron railing like a row of teeth, the hole appeared in this dread street like the mouth of a dragon breathing onto men from the underworld.'

In 1832 an epidemic of cholera, which till then had been thought to be a disease of the past, caused some of its worst ravages in that street and in neighbouring ones, which was presumably why the open sewer was finally closed, though no more fundamental works were done on it then. In addition, the inhabitants became sensitive about a name which, whatever its real origins, evoked the word *mortalité*. They petitioned for it to be changed, and after three years' deliberation the authorities unimaginatively christened it rue de l'Hôtel de Ville – perhaps to remind the unruly, working-class inhabitants of the presence of that seat of authority round the corner. In any case, by the end of the decade, a large part of this street and several adjoining ones had been removed as a piece of early slum clearance, one of the first targets of Louis-Philippe's Préfet of Paris, Rambuteau.

For although the old Paris evoked in many of Balzac's novels and in Victor Hugo's retrospective *Les Misérables* (1862) remained essentially intact, unreconstructed and socially heterogenous till well into the nineteenth century, some development had nevertheless been taking place. The popular conception that nothing occurred till Louis-Napoleon's Préfet Baron Haussmann embarked on a massive rebuilding programme in the 1850s is a much simplified version of events. Paris was a large city well before industrial capitalism belatedly reached it. It is thought to have had about half a million inhabitants when the boundary walls of the Farmers General went up in 1784, but much of the land contained within this new circumference was not yet built upon. Ten years later, after the Revolution and the seizing of properties belonging to the clergy, much of these outlying districts began to be developed. Then came Napoleon, with his own grand schemes. While he was Emperor the interminable rebuilding of the Louvre was undertaken; also the redesigning of the Tuileries, the construction of the rue de Rivoli and plans for the raising of the Arc de Triomphe at the end of the Champs Elysées. The great piles of the Bourse (Stock Exchange) and the Parliament building, which came to be called the Palais Bourbon, date from those years – all the work of men from central France. In addition, the Panthéon – originally planned on the highest point of the Latin quarter as a replacement church under the *Ancien Régime* – was completed as a mausoleum for the Great Men who were to become such an abiding part of French secular mythology.

By the fall of Napoleon, the Paris population was probably approaching three quarters of a million. Estimates vary, but it seems to have increased again by 25 per cent in the next dozen years. The shift from a mercantile and home-industry city into an industrial one was under way and continued through the 1820s. The old quarters, which had always been densely populated, became even more so. Traditionally, social differences within Paris had existed only on a vertical principle, with shops and other places of business on the street level, good class accommodation on the first and second floors and more modest lodgings higher up, ending with the poor in the attics. But now living in the centre of the city became less attractive to the newly genteel, the large old houses were split up into segments, extra storeys were added and courtyards and gardens built over with commercial depots and workshops. Emile Zola's *La Curée* contains a retrospective vignette of just such a large seventeenth-century private house on the Ile Saint-Louis, next to the Ile de la Cité – 'one of those blackened, four-square piles with high, narrow windows . . . which these days are rented out to boarding schools, wholesale wine merchants and soda-water manufacturers'.

So if the gentry and the increasing commercial middle classes were for the first time moving out of the congested heart of the city, where were they going? The answer is that, after the Restoration in 1815, some new districts began to be laid out. These did not just follow the tradition of the piecemeal, semi-rural suburb, but were conceived as symmetrical urban schemes in their own right. The English writer Fanny Trollope, mother of Anthony, visiting Paris twenty years after the Restoration, remarked on 'the rapid increase in handsome dwellings . . . as white and as bright as newborn mushrooms . . . The church of the Madeleine, instead of being nearly at the extremity of Paris, has now a new city behind it.' Some of the development, especially round the Champs Elysées, was for grand, individual mansions. But elsewhere, round the military Champ de Mars in the south-west, and in the north-west towards what became the Parc Monceau, in new streets designed specifically for middle-class occupation, the classic, purpose-built Parisian apartment block made its appearance. It has not changed its form in any essential way since.

At the same period the Arc de Triomphe, part of Napoleon's Grand Plan for Paris, was finally being completed. A ring of tree-lined esplanades was laid out on the site of the old fortifications of Louis XIV, which had been dismantled late in the previous century. Here, the theatres and the smarter cafés were to be found: the familiar Paris of the boulevards was born. In the middle of town glass-roofed shopping *galeries* and bazaars, the forerunners of the department store, were becoming a feature of smart Parisian life. The idea that the centre of town was for business and trade and the outer districts for residence and entertainment, which had struck Louis Simond as peculiar to London in 1812, was at last reaching Paris too, though it was never to take the extreme form that it did and does in the English capital. Already in Paris in 1828 the first omnibuses had begun to circulate – for once stealing a march on London, which did not follow suit till 1830. These public conveyances were changing notions of distance in a city where, till then, almost everyone had lived near their work, frequently on top of it.

The street map of 1834, the year before Fanny Trollope's visit, shows ancient Paris and its network of narrow arteries still intact, not yet eviscerated by town planning: it is nevertheless on the brink of change. The Bastille, of course, has gone, the Canal Saint-Martin (a sign of industrial commerce) is slotted past its site through the developing eastern suburbs. Although these suburbs do not show the classic pattern of triangular street-corners and vistas as in the ones to the west of the city, within a few years they will create another 'new town' there around and beyond the old faubourg Saint-Antoine: on the map a new boulevard (Mazas) is even projected there. Apart from this, no other sweeping *percements* are yet visible; no old streets have yet been widened into great avenues and cross-town routes – but detailed plans for such transformations were even then afoot, long before Haussmann. Two new bridges were soon to span the river. No railways yet appear, but here again they are waiting in the wings. By a governmental Act of 1842 a plan for a network was set out; later in the decade the stations (at first called *embarcadères* on the analogy of ports) would open one after another, though the grander permanent *gares* were not built till the '50s.

The railway lines were to alter profoundly not only the quarters through which they cut their way but the whole meaning of 'living in Paris' and the relationship between Paris and every other region of France. The railways at first made the itinerant workers' journeys far easier, but it was this very ease of movement that, within a generation, began to involve whole families and so brought the long tradition of migrant working to a close.

This, then, was the Paris of the old world, but set to become the new, in which Nadaud arrived as a teenager. He was destined not only to live and form his ideas in the capital of Louis-Philippe (1830–48), but to help construct it with his own hands. Long after, when he was a Member of Parliament under the Third Republic, he firmly corrected another speaker who was suggesting that the transformation of Paris was all of recent date – 'You're not as old as me. I've been here since 1830 and I saw great works undertaken then.' He was better equipped than most *députés* to know what he was talking about.

By these last decades of the century and of his own life, after the far more dramatic impact of the years of the Emperor Louis-Napoleon (1852–70), this Paris of France's last king was to be remembered as quaint and innocent. Its boulevards were still largely pedestrian and white with country dust: you could buy milk there straight from the cow. Its unmacadamed streets were cluttered with people selling things and plying their trades – tinsmiths heated soldering irons dangerously close to the passers-by, mattress-cleaners spread dirty flock out on the cobbles even in good class quarters. Main thoroughfares were lit only with dim oil lamps strung between house-fronts, and when gas began to replace them it took a long time for it to penetrate into the houses for domestic use. It took just as long – till the Second Empire – for water pipes to make their way indoors. At a time when very many houses in London already had mains water laid on under pressure to the upper floors as well as the kitchen, Paris disconcerted English visitors such as Fanny Trollope by lacking piped water even to the most elegant homes – 'The precious gift of nature is doled out by two buckets at a time, laboriously brought ... by porters, clambering in sabots, often up the same stairs that lead to the drawing rooms.'

In the same way, it was not just old and insanitary quarters such as the rue de la Mortellerie that lacked even the most elementary drainage system. Closets were connected only to cess-pits which had to be regularly emptied, men relieved themselves in the streets as readily as if they had been in the countryside, and the contents of chamber pots were still being slung with impunity out of upper windows to join the muddy quagmire of the central gutter. Paris had its own smell: in the words of the Préfet Rambuteau, 'Household water stagnates before the doors, emitting that characteristic odour of rotten cabbage by which a Parisian returning from a long journey recognises his city.'

But even without actual sewage, the lack of surfacing left miry main streets and back streets alike. Fanny Trollope remarked that even in the spacious new quarter going up near the Champs Elysées no provision was made for draining rainwater, so that 'The Board of Works [having] waited for a day or two to see what would happen, and finding that the muddy lake did not disappear, commanded the assistance of twenty-six able-bodied labourers, who set about digging just such a channel as little boys amuse themselves with by making beside a pond ... This muddy channel was left to adorn this magnificent area which, were a little finishing bestowed on it, would probably be the finest point that any city in the world could boast.'

For, notwithstanding all this, the reign of Louis-Philippe was a time of significant progress, when street lamps, public fountains and trees proliferated, when filth was gradually replaced by cobbles and pavements, the first *pissoirs* appeared and a start was made on deeper and more adequate drains. 'In a few years from now, it will be almost as easy to walk in Paris as it is in London', remarked an English tourist more sanguine than Mrs Trollope. It was also during this period that many of the more visionary ideas about what a great city is and what it should be, ideas that were to be so influential for the rest of the century, began to be nurtured.

Revolutions and Other Experiences

The Paris in which Martin Nadaud arrived in 1830 was still, just, under the reign of Charles X, the last truly Bourbon king. Four months later, however, this nervous monarch was noisily deposed and the Duke of Orléans was elected by Parliament as Louis-Philippe. The 'three glorious days' of July in which this took place were among the boy's earliest experiences in the adult world, and were to serve as a beacon for much of his subsequent development. They also, as it happened, brought a financial disaster to his family which was to mark him almost as profoundly.

For eighty-odd years after the cataclysm of the French Revolution the public history of France moves on, or rather is moved on, by a series of further revolutionary uprisings, like secondary shocks of an earthquake. Reversals of power – coup and counter-coup became, for much of the nineteenth century, a set pattern, as if France had learnt that that was a way forward and could not make a further shift to a more evolutionary mode. Over the greater part of provincial and rural France these repetitive shocks were only faintly felt. As Emile Guillaumin put it in *La Vie d'un Simple:* 'In the country, we trouble our heads very little about what Government get up to. Come Peter, come Paul, it isn't our affair.' But in Paris, the highly centralised heart of France where, since Napoleon, all decisions were taken, it was a different matter. Paris was where the earthquakes mainly took place, with some extra tremors in the burgeoning industrial city of Lyon.

It so happened that the first site on which Léonard Nadaud

took his son to work was not within Paris itself but in the then-rural area of Villemomble, some 12 kilometres to the east. (Today, its early twentieth-century suburban villas are, in their turn, being overtaken by the high modern blocks and attendant social ills of Paris's *zone grise*.) There Léonard Nadaud's brother was overseeing other workmen making alterations to a local country house and its park, and also building three houses on his own account. This uncle, the old soldier of the *Grande Armée*, had clearly prospered as a mason and was making the jump from labouring man to entrepreneur; he also seems to have had several members of his family in Paris with him. The summer months were spent there, with Martin Nadaud gradually learning the trade of mortar-mixer under a kindly master mason who did not expect him to carry heavier weights of stone or plaster on his head than he could readily manage. Even so, continuously supplying an energetic master with enough mortar at the right moments, but not too much or it would start drying before it could be used, was an exacting task. Such was the informal apprenticeship system of the time, and an ambitious youngster could look forward to better things by and by. But meanwhile the 'boys' – some of whom were not really boys at all but grown men too lacking in ability to get any further – had all the hardest jobs and were continually ordered about by those a little higher up the pecking order.

'At that time, plaster [plaster of Paris = gypsum] came unprepared straight from the quarries. You had to break it up with a shovel and pass it through a sieve. The remaining bits were left on the ground, and when enough had been collected together the hod-carriers threshed them with a paddle to crush them. This work made us swallow lungfuls of dust –'

It is true that silicosis, known to the masons as *le mal Saint Roch*, was a common fate among them. It is also true that, as the century progressed, lung diseases in general, and more especially tuberculosis, came to figure as an urban plague. Indeed, since TB itself was generally supposed to be the result of 'foul air', 'pestilent vapours', it became a talisman for all the supposed evils of the city – moral and social as well as physical. Dr Villard had a good deal to say, in his late nineteenth-century pamphlets for the Conseil d'Hygiène Publique et de la Salubrité du Département de la Creuse, on the health risks to young masons – on cold and wet weather, on mortar dust, on the dangerous practice of carrying a heavy head-load up a ladder using one hand to balance it. And then there were cholera and smallpox – not to mention racial degeneration . . . But then Villard was an advocate of rural life (suitably cleaned up), regarding it as the moral heart of France. He was opposed to seasonal migration in any case, an attitude that became increasingly marked among the bourgeoisie as their own urban numbers increased.

In the last days of July, when the barricades, that ritual furniture of revolt, went up in the Paris streets and Charles X abdicated, the Nadaud clan were quick to make their way to the city to witness whatever was going on:

'What a picture! For a boy fresh from his village it was indescribably impressive – to see so many people out in the streets, proud of their victory over a king and ministers who had tried to deprive them of the last scraps of liberty they had retained from the Charter of 1815 . . . The final shots had been fired the evening before, but the whole population, both the participants and the rest, were outside, roaring "Long live the Charter! Down with the Bourbons."'

Father and son took refuge in a large wine-merchant's which Nadaud describes as being on the corner of the faubourg Saint-Antoine and the place de la Bastille. In fact that open space was at that time cloaked under a name less redolent of popular unrest and a statue of an elephant stood on the site of the one-time prison, but it was then, and for the next 130 years, the traditional meeting-point of working-class Paris. The saloon was packed with men whose sweat-streaked hands and faces were blackened with powder stains from the breech-loading carbines of the period.

'Their sleeves were rolled above their elbows, and they

were radiant with their victory over the army ... I am not capable of doing justice in words to the impression all this made on me. But this event has remained the one most deeply engraved on my memory out of all those experienced in Paris under the reign of Louis-Philippe which was to be marked by armed uprisings.' He continues almost inconsequentially: 'I except the cold-blooded murders of the horrible days of June '48 and also the massacre of the Commune.'

In this uneasy sequence of phrases is apparent already the contradiction that runs through Nadaud's writing and through his life. On one level, he rejoiced in displays of popular power. He liked a fight, he liked demonstrations, he turned out to be gifted himself at the quintessentially French rhetoric associated with such apocalyptic events – '*Aux armes, citoyens!*' But at another level his humanity and his scrupulous sense of justice made him shy away from the logical consequences of such mass movements, and this inner conflict became more marked as he grew older. In 1871 the man who, as a youngster, had been fired by the revolution of 1830, managed to avoid the Paris Commune almost entirely; his evasive description of it reduces it to the status of a tussle over municipal elections.

Another boy who happened to be in Paris during the 'three glorious days' was also profoundly impressed by what he saw, though his starting-point was rather different from that of Nadaud. Only nine at the time, but very alert, John Malcolm Ludlow, the future founder in England of Mutual Aid Societies and the Working Men's College, was living in Paris with his widowed mother and sisters. His father, who had died in 1821, had been an Indian Army officer with a reputation for going into battle armed only with a walking-stick. John Malcolm had been brought up to revere the father he had never known and so his sympathies were at first with the *garde royale*, but the sight of these being ignominiously routed by the mob made him wonder if a soldier's life was really that glorious. The mob were threatening to fire the deserted barracks, an action which, since the barracks contained a magazine, would have blown up the whole quarter – a new district on the west side of Paris, near the Tuileries Gardens and the place Vendôme. Fortunately a student from the élite Polytechnic, one of many who had taken part in the revolution, a dashing, powder-stained fellow with a sword and a tricolour, appealed loudly to the common sense and better feelings of the mob, who by and by backed down. Much later in his life, Ludlow noted how impressed he had been by this 'magnificent triumph of moral over physical force, of good over evil.' Much later too, in London, he was to meet Nadaud, by then transformed from a Paris working lad into someone quite other, and the two men compared notes on the distant days of July 1830.

During the uprising the soon-to-be-crowned Louis-Philippe stayed in a château near Villemomble, which the innocent citizens and workmen took to be a good omen. However, the effects of the palace revolution were soon catastrophic for the Nadauds. The local landowner under whose auspices they had been working took refuge in Switzerland; all building works came to a halt. The money lost by the two brothers amounted to some 12,000 francs, and their previous agreement with each other – purely verbal, since both men were unlettered – had been that they should take a half share each. Martin Nadaud's restrained comment here is that for an ordinary labouring man, such as his own father, this sum was impossible to replace. An adult mason then earned between 3 and 3.50 francs a day. A boy or an apprentice got 1.80 or 2 francs.

'In simple good faith my father had only drawn enough of his official salary to feed and clothe us. Still worse, he had borrowed from several friends, not liking to bother [the landowner] who was said to be a millionaire several times over. Now, he had no basis for making any demand on this gentleman, since only his brother's name had been on the contract and the latter just kept advising him to wait and see.

'I was present at violent quarrels between the two brothers, which would have come to blows had it not been for the intervention of friends. But the misfortune was there; there was nothing to do but put up with it. To add to our trouble and misery, my father had recently bought out his brother's share in La Martinèche for 1,500 francs.'

The situation was a classic one. Since the breaking of the moulds of the *Ancien Régime*, including that of primogeniture, the Code Napoléon had stated (article 826) that all the sons and daughters of a marriage should inherit the family estate in equal parts. This apparently rational and equitable system (which still lays its dead hand on France today) meant in practice that, to keep a modest family farm intact but not over-populated, one brother or sister had to indemnify all the others. So loans would be taken out at interest, a burden of debt that was often handed on from one generation to another. Peter would deprive himself to indemnify his brother Paul, further debts would be incurred to secure husbands for sisters, men ended up working simply to service the loans and in the longer term no one thrived but the rural money-lenders. The same situation is a scourge of rural life in many Third World countries today, and it is notable that the same solution – seasonal migration to work in the towns – is often seen as the only way of keeping going. The Creusois masons of the nineteenth century find close counterparts in the twentieth-century migratory labourers, dock-workers and factory-hands of the Bombay conurbation.

'"If only"', Leonard Nadaud lamented to his fourteen-year-old son, '"I was younger . . . I would get out of this mess more easily, but in three or four years they won't be wanting me on the buildings any longer" . . . "*Allons, allons, mon père* . . . in a few years from now I'll be a proper mason too, I'll help you. From now till then we'd be really unlucky if we didn't earn at least enough to keep up with the interest."'

They did keep up, but life was hard. Elsewhere in this part of his Memoirs, Nadaud adds that paying off the debts used up all the money he himself was able to save from his earnings between 1830 and 1848.

One reason for the rapid success of the uprising of 1830 was the fact that the bourgeoisie too had been getting restive under Charles X. His final attempt to restore their old powers to the clergy and the aristocracy annoyed the rest of society. A general slump in the late 1820s not only affected the wages of masons and textile workers (the Lyon silk weavers were always a sensitive gauge of economic unrest); it created crises and bankruptcies in the middle classes too. In addition, bad harvests had, by 1829, pushed up grain prices by 50 per cent, at a time and in a country still dependent on the vagaries of local supplies for its daily bread. So people from a wide social spectrum saw the men on the barricades not as resurrected *sans-culottes* of 1791, red in tooth and claw, but as foot soldiers in a cause that was to some extent everyone's.

The Creusois masons were not really very prominent on the barricades that July: only three were reported killed. (It was to be a different story in 1848.) But because they were men who worked out in the streets in any case, and because they had to hand the raw material for barricades – large stones – a whole mythology developed of the Parisian mason as a key figure of Red republicanism. A minor poet, Auguste Barbier, who after 1830 produced poems about a gallery of social types, may or may not have had his tongue in his cheek when he penned the following verse, but it all went to enhance the notion of the mason let loose in Paris as an embodiment of Terror, holy or not according to your point of view:

> *Il est beau, ce colosse à la mâle carrure,*
>   *Ce vigoureux porte-haillons,*
> *Ce sublime manoeuvre à la veste bure*
>   *Teinté de sang des bataillons!*
> *Ce maçon qui d'un coup vous démolit des trônes*
>   *Et qui, par un ciel étouffant,*
> *Sur les larges pavés fait bondir ces couronnes,*
>   *Comme le cerveau d'un enfant.*

('How handsome he is, this giant male figure, vigorous in his ragged clothes, a magnificent workman in a fustian jacket stained with the blood of troops! This mason who, with one blow, demolishes thrones and, under a burning sky, casts crowns down onto the paving stones as if they were the heads of children.')

Meanwhile, in the real world the Nadauds, father and son, returned with debts totalling 11,000 francs to the centre of Paris, to work on without respite through what turned out to be several bad years in the building trade.

They took up their abode in the Champesne *garni* in the quarter of the Hôtel de Ville, where Martin had been introduced earlier. Other areas traditionally favoured by the masons were the nearby Ile de la Cité, where the novelist Eugène Sue set the main action of his *Les Mystères de Paris* a few years later, and the left bank Montagne Sainte-Geneviève, where the relatively new Panthéon reared over the higgledy-piggledy old houses around it. During the next twenty years criticism of these medieval quarters, by those with ideas on what a nineteenth-century city should be, was increasingly heard. Typical of the rising disapproval were the remarks of Henri Lecouturier, written in 1848, in the early days of the next wave of revolutionary change:

'The greater number of streets in our wonderful Paris are nothing but filthy tunnels, always damp with foetid water. Tightly squeezed between two lines of high houses, such lanes never see the sun, which penetrates no further than the level of the overhanging chimneys ... And these streets are the ones inhabited by the better-off workmen. There are, in addition, alleys where two men cannot walk side by side, absolute gutters of filth –'

The pregnant title of the short work in which this passage appears is *Paris, incompatible avec la République: plan d'un nouveau Paris ou les Révolutions seront impossibles* – the insistent suggestion being that the brave new world ushered in (it was hoped) by the Revolution of '48 might be at risk from further dark or uncontrolled forces which lurked in streets too narrow for the forces of Law and Order to penetrate. If Paris was in any case something of a fortress, the old central quarters were seen as a fortress within the fortress. That these undrained streets were a seedbed for germs that then made their way into bourgeois homes was obvious from the cholera outbreak in 1832, which first declared itself in the Cité–Hôtel de Ville area. But the same area in the same year was also the epicentre of the aborted uprising that was romanticised thirty years later in Hugo's *Les Misérables*. The idea of some organic link between overcrowded tenements and extreme political views took root in the bureaucratic mind, and the phrase '*classes laborieuses, classes dangereuses*' gained wide currency. In many mid-nineteenth-century writings these twin concepts, dangerous living conditions and dangerous politics, are so interwoven that at times it is unclear which is being used as a metaphor for which. Naturally the internal arrangements of the old houses, which had earlier been a matter only for the occupants, came under scrutiny also. So, by Martin Nadaud's early years in Paris, the paradox was evolving whereby the masons were seen as potential trouble-makers, harbingers of alarming social change, at the very same time that their daily living conditions (which they themselves organised as a matter of choice and tradition) were being stigmatised as unacceptably backward.

Some *garnis* indeed went on replicating the way of life that had been normal for the mass of the people four hundred years before. Although '*garni*' properly speaking means 'furnished [lodgings]' the masons' preoccupation with saving money made some of them cut expenses to an absolute minimum:

'At No. 10 rue de la Vannerie, near the Hôtel de Ville, was a lodging for masons where, for 20 centimes a night, one had the right to stretch out on a bed of straw laid straight onto the floorboards of a room where twenty other Limousins snored fit to break the window panes' (Memoirs of Canler, a one-time head of the Security Services).

The Nadauds, being at the elite end of the building trade, or at any rate aspiring to it, were lodged a little more comfortably. However, Martin himself, used though he was to one-room life on a family farm where the men used the manure heap to relieve themselves, found the Champesne residence took some getting used to – 'When we went up to our rooms, it was to breathe in stale and impure air. In addition, the only closet in the house, which was used by more than sixty people, was on our landing, and I admit it wasn't easy to force oneself to go in there . . . When the men in our dormitory took their boots off to go to bed, what with their sweaty feet or their old stockings that they didn't always change every week, you had to be well accustomed to that way of life not to hold your nose.'

It was a long way from the sweeping views of the Creuse, the air and the streams and the Druid stones of the Puy Maria.

Nevertheless, his memory of early days in the *garnis*, even if recalled without nostalgia, is also without that tone of nervous social indignation that characterises outsiders' views at this period. He writes with a degree of affection and an absolute understanding of why things were the way they were. Most of the landlords were ex-masons themselves – or the wives of masons, who were some of the first women to break the country taboo that regarded the city as an entirely male province. In the fullness of time, Nadaud's younger sister Françoise, who married an unsatisfactory husband with the ominous surname of Bouteille (Bottle), was to keep a Parisian lodging house. At the Champesnes', the Nadauds were effectively back in their own Creusois village:

'Mademoiselle Rose . . . took me up to the fourth floor of the house, showed me my bed and put my small pack on a shelf. Then she introduced me to the other men in the dormitory [*chambrée*], taking care to tell me they were all nice, decent boys [*tous bons enfants*], which was true, and that in any case they were people either from my own Commune or from Pontarion.

'In that room were six beds and twelve lodgers. We were so much on top of one another that the centre of the room was reduced to an alleyway 50 centimetres wide; I did indeed soon get to know my companions. Night and morning, I listened to conversations on any and every subject, sometimes amusing, almost always trivial – though occasionally disturbing or coarsening for childish ears.

'. . . At that time, no books or newspapers were ever seen in the lodgings: you could say that we just ate and slept without a thought of nourishing the mind . . .

'There were two basic strains of conversation: that of the penny-pinchers and that of the spendthrifts. The penny-pinchers were commonly critical of others, always ready to pass judgement on those whose qualities differed from their own . . . But this type of man was not without decency and loyalty, for he loved his own family and perhaps his friends: it was on himself that he was hard. He set himself to spend no more than 14 or 15 francs a month, excluding the *garni*, where he was lodged and had his evening meal of soup for 6 francs a month, and excluding his bread which he bought "on the slate" and paid for monthly too.'

Bread was an important part of the migrant workman's diet, just as it was in the peasant world from which he came, though in the Creuse it was usually made of rye. The mason striding across town with his two-foot-long personal loaf of bread tucked under his arm was a familiar Parisian sight of the time. He cut off chunks to dunk into the soup his landlady provided and took the rest to work with him, nibbling as he went. It accompanied him again to the *gargote* where he had his mid-morning meal of a piece of meat in broth, and then was stowed away again in any convenient beam-hole in the building on which he was working – 'Sometimes he would keep a bit of his meat to have as a snack in the afternoon, eaten there on the site among the plaster.'

Understandably, a man living with such extreme economy swore if, when he got back to the *garni* in the evening, the soup was cold and had been largely consumed by others. However – 'The landlady did not get cross; ours had a ready tongue and always found a few friendly words to make us laugh. Anyway, we liked our Rose . . . and for nothing in the world would we upset her.

'You did not get bored or wretched in a *garni*, unless you yourself were a melancholy type or plain disagreeable. Some men liked to talk a lot of the *pays*; those who were not married teased those who were with jokes about women left on their own. Then people would fall to praising the boss for his generosity, or criticising him.'

The spendthrifts (by which Nadaud essentially means those masons who had got into the habit of spending a large part of their pay on drink) had a racier line of conversation – 'which amused us a lot. The men who spent nothing had brought to a fine art the trick of getting these others to talk, and really seemed to revel momentarily in the tales they heard of women and other adventures. You might even have said that they were a little regretful at not having taken part in such things themselves.'

In this way Nadaud sidesteps a matter which must surely have been central to the concentrations of single men. The Hôtel de Ville quarter was a prostitutes' district too, and some, at least, of the masons must have been their customers. Large cities by their very nature are erotic, stirring responses, sharpening appetites, favouring anonymous or fugitive encounters. But among the many supposed evils of the city on which commentators like Dr Villard insisted later in the century, venereal disease is hardly mentioned (except in relation to bourgeois female 'victims', which does not seem relevant). There are some veiled references in police reports to other forms of 'debauchery', and disquiet was sometimes expressed about the way men shared beds, sometimes naked in hot weather, but then sharing a bed with someone of the same sex was normal in all classes for most of the nineteenth century, and the almost oppressively 'family' atmosphere of a *garni* must have created its own taboos. There are cases recorded of dormitories turning against a 'dissipated' member and getting rid of him.

Nadaud himself, at a later point in his memories of Paris days, has censorious things to say about the loose women

(*femmes de moeurs légères*) who used to converge on a
particular patch of high ground near the fortifications that
was famed for Sunday revelries – 'On Monday mornings,
these thousands of dishevelled and brazen women trooped
drunkenly back into Paris on the arms of their male
companions, banging into one another and heckling passers-
by with indecent suggestions.' One can see that this kind of
woman was no sexual temptation to the idealistic Nadaud or
to many of his country-born kind. But what of other, more
subtle emotional temptations? Lecouturier does just mention
'concubinage', and the fact that, according to him, one in
every three babies born in Paris in 1848 was illegitimate.
Certainly unregistered but fairly stable relationships (known
in Parisian slang as 'getting married in the Thirteenth
Arrondissement' – which did not then exist) were commonplace. It is impossible to believe that masons, married or
betrothed back in the *pays*, were all impregnably faithful and
never formed second attachments in Paris. Indeed, an old
workman from Lyon, wishing to annoy Nadaud, once
alleged that this was common practice among those who
went to Paris, and the apparently well-worn nature of the
insult tells its own tale. Alain Corbin, the French academic
who has done more than any other scholar to rescue the
obscure lives of the migrant workers from the oblivion of
history, has written: 'The near-total silence of witnesses on
the sexuality of the Limousins of Paris is in itself an
indication of the fallibility of the sources available.' Or, as a
descendant of migrant workers expressed it to me: 'They
must have led parallel lives. Of course they did.'

However, the overwhelming impression given by Nadaud's
Memoirs is that the temptation before the mason was not
sexual entanglement but alcoholism, and one can see why.
Staying together in a troop after work, in unspoken mutual
protection against becoming too assimilated into Paris life,
the men had little to do together but drink. In any case ritual
drinking was part of their work structure: a drink concluded
any agreement to employment and drinks were normally
bought by a new recruit to a site, who was greeted with glad

cries of '*Quand est-ce que?*' and '*Tu régales, coucou?*' ('When's it to be?', 'You buying a round, mate?'). Nadaud places the drink problem nicely in context:

'Some of these other men [the spendthrifts] came in at any hour of the night, and might wake us with their noise, but provided we stayed quiet ourselves and said nothing sleep soon overcame them. And, after all, these men were not wasters, they stuck to the habit of hard work. If you were friendly to them the next day that made them happy, for it is indeed true that a man needs to be respected by his own kind to bear the burden of living.'

Among other scraps of information that have come down to us on the real lives of these men, as distinct from the lives they were supposed to lead by their detractors or their self-appointed protectors, is a small book by Pierre Vinçart, *Les Ouvriers de Paris*, which evokes a *garni* the author visited. On the sloping attic ceilings were 'innumerable grotesque drawings, done not with a pencil but with a candle flame'. On the walls were simple inscriptions – 'a yearning for the village at home, the hope of returning there soon, a thought for the wife and children'.

Some of these old, high Paris houses with attic rooms survive today. As you perch in your left bank hotel room, with its polystyrene ceiling tiles and miniature bathroom, or in someone's rather smart studio-apartment that has been hollowed out of a beam-crossed roof space in the Marais, spare a thought for those homesick inscriptions that may still be *there* on the ancient walls, though long since covered by layers of plaster, paint and forgetting.

As soon as any commentator began to look beyond the stereotype of the Red devil migrant worker, the conclusion was the same: the Creusois masons were in Paris but not of it. Far from making common cause with disaffected Parisian working men in other trades, they tended to live among themselves. Indeed they were resented by native Parisians for *not* joining guilds or mutual aid societies (at periods when

these were permitted). They were also said to be mean –
'chestnut eaters' was the usual gibe. The Creusois got into
ritualised fights with Parisian labourers, but also between
themselves; men who hailed from one district would square
up to those from another, 'glaring at each other like china
dogs' – country rivalries simply transported to the city. But
few of them, in proportion to their large numbers, acquired
criminal records.

Since the masons were in Paris first and foremost in order
to amass money to take home, they did not regard their
salaries as their own to spend. Some sets of men in *garnis*
even paid their living expenses out of a common kitty. Most
men consciously kept themselves apart from the more
obvious urban temptations, against which they would have
been warned from earliest childhood. Hence too the defensive
solidarity of the lodging shared with men from the home
group of villages, all speaking the same *patois*: it provided
protection, both material and emotional, but also a system of
mutual surveillance. Tales of bad behaviour would be carried
back to the *pays*, and this might influence one's standing at
home and thus one's chances of making a good (i.e.
financially sound) marriage. Far from joining that melting-
pot which is the history of cities, these temporary Parisians
maintained, for most of the nineteenth century, their rural
identity. The fact that, till late in the century, few wives came
to share this exile, had an economic and practical reason –
there was the farm to be tended at home – but also a
psychological one. There was an unspoken fear that once the
wife was part of city life the couple would make a proper
home there and be lost eventually to the *pays*.

On the buildings, out in the open air unlike the mass of
urban workers, the masons continued to live their lives at a
country rhythm. The walk in the dawn to the current site
paralleled the country walk to the distant field to be ploughed
or sown. The length of the working day depended similarly
on the season. The 'long day' of summer lasted from 6.00
a.m. to 7.00 p.m., with an hour off for a meal between 9.00
and 10.00 (much earlier than the then-standard Parisian

dinner time) and another break between 2.00 and 3.00. At other times of the year the day began at 7.00 and went on till dusk, with one break between 10.00 and 11.00. It seems clear, however, from Nadaud's descriptions of work, that though the hours were long the men were not strictly regulated, except by each other. It was possible for an adult mason, as for a peasant, to knock off from time to time for a smoke or a drink or simply a rest.

When work was over they would set off back to their own quarters, often in large groups, not stopping on the way, not even talking among themselves, making no noise but that of their heavy footwear on the cobbles. When they did talk together, townspeople were struck by the long pauses in group conversations. Like the Limousin peasant, the immigrant worker did not often whistle or sing; the demeanour was thoughtful, a shared silence punctuated with proverbs. Their stoicism – considered an almost 'oriental fatalism' – in the face of hardship, accidents or sickness was also commented on. In other words, although each man might be seeming to exercise initiative in making the long trek to Paris to 'better himself' and his family, in practice he simply imported to Paris the acceptance of his lot which is part of a peasant world. Nadaud's own retrospective comment is: 'his destiny, however unfortunate, appeared to him unalterable'. This attitude in itself tended to prevent masons from making their way up the social scale as immigrant groups traditionally try to. Even those who became entrepreneurs employing others, and who were celebrated in the Creuse for the amount of money they had earned, retired back again in middle age to the life of small farmers. When Léonard Nadaud ended his last campaign in Paris at the age of fifty-four (having stayed on a few days more in bitter winter weather to see the remains of his hero, Napoleon, laid to rest in the crypt of the Invalides) he never again returned to the city. His son, starting 'in the mortar' but rising to a quite other level of society, was indeed an exception in every respect.

One of the homespun proverbs repeated among masons was *la distraction c'est le repos* – 'a rest is enough of a change'. When the masons did go out, perhaps to an open-air *bal*, it was often to watch the dancing rather than to participate. They were shy with the city girls, who preferred smarter types. In any case, *bals* were mostly held on Sundays, which, after 1830, was often not the masons' day of rest. The Monday-off for workmen was officially favoured under Louis-Philippe (in order to make a distinction between Church and State, that recurrent nineteenth-century preoccupation), and many masons preferred this as it meant they did not need to run to the expense of a Sunday suit. On Mondays they were to be found, in small groups or alone, sitting smoking and watching the green, still-countrified river flowing between its unembanked shores – 'And what do you suppose he's dreaming of, there leaning on a bollard outside your door? . . . He's dreaming of the small field of rye or the patch of grazing that he'll buy when he goes back to his mountain home. It'll take him ten years to save up enough! Never mind . . .' (Henri Michelet, *Le Peuple*, 1844).

And yet, of course, Paris was not the Creuse, and certain things did rub off on the masons, at any rate sufficiently for them to bring new clothes, tastes and even ideas back to the *pays*. Their diet was different and often better than the traditional country one. The standard foods of the Creuse were rye bread, usually cooked hard and still eaten when stale, buckwheat pancakes, dripping, potatoes and the all-purpose chestnut. There was no concept of variety, any more than there is over much of the Third World today. The only regular meat was a little salted pork or black pudding. In many families, the butter and eggs and meat they produced were to sell in the local market, and an omelette was a treat. But in Paris the men got used to beef and wine daily. Nadaud, who was hard at work during his first autumn in the rue de la Chaussée d'Antin (part of that 'new, white town' rising behind the Madeleine of which Mrs Trollope wrote), took a while to adjust to this:

'In the evening, when I got back to the *garni*, my father would take me to the wine shop for a drink; he had bread and cheese brought too, and encouraged me with kind words. What bothered him was that I did not like meat and that, in the *gargote*, I used to exchange my slice for vegetables with Neuf Heures [the nickname of another boy]. "You won't be able to hold out if you go on like that." The thing was, at home my mother had brought us all up on soup, bread, pancakes, potatoes and dairy products.

'For more than a year, instead of beef, I took to eating Italian cheese that I got from *charcuteries*. I ate so much of it that, ever since, I have quite gone off it.'

The extent to which the masons brought back other acquired tastes and views to their country districts was, in the nineteenth century, a matter of debate among the more articulate classes. The sparse local aristocracy of the Creuse, the bourgeoisie such as Dr Villard, Louis Bandy de Nalèche, the Sub-Préfet of Aubusson, and other back-to-the-land romantics such as Lecouturier and Lavergne, all tended to complain that those who stayed on the farms had old-fashioned ideas and wouldn't adopt new methods of production – but at the same time they felt that masons who went to the wicked city lost their taste for agricultural labour. The masons were not, in any case, in the country at harvest time, and they were said to become impatient with the slow rhythms of the agricultural year, eternally in thrall to the vagaries of drought, sun, storm, floods or frost. In other words, quiescent as the well-behaved mason might seem by urban standards, concepts of individual effort and thus of individual choice were inevitably implanting themselves.

There were also upper-class murmurs about masons with town sophistication attempting to limit their families, though it does not seem they really had much to teach their peasant cousins in this respect. Over the French countryside for the whole of the nineteenth century, birth rates were low – considerably lower than those of either Britain or Germany – for reasons that have never been entirely explained, but probably relate to the desire not to split the small family property into too many shares. The birth rate in the Creuse was consistently slightly lower than that of France as a whole, and lower than that in the next *département* south, but this would seem amply explained by the men's long absences. (Léonard Nadaud and his wife had only three children, with a gap of three years between Magdelaine and Martin and then nine years between Martin and Françoise. From the local Birth Registers, it does not appear that they had any other child born and dying in infancy during those years.) It would seem that when a baby did arrive in the Creuse it was usually valued, as the infant mortality rate too was significantly lower than the national average.

I have mentioned already that, because of the long periods husbands and wives spent apart, literacy rates in both sexes were higher by the mid-century in the Creuse than elsewhere. Naturally this new literacy was feared by the traditional rural upper classes as being a vehicle for new (read 'dangerous') ideas. Nadaud remarks in his Memoirs that when, towards the end of the 1830s, young masons who had been through the new schools set up under the Guizot Law began coming to Paris, they bought newspapers, and conversations in the lodgings and drink shops became more interesting. Meanwhile, country clergy, already insecure from decades of Revolution and counter-Revolution, muttered about 'de-christianisation'. The spectre of Red republicanism stalked. The fact is, however (though Nadaud may have interpreted it differently with the hindsight of a Member of Parliament), the Creusois developed their own sort of pragmatic republicanism that probably owed more to long-standing local traditions than it did to urban socialism. As the century continued, religio-pagan festivals were given further dimensions of meaning, as when (for example) an unpopular royalist mayor was guyed in the form of the Bad Devil. But the independent small-holders of those central regions were never going to be the stuff from which ideological movements are created – a fact with which Nadaud himself never entirely came to terms.

It was apparently in the rue de la Chaussée d'Antin that he first encountered what was to be his life's faith. On that same street was living General Lafayette, who long ago had been the darling of American independence. He was by then old but he had been a popular hero in 1830 and was chief of the National Guard, the citizen militia that at various times in the nineteenth century acted as a counterweight both to dictatorship and to mob rule. Some of his NCOs used to come and eat in the *gargote* the masons used; old soldiers of Napoleon, they told tales of battles and attacked Louis-Philippe and royalism in general. One or two of them even remembered the January day in 1793 when Louis XVI had been guillotined near by, on the open space that later became the place de la Concorde.

'This was the first time I heard talk of republicanism – and as the speakers spoke with fire, we [Nadaud and a new friend, Luquet] became followers of this great and noble cause, to which we later devoted our whole lives.'

During the mid-1830s Nadaud and Luquet formed the habit of making off, when work was suspended on wet days, or in winter seasons when work was slack, to sit in on trials at the Palais de Justice. It was there that Nadaud first saw Isaac Adolphe Cremieux, the liberal lawyer and republican, and was fired by his example with ambitions to oratory. Of the two young men, Luquet, whom Nadaud elsewhere refers to as 'the founder of the Republican Party among the workers of the Creuse', was the more trouble-prone. He was arrested while building a barricade during the uprising of '32 and again in '34, when he spent three months in Sainte-Pélagie, a prison that Nadaud was also to know. Later again, when trying to steal a mould to make bullets, he was chased by the police and had to escape over rooftops and leave Paris. He was one of Nadaud's supporters in 1848. In 1852 he saw him off on the road into exile, and 'we were never to see one another again. He died in Vaugirard [then a village on the edge of Paris] in the arms of a woman who was unworthy of him, having married at a late age.'

Evidently there is, there, a whole other story to tell.

· 5 ·

Life on the Buildings

Apart from the endemic risk of slump and unemployment – pawning your only respectable clothes, staying in bed so as not to get too hungry – two particular dangers haunted the lives of the masons and their families. One was the risk of a disabling or fatal accident, in a time long before employers' insurance, subsidised medical schemes or pensions, and when building sites were organised by labourers themselves unhindered by any safety regulations. The other was the risk that a promising youngster, just becoming a skilled workman, would 'fall' to the military lottery.

From the days of Napoleon till almost the end of the twentieth century, France maintained obligatory military service for young men, but, till 1870, this depended on the drawing of lots. Except in time of war, only about a fifth of those called up at the age of twenty were actually required to serve. In theory, the lottery was an impartial system; in practice, however, families could pay a substitute to take their son's place – if they could afford to do so. Prudent fathers of the commercial classes set money aside in case the need should arise. Sometimes in the countryside a group of neighbours would band together, all contributing collectively to a mutual insurance scheme for their sons. This meant that one way or another the conscripts who actually served were mostly from the poorest classes. Really needy families with many sons might find 'selling' a boy as a substitute to a wealthier neighbour a useful resource, but for a respectable peasant or labouring family to have an only son spirited away by the army could be a disaster. The length of service varied with the decades, but in the 1830s it was a full seven years; a young man who was away for so long had to be reckoned lost to the occupation for which he had been destined. His manual skills as a mason, metal-worker, weaver or whatever he had been trained in, would have wasted from lack of practice. Psychologically, too, the roving life of a soldier would have claimed him, in an era when military service was deliberately conceived by the authorities as a crucible in which men from disparate areas, cultures and language groups made common cause and became proper French citizens. The family, of course, never received any recompense.

It so happened that both accident and the military lottery almost ruined Martin Nadaud's prospects, but the one, as it turned out, became the escape-route from the other. Had he been forced to abandon the tools of his trade to follow the flag in the mid-1830s, it is curious to reflect on the alternative life he might have led. With his intelligence, his courage, his romantic taste for action and his literacy, he would surely have risen to a position of responsibility but, given his political leanings, he would surely too have gone over to the side of the insurgents in 1848. If he had avoided a hero's death then, he would probably have had to escape beyond France's borders and would have found himself in exile just the same – the identical destination arrived at by a different route.

The Nadauds did not go home in the autumn of 1830: there could be no question of doing so with all the money gone. They worked on in Paris through a particularly cold winter, fingers frozen and cracked with mortar-dust. Martin Nadaud was hod-carrying for a master mason called François Thaury, who did not spare himself or the boys under him either. (He was one of those who earned a good deal of money eventually, but retained into old age the outlook of a day-labourer.) Then, the following spring and summer, the boy was back in the rue de la Chaussée d'Antin, working for 'the worst-tempered, most bitter man I have ever met in my life'. One day, irritated because a scaffolding pole was not produced instantly, this man chucked a small stone at his boy. Angry now himself, Nadaud lunged to seize a pole he could see across the hole in the building left for the stairs – 'but unhappily I got the end of it between my legs and fell from the third floor into the basement.

'The cry went up: a boy has fallen! It was for the first down the ladders to come and pick me up. A man called Michel Dizier leapt from the ground floor into the basement and tried to lift me. I was already covered in blood [from head wounds] and both arms were broken. In this state I was carried up and laid on the flat place where the plaster was mixed . . . In an instant, everyone had stopped work to come over to me, and all found it a miracle that, falling from such a height, I hadn't been killed on the spot.'

Taken back to the *garni* in a cab, he fainted with pain and finally a stretcher was procured, but he still had to be got up four flights of narrow stairs on his feet. His father was summoned from the different site where he was working, also a doctor used to attending to such injuries. Should he or shouldn't he go to hospital? '"He shan't go there," declared my father, "even if I have to spend my last penny."'

Nadaud did stay in the *garni* and this was when he was cared for by Rose Champesne. Evidently the decision was the right one: the doctor came each day to re-dress the splints on the boy's arms, and gangrene, the killer that often followed such accidents, was kept at bay. Gradually Nadaud got better, and after three months he was able to do light work again, watched over by his old task-master Thaury, who proved extremely kind. In illness and misfortune the solidarity between masons was their great, indeed their only, protection. In time the boy recovered fully, though ever after there was a slight weakness in his right wrist, which was the more seriously injured. He used to brace it at moments with his other hand, which amused his work-mates. Nadaud does not say so in his Memoirs, but in a letter he wrote many years later from England he mentions being left-handed. So he was doubly fortunate in his narrow escape – to avoid not only death but also lasting damage to the arm that, to him, was the more important.

He must have been a healthy boy. This was to protect him again the following spring (1832) when the cholera epidemic broke out in Paris. His father and many of the other men from the Hôtel de Ville quarter decided to retreat to the country, but he was growing up now and declined to go with them. Further works were being undertaken just then on the Tuileries Palace, for Louis-Philippe – it was to disappear finally in 1871, fired by the Communards. Nadaud worked on the site for months 'doing more or less what I wanted. What was mainly asked of me was to have a shovel in my hand, especially when the inspectors from Fontaine, the architect, came by.' One day the king, too, visited the site, to view a planned bathroom. 'What struck me about him was his straightforward, ordinary manner and the large watch-chain he wore across his white waistcoat.' This was Louis-Philippe in his role as middle-class, constitutional monarch with his trade-mark umbrella.

On this easy job, Nadaud gradually got back the strength in his arms. He did not get cholera either, though he saw several work-mates die: in all, nearly twenty thousand people in the city perished – 'Paris was lugubrious. At one point people were convinced the water fountains were being poisoned, but others claimed the awful sickness was in the air. Those you saw about in the streets held handkerchiefs to their mouths and were hurrying, hoping to escape the plague.'

These two opposing theories of the genesis of cholera were to compete with one another for some time to come, both in England and in France. (The older theory that it was God's punishment for sin, especially working-class sin, still had some proponents but was losing ground.) It was to be seventeen years before John Snow famously removed the handle from the Broad Street pump in Soho and so demonstrated by the drop in cases that followed that cholera was water-borne. However, the 'miasmic' or poisoned air belief did create a general concern about unhealthy living conditions: in Paris as well as London the concept of slum-clearance was born. But whereas in London a sanitary commission under Edwin Chadwick eventually came to the conclusion that a comprehensive drainage system was what mattered, in Paris the preoccupation was with street-widening. It is sometimes supposed that this was a military, essentially right-wing initiative, but it was a left-wing idealist called Perreymond who, after the cholera, first proposed the drastic solution of demolishing completely the districts of the Ile de la Cité, the Ile Saint-Louis and a great swathe of little streets on the left bank. One may be thankful that only the first of these plans was eventually carried out.

Typically, plagues such as cholera were believed to have been brought by strangers from elsewhere. Also, the middle classes felt threatened by the squalor of working-class life, and thus cholera was generally connected with those other feared contagions, immorality, irreligion and dangerously radical ideas. All these elements were present in the attitude of rural France to the epidemic in Paris, though cholera had always existed in the countryside too. Cholera was seen as the embodiment of the Wicked City, and in central France there was much alarmed middle-class talk of the itinerant masons carrying it home with them (like republicanism and fancy clothes) and contaminating decent country folk. However, an inquiry instituted by the *Gazette Médicale* at the end of the year revealed the true pattern:

'There was some contamination in Seine-et-Oise, the Loiret and the Loire-et-Cher and even, at the last gasp, in the Indre. Essentially, from the gates of Paris onwards, men were seen to collapse by the roadside ... Some, who had taken the coach, only succumbed beyond Blois, in the region of Châteauroux. In the end none brought the cholera into the Creuse. The carriers of the sickness had all died on the way.'

There was, after all, something to be said for travelling at foot-pace. Quicker journeys would have produced a different story. The plight of the men who died on their feet of excruciating stomach cramps and uncontrollable diarrhoea, impelled onwards by a mental vision of their beloved home village, hardly bears contemplating. They must have needed all their well-known stoicism.

A couple of years later, in 1834, Nadaud had another accident, more minor, but which affected his left arm again and upset everyone. This time his emotional father lost his temper: 'If I go up to see him, I'll strangle him. If he's going to kill himself, why doesn't he do it, once and for all and be done with it. He's reckless and he doesn't listen.' Once upstairs, he glared at his son in silence and then left. Nadaud, deeply pained and equally emotional in his way, demanded to be taken to hospital, and was – after a heated argument with Rose.

This hospital was the notorious Hôtel Dieu. Originally founded in 660, for nearly twelve hundred years it had been caring without charge for all who presented themselves – but had killed a great many of them with hospital infections. The huge building by the same name that today occupies a substantial chunk of the Ile de la Cité is the one planned under the Haussmann rebuilding of the Ile and constructed in the 1870s. In Nadaud's youth a medieval building was still in use. It stood on a cramped site between the square in front of Notre Dame and the Seine, with the river at that point acting as a general sewer for it. A covered wooden bridge led over the water to the little church of St Julian le Pauvre on the left bank (today the home of the Russian Orthodox church) which served as its mortuary chapel. It was much in use.

However, Nadaud, true to form, found a nursing sister who 'seeing that I was very down, welcomed me with gentle and kind words. I was undressed and put to bed ... I was given every possible care and I slept all through the night.' Meanwhile, Léonard had been scolded by Rose and cold-shouldered by other men in the *garni*, and arrived the following day in penitent mood to see his son – 'I was perhaps the only one who understood that his fury had come from the strength of his love rather than from any other cause.' The quarrel was made up. The arm was not broken this time, merely swollen – possibly dislocated – and within a few weeks Nadaud was fit to work again. Probably the most significant memory of the episode for him was that, while in the Hôtel Dieu, he was several times taken across the wooden bridge to the old church – 'there, I had to make my confession to a priest, a middle-aged man, who did not give me bad advice at all'. What was that advice, one wonders, and on what subject?

Nadaud's Memoirs contain passages about priests imposing on superstitious villagers that are in the central tradition of anti-clerical republicanism. However, by temperament and upbringing he was far more inclined to respect a figure of authority than to view him with cynicism: this strain ran throughout his life. Many years later, when he re-encountered organised religion in the form of the Church of England, its orderly and pragmatic spirit appealed to him. Protestantism had previously been quite strong in the Creuse: Huguenot Flemish weavers had settled there in the fifteenth century, Nadaud would have been aware of their reputation for integrity – for 'protesting', indeed, against an entrenched and corrupt order. Like many of his fellows, including François Michaud the sculptor of strange beasts, he was not so much an unbeliever as an unofficial believer – pantheistic, progressivist, faithful to a concept of the essential good of mankind.

In Nadaud's twentieth year, the two accidents proved to have been a blessing in disguise. He and his father, having been through good times and bad times, were just reckoning that together they would soon manage to save money to pay off their burden of debt. Then, in the middle of the summer, word came from Nadaud's mother that she had 'drawn a bad number' for him. When a young man was away from his native locality, his father normally drew the military lot for him; if the father were absent too then the mother did it. Poor Marie Nadaud had drawn a six, a number so low that it would inevitably result in their son's departure into the army – unless a doctor could be induced to take the view that he was unfit. Léonard Nadaud had never been able to afford to join an insurance scheme, and the thought of increasing their debts still further by paying outright for a substitute was one they dared not consider. Martin Nadaud was to present himself before the military authorities in Bourganeuf.

As ever, other masons from the Pontarion area rallied round. Money was lent for the boy to return quickly to the Creuse by coach. Before leaving, he armed himself with a letter from the Paris doctor who had set his broken arms. At home, his mother had remembered a cousin of hers who had worked all his life for the local doctor who was a member of the Army Board. So, the wheels turned. A long tramp was undertaken to see this doctor in Guéret.

'Monsieur Cressant had me take my jacket off. He examined my healed fractures with care, particularly the one on the left, without saying a word to me. Then he moved onto another subject of conversation, recommending us to have a good dinner. So we took the road back to Pontarion, quite satisfied with the way the doctor had received us.

'On the day of the Army Board I hardly recognised my doctor, all dressed up as he was with gold braid. I held out my other doctor's certificate to him and he took hold of my right arm. I barely even heard the word "Unsuitable" [*impropre*]. I was so happy I rushed out still half dressed to my mother, who was waiting for me on the stairs. Naturally she was happy, for she knew that I was to be the saving of our poor family.'

I have traced this occasion in the large, tattered stack of papers that make up the army archives for the Creuse in the year 1835. Martin Nadaud's lottery number was indeed six, he is marked 'exempted' and there is a reference to his having broken both wrists. However, there is also a mention of his being absent in Paris and having asked to pass before an Army Board there.

Is there more invention in his account than one would suppose? Or did he, in fact, make a request to be seen in Paris and then decide that he would have a better chance of getting off in the Creuse? The men who made up the local Board in Bourganeuf do seem to have been liberal with their exemptions. More than half the young men who were called on to present themselves were found 'unsuitable' for one reason or another. Sometimes the prospective soldier is let off as 'the only son of a widow' or as the brother of a man already serving, but large numbers are listed as 'feeble in constitution' or 'feeble in complexion', as having flat feet, varicose veins, weak stomach, chronic malaria, or simply as 'too short'. It is hard to imagine that many of these immensely tough and muscular, if small, men would not have coped with military life just as well as they did with heavy manual labour behind a plough or on a building site. Presumably local doctors, mayors and retired army officers in country areas took a relaxed and benevolent view of their duties.

Martin Nadaud's return for the Army Board was not his first reappearance in the Creuse. Because of bad times in the trade and the further debts brought about by his first and worst accident, he had stayed in Paris without a break for three full campaigns and the two winters in between. But by the winter of 1832–3 '*la maladie du pays me gagna*' – a phrase which translates, with a different nuance, as 'homesick'. In England, it is the personal home that is said to tug at the heart-strings. In France, it is the native territory, its earth, its vegetation, its accents and customs, that are quintessentially missed.

Before leaving Paris, Nadaud went with a good friend from home, Jean Roby, who lived in the same *garni*, to buy a set of clothes in the Temple market. 'At that time all the materials that our new manufactories were beginning to produce were introducing the idea of fashion into the minds of working people. Before, we had never known anything but the felted cloth that made us move heavily and clumsily . . . Now we wanted to be seen as well-brought-up young men, tastefully arrayed.'

A rather different view of this aspiration was taken by

some of the local Creusois middle and upper classes, as this passage (from later in the century) shows: 'Back they come, dressed up in the costumes of the bourgeoisie in which they shiver in winter, garments against which they have exchanged with some old clothes dealer their solid outfits of country wool' (Le Comte du Authier). Of course what was really being objected to was the 'propaganda of Freemasons and free-thinkers' that might have been picked up along with the new clothes. The supposedly educated middle classes, who had never moved far from a small town like Bourganeuf, felt threatened when confronted by masons who might still be illiterate but whose journeys had exposed them to a far wider world. A similar tension sometimes informed a mason's own attitudes, strung out as he was between town and country. Nadaud admits that his own view had become ambivalent: 'You have odd thoughts about your own countryside when you hear people running it down . . . [In Paris] we did not like to be taken for Limousins . . . We tried to alter the way we spoke. To talk affectedly, without our natural accent, seemed to us the height of distinction.' Yet once back on home soil – 'everything changes, you find your own people again and, as you hug one another, the sense of hostility and scorn changes to passionate joy.'

A similar ambivalence about the city afflicted those who had been left at home. They wanted to get their menfolk back unchanged; fancy city ways were not welcome, yet – 'Everyone wants to know what he has done and seen and what he thinks. His slightest word is listened to with goodwill.' So much extra respect was accorded to a man returning from work in the town that even when not forced to go by their family's economic situation, some men chose the migrant life anyway to boost their local esteem. Thus a double wariness underlies the joke played by Nadaud and another friend when they got back to Pontarion. The two young men went into the inn that had been the meeting-point for the journey to Paris three years earlier, and pretended to be Parisian gentlemen. They were unrecognised, even by the innkeeper's wife who was the other boy's godmother. She served them politely, but then went round removing the keys from the drink cupboards, since with strangers from the town you never knew ... Not till they spoke to her in *patois* did she realise she was looking at boys she had known all their lives.

When Nadaud finally got back, in good spirits, to La Martinèche, his mother too found that in place of the child she had kissed goodbye a strange man had returned:

'"How you've grown! My poor boy, I was so afraid that after you fell from that great height I'd never see you again."'

New Parisian clothes or not, she reasserted her authority by having ready for him a fresh suit of country wool – 'The tailor made it to the measure of Michel Vergnaud, who's a year older than you.' Then she asked him if he would give her for safe-keeping the bag of savings she confidently assumed his long absence in Paris would at least have filled. So, the awful revelation had to come: any savings that the boy had so far been able to make had been spent at the time of the accident and the months off work that had followed.

'She burst into tears then. Still weeping, she told me what trouble we were in.' There had been the Villemomble business that had ended in heavy debts – 'and, as well, the harvest had been bad, we didn't have enough corn to last till the following summer, the cows had no more milk, she hardly knew where to turn to make the daily meals – "And another thing: your sister Magdelaine is twenty now; she's been asked for in marriage and we must make up some sort of little dowry for her." I listened to all this in silence, but my heart was very sore.'

When she recounted this conversation to Léonard Nadaud, who was already in the country, his son heard him say: 'I was waiting for this. Above all, don't reproach him. He's a good lad, he has a lot of heart, but he's sensitive and at the same time gets into states [*en même temps vif et emporté*]. You must work through his feelings, make him feel again that this is his home and I don't think he'll let us down.' One senses in this thoughtful remark all the pregnant fear of the rural world that the city will take their children from them. Two generations later, when the trickle to the cities had become a flood and the migrant worker had insidiously become the skilled man who goes away with his wife to found a home elsewhere, Daniel Halévy was to write in *Visites aux Paysans du Centre*: '[Some] come home on a visit. They are welcomed, fussed over; it is keenly desired that they should go on loving this corner of the earth that has nurtured them. But they don't care for it any longer – or care only a little . . . They do not take pleasure in seeing the countryside again so much as in being seen, in showing the town ways they have acquired.'

The family closed ranks. The father asked his son to help with the wheat-threshing, a tiring task but one which, in the circumstances, was undertaken with relief. Soon the winter round of *veillées* and parties began. At a dance in a remote village called Vidaillat Nadaud's new, tight trousers, with a strap beneath the foot, let him down by splitting in several places. Fortunately a handsome smock with a tricolour belt ('very fashionable at the time') covered the damage. The returned masons went from village to village by torchlight, finding childhood friends they had not seen for several years. Round fireplaces the older generation compared notes, asking one another what so-and-so had said about his campaign, calculating what money he might have saved – 'But where the migrant figures most importantly is with the women, especially the unmarried girls. A mother praises a certain young man of an evening; her view influences the father and then, if the aspiring young man is well dressed with a nicely tied cravat, the young daughter readily falls in love with him.

'Four or five weeks after these preliminaries, the marriage has generally taken place. It is as if an external pressure forces the pace, for the month of March drives us away again from our villages. Paris and other towns call us to build their houses. This is why an agreement to marry that is not brought to a satisfactory conclusion in January or February has to be put off till the following winter.'

That winter, indeed, Magdelaine Nadaud was married off to Louis Soumis (or Soumy), after a certain amount of hectic bargaining over the money that she was to bring and after Léonard Nadaud, grieving when alone with his son, had to borrow yet again to cover the expense. Martin Nadaud put his own name to a promissory note, even though at seventeen he was legally under age. Contrary to what modern thinking might predict, the marriage turned out a long and happy one. Soumis was the best of sons-in-law, help and *confidant*, and it is in his hand that most of the surviving letters from Léonard Nadaud to his son are written. For by the time Léonard was old that son was far away in another country, and even had he been in Paris he would not have remained physically close to his father as Soumis did. By a familiar irony, Martin Nadaud's success in life was to separate him from the very people to whom that success was a matter of such pride.

'Three or four days after the marriage, I borrowed 60 francs from one of my uncles . . . I gave 20 to my father and, with the rest, I disappeared again to Paris to begin a new campaign.'

The texture of Nadaud's Memoirs of these early Parisian years is so closely woven, so full of colour and detail, that you feel an entire life is being put before you. It is only after several readings that problems become apparent. For one thing, although the account has a chronological framework, in practice, as the 1830s go by and give way to the 1840s, the author moves backwards and forwards in time so that it is not always easy to work out exactly when a given development occurred in his life in relation to other events. The French use of the historic present, also, casts a dateless glow over many descriptions. In addition, when he does place two events in conjunction, other sources of information sometimes reveal that his time-scheme is faulty. Is this simply because, writing as an old man sixty years later, he got some details wrong? Or is it that to make the story more dramatic or perhaps more morally effective, he deliberately conflated certain things and obfuscated others? It wasn't that he was always concerned to present himself in a good light: he mentions discreditable incidents, like the Bayle business in childhood and others in young manhood, of which he was not proud. The tendency to write only of the more satisfactory and anodyne aspects of his life, which makes the later part of his Memoirs so unreliable, is not at all apparent in the early days. And after all, though it is clearly his own story he is telling, it is ostensibly that of 'Léonard': no implied contract with the reader has bound him to tell the whole truth and nothing but the truth. To expurgate details that might seem untypical, redundant or merely confusing would be quite in order.

Yet in presenting himself as typical Nadaud has created a problem for himself which gradually begins to surface. For the typical mason of the 1830s was not, to start with, literate, nor did he go on to educate himself further, nor did he become known to the politically minded bourgeoisie, still less was he elected to Parliament. Nadaud was not a writer by vocation but, rather, a teacher and orator, and I do not think he ever quite confronted this conflict of purpose at the heart of his Memoirs. On the one hand he wanted to show what his life had been like as a man among many others, working, hoping, saving, getting into fights, marrying, settling down. But on the other hand he also wanted to show, in the classic way of a self-made man, how his early struggles gradually led him into new worlds and into a position of power and influence to which an ordinary young man would not even have aspired.

This contradiction in intentions leads to a disconcerting unevenness of style and tone. The experiences of the ordinary young man are recounted with the limpid clarity of things enshrined in a past life – 'I seem to see, even as if standing before me now, some of the workmen and master masons of that marvellous time.' But even the early days of his life as a political figure, when he was still working on building sites, are not depicted with anything like the same sense of vivid reality. One reads: 'I began to go to such-and-such a café – this or that organisation' – but not what these places were actually like. Nadaud has let us see the inside of a farmhouse, a workmen's tavern, a squalid lodging, but he never shows us the inside of the Palais Bourbon where he sat for years as a representative. He does not even take us into a republican meeting in someone's house. We hear: 'I met So-and-So, or Such-and-Such – or X (whom I had already met) was kind enough to say to me –' but they remain names. Even Louis Blanc, one of Nadaud's closest allies, who was to be a good friend to him throughout his years in England and whose house he often visited, is not described so as to become real to the reader, not as the fellow masons are.

I think there are several reasons for this arbitrary curtailment of descriptive power once his career as a republican is under way, but one is his shifting viewpoint. In later life, he moved so far, geographically and then socially, from the scenes and experiences of his obscure youth, that those memories remained safe, uncontaminated by later perceptions. In contrast, he viewed his public and political life, even its beginnings, with a hindsight that affected many recollections and is, as well, shrouded in caution and in things not fully admitted even to himself.

There were different strands in Nadaud's life, even from quite early in his Paris days, which at first are entwined but gradually separate. There is the labourer sharing the lot of other labourers while at the same time trying to work his way up to becoming a master mason and perhaps even – one day – an entrepreneur, the sum of his ambitions for the moment. There is the tough boy joining the confrontational culture of men alone in the city. There is the good son obsessed with the need to clear the family debt. There is also the youngster who goes to evening classes initially to acquire further skills in draughtsmanship and accountancy, but who by and by is fired with the idea of self-improvement for its own sake. There is the young man, by now slightly better equipped, who starts passing on his literacy to others and who discovers in this way his own talents for teaching and speaking. And through all these runs the thread of nascent political awareness, the Nadaud of the future.

It is obvious that his experiences in and around building sites shaped ideas that were to be with him for life. He developed an abiding interest in justice for workers, in trade unionism (illegal in France in one way or another for long periods of the nineteenth century), in working conditions, in pensions, in the abolition of the *livret* – the much-disliked workers' police papers without which a mason could not move about freely, and which could keep him bound to an employer who refused to give them back. The concern Nadaud showed, his life long, for the conditions of working-class existence, for the destitute, for unprotected women and children, clearly had its roots in what he had seen at first hand when young. In the same way, in the aggressive young mason settling a score with an unpleasant work-mate or challenging some cocky Parisian, one may see the combative electioneering figure of later years 'with the broad shoulders and neck of an old fighter'.

Nevertheless, my impression is not so much of coherent evolution as of a man who by and by came to lead several different, encapsulated lives at the same time. Most masons already led two lives, their Parisian one and their one rooted in the *pays*, let alone any other hidden worlds in which they might be venturing: Nadaud was simply extending this pattern. In contradiction with the apparent frankness of the early chapters of the Memoirs, after a certain stage his domestic world becomes private and almost disappears from view. It is as if the habit of keeping the various dimensions of his life in different compartments grew on him only gradually, perhaps as a way of coping with the varying social roles he felt called upon to perform, but then became a fixed attitude, almost an obsession. For the real Nadaud of the later years one has to look elsewhere than in his published writings.

It was bad luck on the Nadauds that they were struggling with their burden of debt in 1833–4, just when France was undergoing the worst slump in the building trade for many

years. Each day, on the place de la Grève, groups of
unemployed masons stood about 'shivering with cold under
thin smocks or threadbare jackets, stomping their feet on the
stones to try to warm themselves.

'When, about nine in the morning, they left this place of
desolation and poverty, some used to make their way to the
army barracks to get a few spoons of soup thanks to the
generosity of the soldiers . . . But most went back to the
garni. They were far from being the worst off and I soon
found myself among them. We, after all, could usually get
bread on the slate at the baker's and the landlady gave us
credit.' One understands the extreme importance, for a
worker, of keeping up a reputation for sobriety and prompt
repayment in prosperous times so that, in bad periods,
friends might help out. Even when a man did find a job, he
had to work for a week till he could touch a sou, for the
advance on wages from an employer that became commonplace much later in the century was then, says Nadaud, an
unknown practice. He was particularly grateful to a master
mason who, providing him and another youngster with
work, also gave them a hand-out to tide them over. Later,
when he himself was hiring a boy on the Grève to mix mortar
for him, he realised that he had to give the teenager money to
eat before he was fit to work. A Parisian doctor of the period
remarked: 'For a working man, to live is simply not to die.' It
was a disparaging outsider's view of existences that were in
reality more complex, but it was sometimes almost true.

The high hopes with which the masons had initially
greeted Louis-Philippe, and his intention to complete the
Napoleonic plans for Paris, were dashed. Rules about
workers banding together in unions were tightened again,
strikes were illegal and punishable by prison, morale was
low:

'No, there is no torment like it, no distress harder for the
workman than the one he feels during acute crises such as
these. He goes out in the morning in search of work; in the
evening he comes in again, having trudged the city streets
from end to end, talked to master masons, bought drinks for

Peter and Paul – his pockets are empty and he is exhausted. He feels that the next day is going to be just the same. His anxiety, far from abating, gets worse and worse because he has no way of telling how long the spell of bad luck is going to last.'

Here is the desperation of the jobless in every era. Nadaud had had three weeks of it when his father returned from the country. Finding his son sad and demoralised, Léonard managed to get work for both of them together. In this way, though nominally back to hod-carrying, Martin Nadaud was able to learn from his father and perfect his skills as a plasterer for a new job of his own. All went well for a bit, but it was round about this time that Nadaud had his second accident, with another period of enforced idleness – 'I saw the year 1834 trickle away, without having anything put by.' The scarcity of good jobs forced him to seek work one and a half hours on foot from his lodging, out on the fortifications and the quarries on the edge of Paris, the rough zone of disorderly wine shops and shanties built by the wretchedly poor. (Ten years later, when a new wall had been built right round Paris, taking in both recently risen suburbs and rural villages, the *zone*, as it is always called, military fashion, simply displaced itself, with its drink shops, prostitution, etc., further out.) On one of these far-off jobs Nadaud had to take poorly paid work driving the cart carrying stones to the new site, and felt that his ambition to become a skilled man was getting nowhere.

But there were other aspects to life, even in unemployed times: 'Each morning, after a trip to the Grève, we used to come back to the *garni* and pile our beds up to turn our rooms into spaces for boxing or *chausson* [a ritualised kick-boxing, resembling present-day martial arts]. These contact-sports brought us some moments of fun.' Sometimes, too, when they had money, the young masons went to professional gyms – 'So I developed a taste for this kind of exercise and became quite strong.'

References to *chausson* crop up frequently in the Memoirs in these years, though Léonard Nadaud disapproved. In

France at that period, athletic sports had absolutely none of the social cachet of 'manliness' they were beginning to acquire on the other side of the Channel. But as a general mental and physical discipline and source for self-esteem, boxing and related skills have been a route out of the ghetto in many cultures and periods, and the Creusois in Paris were perceived as members of an ethnic out-group. Nadaud himself linked the cult of physical force among his kind with their need to stand up for themselves and 'teach a lesson with our fists to those who despised the chestnut eaters of the Limousin and Creuse'. But at other moments he seems undecided as to whether 'backing up right with might' was a moral occupation or whether these endemic hostilities were a sad reflection on the lack of working-class solidarity then and on the lack of other occupations for these uneducated men. 'We followed one another around in groups. At the smallest gesture, the slightest word, we resorted to our fists.

'The police did not often intervene. But it did happen once or twice that I got picked up and spent the night at the police station. I admit that I did then feel much ashamed of myself' – though his shame seems to have been mainly on account of finding himself in the company of the dregs of Parisian night life, who made scenes and vomited on the police station floor.

More serious was an occasion when he was chosen by his mates to settle the score with a Parisian labourer who had (like Bayle) provoked them by peeing at them. Kicks and punches were exchanged in *chausson* style in the middle of a circle that grew and grew; the police appeared. Nadaud and his adversary were taken into custody, where fortunately 'My foreman did not leave me for long. He came to get me out and spoke up for me before the magistrate.' This did not prevent him from getting into a fight later on another site, with a carpenter who was rude to him. Nadaud pushed a handful of wet plaster into the man's face, and both of them were sacked.

His comment on all this, made with a lifetime's hindsight, does not ring entirely true: 'Today, after the great transformation that has occurred in our social behaviour [*nos moeurs*] one can say, with the famous English statesman Gladstone, that our century really has been that of the working man.' Certainly Gladstone was exactly the sort of humane, reforming, bourgeois liberal who came later in life to appeal to Nadaud, representing everything that he found congenial in England. But there is still an insistent counter-suggestion that these youthful fights had something to do with Rights, that very French preoccupation, and that they were a preparation for the republican demonstrations on the barricades that were to come.

Nadaud's worst scrape, described by him as 'the most reprehensible and culpable of my life', occurred soon after and had nothing to do with Rights or yet honour (his other preoccupation). He and a master mason, delicately referred to only as 'F.', found some old iron on a site and made plans to take it off and sell it in the rue de la Mortellerie. At the same time they got drunk on wine someone had also 'found' in a cellar. The evening ended with supper in a restaurant, with women primly described by Nadaud as 'frivolous and of light morals'. The next morning he was hung over, and so full of remorse that he confided in his father and the other senior mason, Thaury. 'As they listened to me, their faces changed and my father became pale with fury and began to tremble: "*Malheureux*, what have you done? Tomorrow, first thing, you make sure you fetch your tools away."' (That is, leave the job).

'It was lucky I did. F. was almost immediately picked up for theft. He was given a two-year sentence and he died in prison. As F. was almost a neighbour of ours, and as all our work-mates knew him to be good-hearted, friendly and obliging, his humiliating end distressed us, even if it was deserved. Besides, he belonged to a very decent peasant family.

'Just to add to it, he was married to a very nice type of girl [*une jeune femme de conduite exemplaire*]. She is still alive today [Nadaud was writing in the 1890s], well-esteemed in the village where her honourable old age has been spent.'

One cannot help contemplating the bleakness of a life in

which a retreat into an honourable background role was forced on her so young, with little to remember her husband by but his disgrace and his lonely death far away.

This obscure tragedy, which would have been long wiped from history and from human memory were it not for Nadaud's passing mention, underlines the sheer fragility of life then, even among the young, the strong and the happy. Their flowering was often brief. An unlucky fall, a temptation to stupidity, an infectious disease, slack times in the trade, a failed harvest, a burnt-down barn, a low number in the military lottery – any of these blows could blight or destroy a life for ever, for there were few second chances. The modern perception that life lasts a long time, and that a run of bad luck may reasonably be counterbalanced by a better period at another time, was largely alien to our ancestors' experience. In living such a long and varied life, in the course of which he was to pass through several different identities, Nadaud was an exception, a harbinger of a world that was still to come.

Although he does not date this perilous episode with F., it seems to me likely that it was one of a series of events that finally provoked a confrontation he actually describes earlier. He was cornered by François Thaury, Jean Roby, with whom he had bought his second-hand trousers, and another master mason called Giroudon the Lyonnais, the man who had advanced him money on his wages. Léonard Nadaud, who had become sick of giving good advice that was not followed (not, one feels, that he would necessarily have followed it himself), had asked these three men to give his son a talking-to.

'They were fond of me, because I liked to be with them. They called me into Bertuzi's wine shop near our *garni* . . . The remarks that followed were fairly sharp, particularly from François Thaury, but showed a true concern for me. I listened to them with my nerves on edge, and told myself inwardly that I was worth more than they believed. They accused me of hanging around boxing saloons and getting into fights about nothing, but their most serious charge was that I got mixed up in the street demonstrations that were happening a lot then and that I talked too much about republicanism.'

We have not, till now, been told much about what Nadaud got up to in that area of life. Only considerably later in the account do we hear he was present in 1831 when a mob sacked the Archbishop of Paris's palace, and that when he got back to the lodging his father was so annoyed that he hit him. However, he has already mentioned at that point what was clearly, for him, a very significant moment, and one that sprung directly from the fact that he could read when most men could not. 'Newspapers were by then being sold in the streets. Each morning in the wine shop people would ask me to read aloud to them Cabet's *Populaire*.'

A medical student who sometimes came to that shop complimented Nadaud on his energetic delivery. Understanding that he had republican leanings, he asked him, along with the ill-fated Laurence Luquet, if he would like to join the Society for the Rights of Man.

'This was the first time an educated man shook me by the hand and I was very flattered.' This comment, made so long afterwards, is revealing both of the social gulf between classes that was then taken as a matter of course, and of Nadaud's own nervous awareness, which never seemed to leave him, of how far he had come.

The Society for the Rights of Man was a prominent republican association. It was then much involved in supporting those workers who, in a long-drawn-out trial that lasted through 1834, were being arraigned for strikes and riots in Lyon in 1831–2. One often has the feeling that decent compromise, the *monarchie bourgeoise* that Louis-Philippe was initially trying to incarnate, might really have been more to Nadaud's natural taste than revolutionism. However, under a reign that still gave the vote to only five Frenchmen in every thousand – less than one sixth of those enfranchised in England under the 1832 Reform Bill – it was inevitable that the energetic and voteless such as Nadaud should be driven into a radical stance.

He says that from then on he used to meet up once a week

with others from the Society for the Rights of Man, and that this was something he could not admit to his father's unpolitical friends. But their essential advice – to move out of his present *garni* and to be more selective in his choice of company – was undoubtedly good in wider terms, and he took it. Jean Roby had a room in the rue des Barrès, off the Mortellerie, which he shared with only one other, and he invited Nadaud to join them.

'It was an odd place I came to. It was at ground level and the ceiling was so low that you could hardly walk upright. In this space, which was also used as a sort of store, were mortar-troughs, measuring rods, planks and old iron; let me add that it was hardly ventilated at all and that half the floor tiles had gone missing.

'Today we have regulations about insalubrious lodgings and the police would have a hovel like this condemned. But at the time workmen all over lived in rooms not much different from ours.'

After a few days of this, he persuaded Roby and the other to move – 'So we rented ourselves a really large room, at No. 23 rue Saint-Louis en Ile, on the third floor, at the back of the courtyard.'

This distinct but inconspicuous social shift – from the dormitory to the room shared with two chosen friends, out of the Mortellerie quarter and into the quiet backwater of the once-aristocratic island – was a turning-point in Nadaud's career. For the next fifteen years he was to share quarters with Roby, a man from a landless peasant family who had been sent to Paris very young in Léonard Nadaud's charge. He was, says Martin Nadaud, puny in size, not strong for a builder, but much prized by his friends for his human qualities.

The move to the Ile Saint-Louis was also to be the beginning of Nadaud's further relationship with education. Renouncing street-life (at least to some extent) he began in fits and starts to go to a teacher in the evening, replacing, as he puts it, the 'honour' of street-fighting for Creusois pride with the ambition to succeed in another way. More prosaically, he needed to do something with his evenings other than fight. Later, the happy chance of the large room was to provide the locale for the lessons he himself gave.

I have found this building, for I do not think that the street-numbering there has been changed since. It is one of a pair of high, old stone houses. No. 23 has been done over in the standard style of the late nineteenth century—wrought ironwork, *gaz à tous étages* – but its neighbour has been more authentically restored to its old appearance and an engraved stone is on display: '*1645, maison construite par Gilles de l'Epée, Maître serrurier.*'

With the long hindsight of history, which blurs detail and immediacy and shows only the general view, Nadaud's lifelong conviction that republicanism was synonymous with a high moral tone, Rights and a concern for the welfare of the individual, now seems simplistic. But in the words of an English commentator (Lowes Dickinson) writing towards the end of the century, 'Republicanism . . . meant not merely a machine but an impulse; not merely a form but a spirit . . . It was to be the symbol of fraternity, the pledge of equality, the guarantee of liberty. It was to purify every passion and solve every problem.' Naturally, no mere system of government can in itself fulfil such a dream. However, it is perhaps something of an achievement that in France, by the late twentieth century, to be a republican has simply become a matter of course, a benchmark of sound if uninspiring principles. '*C'est pas républicain, ça*' is now used as a set phrase with which to dismiss more exotic political views.

Nadaud's idealistic conviction was no more unrealistic – in fact, considerably less – than the middle-class conviction of the 1830s and '40s that republicans were dangerous Reds and, by some emotional association between that colour and blood, probably criminals as well. As Nadaud says, when mentioning the first stirrings of bourgeois republicanism in the Creuse (two lawyers in Bourganeuf whom he encountered on his visits home) – 'It needed a certain courage at that time to proclaim yourself republican.' Later, when he himself was standing for election there after the revolution of 1848, some of the minor gentry of Bourganeuf put it about that he was a drunken pimp. Long after, in Paris during the Commune, he was to see his own police dossier from the early 1840s. This included a note from the Préfet of the Creuse (the occupant of the post he himself was to hold in 1870) describing him as a 'dangerous man'. By the '70s, of course, the liberal republicanism of the vanished 1840s was no longer an eccentric stand but a reassuring middle-of-the-road one. The more extreme territory had been taken over by people whom Nadaud himself tended to avoid, with unspoken wariness and some degree of pain over lost fraternity.

6

Country Matters

It took Nadaud a while to find a teacher who really met his needs. Eventually he worked out that, according to his present life plan, it was not the niceties of grammar and parsing he required so much as technical drawing and geometry. Ten years later, when he was elected under the short-lived Second Republic and found himself for the first time having to write letters to people who might sneer at faults, he had to repair the deficiencies of his formal French education with coaching from a medical student. But in the late 1830s he was content to feel he was making general progress and opening new doors.

'I discovered in myself a will-power and capacity for intellectual effort that before I had not realised was there. I also found for the first time that, alone in my room, I could create joys of the spirit for myself which were enough to drive away both worry and the need for other distractions.' However, in developing this new dimension to his life, the specific troubles of his family appeared to him 'in all their poignant reality. I began to see clearly that I would never be able to pay off all the debts out of what I saved as a working man, for we had no less than 500 francs' interest to pay each year.' His perception was surely right, for 500 francs then represented well over half his own average annual earnings. It was not till he became a master mason in the 1840s that his daily rate crept up above 5 francs.

'What could I do? Finally I said to myself that as I was surrounded by decent and hard-working lads who could not even sign their names, it would be easy for me to gather a dozen of them together in my room to teach them what I knew.'

To understand the originality of this thought, one has to run time's reel backwards to a point before the whole edifice of workers' educational movements was constructed. Nadaud had to start from first principles. The idea was well received and he computed, with a nice blend of altruism and materialism: 'I reckoned to charge my pupils 4 francs a month, which would give me the 400 to 500 I needed a year to keep up with our debt. Also, since my own wish to learn was still strong, I said to myself, "Teaching others will be a way of teaching myself too."'

However, he did worry, when he thought about it, as to whether he could stay the course. To get up at five in the morning, walk to work, plaster for the next twelve or thirteen hours, hurry back from the site to his father's lodgings off the Mortellerie where he was currently having his evening *soupe*, then back to the Ile Saint-Louis to devote himself to teaching till eleven at night, then only a few hours of oblivion till dawn came again – would he have the strength to do all this for long?

Roby too had his doubts and warned his friend not to embark on something he would have to abandon. But he generously said that he himself did not mind the room's being filled up each evening with an extra twelve men.

In fact the classes were a success. Nadaud found no shortage of pupils, and remarks that, as adults eager to get on in the world, they were far more highly motivated than the middle-class schoolboys he was later to teach elsewhere. 'From eight until ten or eleven in the evening I did not sit down, I went from one pupil to another round and round the two tables we had ... After a few months men who hadn't even known their letters began to write passably ... Then, each evening, half an hour before the end, we would shut up the books and talk about building works.' He had a series of plans of a house, from cellars to attic, pinned up round the walls. 'Since those days, some of those hard-working young men who went through my hands over the course of ten years have become good master builders, and even wealthy entrepreneurs.'

For ten years, from 1838 till he was caught up in the events of 1848, Nadaud ran his classes. Though the Memoirs covering those years criss-cross back and forth over time and over themes, every so often there is a cheerful reference to an improving financial outlook and diminishing debt. It helped, too, that by the late 1830s and into the '40s, building work had picked up again. Perhaps this is one reason that Nadaud always had something of a soft spot for Louis-Philippe, even though he was among those who rose against him. He once refers to that king as *le roi du bâtiment*, on account of all the profitable embellishments that Paris underwent during his reign. Victor Hugo, more critical, complained, 'Our fathers had a Paris of stone. Our sons will have one of plaster.' Many masons, including Nadaud, were plastering then seven days a week.

'For the first time for several years we were so busy we had peace of mind. Having fewer worries, we did not get so tired physically . . . I still remember how, on the walk home in the evenings, in spite of our weariness we would stop on the quais where there used to be crowds of street-sellers, acrobats, tumblers and card-tricksters who half deafened us with their cries.

'In those days there were many more of these hucksters aiming to extract money from the working man's pocket than there are today. The outlook of the masses was more earthbound; idealism did not really come into it. And the notion of a better life in another world, as promised to them by the priests, had never taken root in their heads.'

This remark amounts to something more than just Nadaud's lifelong anti-clericalism. His wish, which was the main-spring of his existence, was always that the kind of people from whom he himself had sprung should aspire to something better – that a man's destiny should not just seem to him 'unalterable . . . however unfortunate' – though the form in which he conceived these aspirations changed as his own life passed through its different stages.

For three years he had good jobs with one Delavallade, a Creusois who had been educated in Paris and so represented a new breed of men that was then emerging. Delavallade was beginning to undertake work on his own account and took good care of his workmen. He had some houses going up in the rue Neuve du Luxembourg (today rue Cambon), the very street in which the boy John Malcolm Ludlow was then living. So Nadaud was then, unawares, very near his future friend and archetypal encourager of a man's desire to better himself. Later, again thanks to Delavallade, he worked for eighteen months in a responsible overseeing job on the building of a school in the rue de Pontoise on the left bank, earning 150 francs per month. Delavallade's trust was important to Nadaud, who was beginning to be avoided by some entrepreneurs, since his reputation in republican circles was growing and they were afraid he might be a trouble-maker. (Since he took to wearing a red woollen cap on site, or so he says, one can understand why they might have been wary.) He always supposed Delavallade, like most bosses, to be politically on the opposite side from himself; and was surprised and grateful, when he was an exile in London in the 1850s, that Monsieur and Madame Delavallade sought him out as a friend when they came on a visit. (He took them to see Hyde Park.) His life long, Nadaud respected those who managed to make money, in a way that sometimes seems naive, but he had seen too much of the ugliness of poverty at first hand not to appreciate those who made a success of life.

His own savings were gradually growing. On one occasion, which he situates in 1840 but which I suspect occurred rather later, he made a sum of 1,300 francs after doing piecework for an employer and hiring his own labour. 'I was very pleased, and felt I had come into a fortune. But then I began to worry. Where should I hide my hoard? I had no idea about savings banks [these were being introduced in France from the end of the 1830s] and I was sharing the room with my good friend Roby and with Jacques Lafaye of Saint-Hilaire, who were both as innocent as I was.'

Having thought, classically, about putting it in the mattress, the three men eventually hid it in a network of plumb-lines that were hanging up by the ceiling. Apparently the money stayed safe there, but the anxiety was a familiar one among masons, particularly when they had to carry their precious savings back to the *pays*. A Creusois newspaper of 1835 tells a dreadful story of four masons on the long march home falling into company with two strangers in an inn, who spiked their drinks with what seems to have been a paralysing poison and robbed them of all they had. The episode is recounted in apocalyptic terms, almost as if the men had been the victims not of humans but of devils, and had been charmed. It was reported that afterwards, as in a story of fairy-visitation, their vision was altered and they saw things strangely, believing themselves to have deformed heads and their bodies to be covered in hair.

By the following decade, when a network of proper roads was at last spreading across France, migrants were becoming more sophisticated and cautious of who might be after their hoarded money. The increase in mail-coaches also made it easier to send small sums of money home. In the mid-1840s Nadaud was using the time-honoured method of remitting sums to his family via any trusted friend who happened to be travelling to the Bourganeuf district. But during the 1850s the coming of railways and post offices brought in further changes, and the Sub-Préfet of Boussac, in the north of the Creuse, could write: 'Never before the last two years have the post offices had to deal with so many postal orders.' In fact those who still carried their savings home all at once in the old, grand style tended to be those whose families were less desperate for cash. The postal order was the greatest boon to a wife who, with the new literacy of those times, was able to send a private word to her husband that she really could not manage. It was also perhaps a way for a husband to pacify a wife who was getting sad and querulous on her own –

'*Cher époux, tu me dis que tu veux rester au pays là où tu es . . . Tu sais que voilà déjà longtemps que tu es parti d'ici et tu sais que je ne suis pas bien argenteuse, au moins si tu envoyais l'argent pour les affaires et encore dans l'hiver il fait si mauvais travailler que tu ferais seulement un petit tour au pays . . .'* (Marguerite Tixier, 13 December 1861).

('Dear husband, you tell me you want to stay on there in the place where you are . . . You know it's been a long time since you left here, and you know that I haven't much money about me, if only you'd send money to settle some things, also it's so nasty working in wintertime that if you could just make a little trip back home . . .')

Nadaud says that he did not keep his father continually informed of his own growing savings. 'He visited me from time to time and, seeing me cheerful, wanted to know how much I was earning; I kept him in suspense, so that he would get a nice surprise at the end of the year.' By the early 1840s the family were still far from paying off their burden of debt entirely, but Martin Nadaud had worked out that, with his money from teaching added to his pay, now, as a master mason, the idea of doing so one day was no longer impossible.

By this time the balance in the relationship between father and son had tipped. The man who had hit his son for getting mixed up in the sack of the Archbishop's Palace in 1831, predicting that he would end in prison (as indeed did his friend Luquet) had now, with his usual fervent emotion, been won over – 'What strengthened . . . my will-power and my energy for work, was that I knew my father had developed a total confidence in me.' The hopes and hard-earned money that Léonard Nadaud had invested fifteen years before, in getting the rudiments of an education for his bright boy, were being vindicated.

In the 1830s Nadaud had not been able to return home each year. There had been the return in '33 with the tight Parisian trousers but no savings, and then apparently the impromptu summer return for the Army Board in '35. After that, he claims, he stayed home for four months, time to help with the harvest and also to make republican acquaintances in

Bourganeuf – though a few pages later he locates certain events from this visit in the winter of '36–7, which does not accord with the Army Lists:

'The winter season, always joyful for the migrant come back to see his family, had gone by ... Such is the strength of old habits that we were laughing and singing as we began the hundred-league trek on foot that separates the Creuse from Paris ... It was my third time. I was stronger now, my legs were sturdier and in the evenings the exhaustion weighed on me less.'

There seems to have been another return at the end of '37, he and his father travelling together with a respectable bag of money for the first time. The following year, winter '38–9, was the occasion of his marriage.

For several years the subject had been in the air – as soon, indeed, as it was established he would not be spirited away for seven years' army service. In the world of the migrant masons, rooted as it was in enduring peasant culture, marriages took place young. At twenty or so, a boy who was shaping well was almost a grown man with a man's skills and earnings. It was no doubt thought that if he were left on the loose for many more years he might become too accustomed to the bachelor life. A prudent marriage, on the other hand, would tie him to the *pays* and to family responsibilities.

There could also be pressing financial considerations, though these tended to be bound up with more general perceptions of who would make a good husband or wife and who would not: such marriages were not really the exclusively materialistic arrangements they may appear today. The first marriage suggested for Martin Nadaud fell into this category. A country friend of Léonard Nadaud's, dying in Paris (apparently with fatalistic acceptance of his lot), had sent word to his wife that she should marry their daughter to Martin Nadaud and come to live with them at La Martinèche herself. The family had some 7,000 or 8,000 francs saved – 'That way, we would have had the money and the two women as well [for the farm work, the implication is]. This combination appealed to my family, much in need of money as they were.'

However, when Nadaud went to visit the girl she would not look at him. 'Either I didn't appeal to her, or perhaps she was already promised to some boy in her own hamlet. When I spoke to her she ducked her head and was as dumb as a carp.'

Another scheme was cooked up by family friends concerning a girl supposed to have a dowry of 4,000 or 5,000 francs. (Such sums seem handsome in comparison with a mason's wages. The perspective changes, however, when you remember that the bourgeoisie of Balzac's novels of the same period count dowries in hundreds of thousands.) Once again Nadaud paid a ritual visit. He says that ever after he laughed when he thought of it and made others laugh in telling of it, but at the time it must have been nerve-racking. He found the house filled with women, variously knitting and spinning. 'Whether they always spent the evenings there, or whether they'd come specially to see Marie's suitor, I never knew.' When he sat down at the fireside all those female eyes turned silently towards him, and after a few polite remarks he ran out of things to say. Then the grandfather, 'who was lying ill there in his bed, wearing a large cotton nightcap that left only the end of his nose showing', took over. First raking up supposed debts contracted by Nadaud's grandfather, he then moved on to the topic of the family's current commitments – 'Maybe he wasn't consciously trying to offend me but, as an old Lyon-hand, he was opposed to those who went to Paris. Such was then the state of our society: jealousy and enmity between one working man and another.'

For good measure, the old man added that the Paris lot earned good money but spent it all and didn't hesitate to leave their wives to live with good-time town girls (*des coquines*).

The mother and daughter followed Nadaud out into the dark when he left and begged him to pay no attention to grandpa, but the visit had hardly been a propitious one for a future union of the two families. In any case, Nadaud had already complained to his father in private at being pushed into marriage just to solve the family's financial problem. 'Since I was only twenty-one and liked running about with young men my own age, my distress [at being turned down] did not last long.'

As if to underline this, but also to draw a moral, the section of the Memoirs covering the following campaign tells of some drunken evenings and a further fight, for this was the year before Nadaud started on the hard grind of his classes. He had a particularly good job and was keeping the tally of days and the accounts for the rest of the men on site; he was friends with the son of the boss – 'a well-turned-out young man, handsome and very nice, whose father had given him some education'. This boy's way of life, however, became a problem: 'What he really liked was going to a café in the evening to make his mark with the serving girls . . . He was always glad to have me along too and didn't often let me pay, but from time to time of course I had to stand a round and at the end of the week I noticed the difference. At that age, and in that sort of company, you never like to say you're hard up.

'In the mornings, going to work, remorse often caught up with me, especially when I thought of how my family were placed.

'On the day after one evening with these cheerful young men my discontent became more acute. Their silly laughing and their worse than silly songs had finally pricked my common sense and my conscience.' He left the job. The reader will not be surprised to hear that the nice young man ('really good-hearted and affectionate') went to the bad later, that his less-than-amiable father also suffered catastrophic business failures and that 'the family was completely ruined'. In Nadaud's taste for life, fun and good company, there is a strong thread of puritanism also, otherwise he would hardly have become the political idealist and leader that he did. He does not make the point himself, but clearly, with his ambitions and his taste for self-improvement, he was at this stage having to work out as he went what constituted genuine social advancement and progress and what was the more equivocal seduction of the city.

Nadaud's account of the marriage he finally made seems impregnated with the sense of a lost idyll, though he does not at this stage tell the reader what happened after. It is hard to tell how much he and his contemporaries really did aspire to marriages that would be matters of romance and individual compatibility as well as of general family comfort. During the next decade the Paris of Louis-Philippe was to become that of Alfred de Musset's fashionable love-stories and Murger's *La Vie de Bohème*. In the personages of students and their working-class girl-friends images of romantic love were being democratised (and commercialised) for the first time. But at the end of the 1830s this cult, along with a sizeable reading public, was still to come. It is with a slight shock that we encounter Murger's actual Café Momus in Nadaud's Memoirs – 'at the bottom of the rue Saint-Antoine, a little house, a sort of dairy-shop . . . Bonapartists and republicans met there on good terms with each other.' Nadaud seems to have been drawn there by 'political discussions, always lively and interesting' rather than by a Rodolfe or a Mimi, with her tiny frozen hand and her silk flowers.

There are sentimental references in the Memoirs to 'our lovely young Creusois girls' having no one to equal them for long black hair, but such remarks would also have been the standard possessive gallantries of the Creusois males as they arrived for dances in barns. (It was true about the hair; many farm girls from that part of France used to sell their locks once a year to wig-makers, who travelled round the fairs and markets with their shears.) The basic assumptions still seem to have been those of the world of subsistence, perpetually in fragile balance between survival and disaster, in which the question of a couple having special interests and views in common would hardly arise, since everyone shared in any case the same hardships. Ideas about life were hardly likely to differ very much from one household to another, nor would a girl's own opinion as to what constituted a desirable husband have differed much from her parents'. The notion of distinct generations in one house inhabiting separate social contexts belongs to our own more fragmented world. Louis Bandy de Nalèche, the liberal and compassionate Sub-Préfet of Aubusson who wrote a little book on the masons and their lives and was in favour of more education all round, remarked of the dark clothes and caps worn even by the younger woman – 'She knows that her husband loves her for her hard work, not for her beauty.' However, de Nalèche was seeing these women with an upper-class eye and taste: Nadaud's own view may have contained more subtle perception. He mentions at one point that it was, rather charmingly, the custom at barn-parties for the young men to invite the older women for the first dance – 'You should see the faces of these women then; relaxing, they become attractive and eager, which goes to show that dancing means more to them still than people like to think.'

When he returned to the Creuse at the end of '38, another match that had been mooted came to nothing because of the public knowledge of the family's debts. One unpleasant creditor took pleasure in crowing over them, though Nadaud does not admit this till a later stage in his account. His uncle comforted him with what was surely sensible advice: '"You're a good mason now. Show people how much you're worth in yourself. That'll stop them tattling."'

In fact François Thaury, Nadaud's first master and also one of the family's chief creditors, was sufficiently impressed by the young man to want to marry him to his niece, another arrangement that would have neatly liquidated much of the debt, then still around 6,000 francs. However, once again the girl in question had already given her heart to a different boy. It becomes clear that, in spite of the apparent resemblance of the situation to the arranged-marriage-and-dowry system current in other parts of the world today, the Creusois girls did enjoy a degree of autonomy within their circumscribed lives.

Nadaud felt discouraged, and resented it when acquaintances teasingly suggested other girls – 'naturally always ones who were none too respectable in their way of life. I was being laughed at.'

The meeting that put an end to this period is described in classic romantic-story terms. Nadaud and a friend were walking to a distant place when they called at the inn in Monteil-au-Vicomte, a village about 9 kilometres from La Martinèche going across country.

'In the corner of a huge open fireplace was a tall and beautiful girl accompanied by her mother. She seemed so quiet, so nice-mannered and so glowing with youth that we both looked and looked at her. Both of us had the gift of the gab that one does at that age, especially after several years in Paris ... I was later to learn that we had found favour.'

Of course, this being the depths of the Creuse, the girl did not long remain a mysterious stranger but turned out to be a niece by marriage of one of Nadaud's friends who had anyway been thinking of suggesting a union between the families. A visit was made to the family home in the hamlet of La Chaux. 'The mother took me to a byre where her daughter was busy slicing beets for the cattle to eat. At the word "marriage" she bent her head and said nothing. I admit I must have seemed stupid to her, for I couldn't think how to get a conversation going. The mother helped us out, asking me some questions to which I replied as best I could. The girl remained silent ... But when I asked if I might kiss her I was allowed to.'

Another work-mate contributed his good opinion of Nadaud, initial family resistance to marrying off the girl that year faded. The Aupetit family (such was their name) came on a ceremonial visit to inspect the property at La Martinèche and to discuss a dowry. This was finally agreed at 3,000 francs payable in instalments, one or two pieces of furniture, linen, a feather mattress, six ewes and their lambs and one heifer. 'One brother, not much in favour of me, wanted to raise the subject of debts, but the mother told him quite fiercely to hold his tongue, saying that if she hadn't believed in my worth she wouldn't have let matters get this far.'

As with his sister's marriage a few years before, everything had to be packed in before the departure for Paris at the end of the winter. So Nadaud took to visiting, ostensibly, the father, Jean Aupetit, three or four times a week (a 10-kilometre tramp there and back again each time) 'hoping to spend a few minutes with the young and pretty peasant girl who was constantly on my mind'. On one visit, leaving when dark had already come, he became caught in a snowstorm and lost his way. One recalls what a trackless, wolf-haunted waste much of this country was then; even Nadaud himself remarks: 'there are few parts of the Creuse that are more alarming at night than these.

'. . . I must have wandered for seven hours, across meadows, hills and steep valleys, without knowing where I was going. At one point despair gripped me, for it seemed to me that whatever I did I would not escape death, especially if cold and exhaustion got the better of me before dawn came.'

Did he, in those hours, think all the time about his Julie? No, apparently not – although there were hearty jokes in her family, once the tale was told, about her escape from premature widowhood. He says that it was the image of his combative and well-loved father that came before him and kept him going.

At last, hearing barking and deciding that they were dogs this time, not wolves, he found his way to an isolated hamlet, Masdarier, where he was readily identified: in that country-side all families knew each other by reputation at least. A big fire was stirred up to warm him and a bed found for him in the stable. Near the end of his life, he was to write: 'Hardly two months ago, on one of my walks around my home, I met a son or son-in-law [from the family] and reminded him how, fifty-three years before, I had had such a near brush with death and what hospitality I received . . .'

The wedding took place on 23 February 1839 in Monteil-au-Vicomte, in a dark, plain little church with few ornaments that seems to have changed little between then and now. The necessary civil ceremony, according to the records, was three days later. The bride could not sign the register, nor could her mother, nor either of the elder Nadauds, though of course the groom could and so could his young witnesses. Nadaud does not say how his bride was dressed; one must assume the same standard applied as it had for his sister five years before. This was just before the era when much cheaper, factory-made lengths of patterned material began to be carried along the new roads by pedlars:

'At that time, the idea of fancy clothes hadn't really spread in the country. A dress of ordinary black cloth, a kerchief on the shoulders instead of a shawl, a cap with or without lace, clogs with nice straps, one or two silver rings . . . That was the wedding dress of our young peasants.' Often it was also to be her Sunday-best dress for the rest of her life and the one in which she was laid out in death.

On his purchases for his own wedding, Nadaud remarks that when Julie's family and he went to Aubusson (the tapestry town some 20 kilometres distant from La Chaux) to sign the marriage contract before the lawyer and to buy her clothes – 'the girl was the least demanding person there. For when it came to jewellery, she told her mother to say that she wanted only a couple of rings and that we would see about other things later.'

I record this scrap of evidence about Julie's personality, for it is only at rare moments that it appears at all between the crowded pages of her husband's life story.

The next day, more prosaically, Nadaud and an Aupetit brother set off elsewhere to buy 'an old cow' for the wedding feast. In country style this lasted two whole days, complete with a procession of the young and handsome from all the villages round, fusillades from shotguns and 160 persons dancing their hearts out. At one point the happy couple retired to bed, to be disturbed two hours later for 'the chicken ceremony':

'The young crowd offer the pair a chicken leg and a bowl of mulled wine. There are hearty handshakes and one by one the girls kiss the bride, who stays sitting up in bed. Then everyone sings the wedding song. The words are so free and easy [*échevelés*] that you'd think you were still in the time of Rabelais, when they called a cat a cat and a blackbird a blackbird.' (One hears here the tone of the frock-coated figure of later years). 'Then, after this burlesque show, everyone goes to bed and to sleep wherever they can.'

Two days after the wedding Nadaud received word of a good job in Paris, which could not wait for long. 'When I told my wife about this she cried a good deal.

'It was an odd fate that befell the women who married masons. Today, some of the masons bring their young wives with them to Paris or elsewhere, but at that time this practice did not exist. Apart from the winter breaks the couple lived their lives separately, often till the age of fifty . . . Such was the tradition among the migrant Creusois. You conformed to it without complaining over much: to console yourself you just said, "The sons must do as their fathers did."'

In fact, tradition or not, within a few years Nadaud was to bring Julie to Paris with him, another of those signs of individual choice and decision that were increasingly to mark him out from all the others busy on the scaffolding of Paris. But for the moment there was no affordable home fit for her in Paris and no railway line for her to get there, and she was left to her accepted fate. She must have expected it, for it was the custom of her family too: she had brothers of her own at work in Paris.

'There are countries where . . . women marry in the hope (often realised) of not working at all except inside their own homes; in France nothing like that happens, indeed it is rather the opposite.' Nadaud at this point was, I suspect, thinking of the large English lower middle class of tradesmen and skilled working men with which his later life had made him familiar, in which the wives led more genteel lives than their less prosperous French counterparts. 'My own wife, like all country women, had been brought up to labour from dawn till dusk in the fields, and after marriage she worked just as hard if not more.'

There was always the next winter to look forward to. Nadaud had a good campaign as a trusted man on jobs where his literacy was beginning to be an advantage to him. He saved 550 francs from his mason's wages and 300 from his teaching. To this, his father, who was apparently staying in Paris for the winter on what was to be his last-ever campaign, added 500, so Martin Nadaud set off for home with 1,300 francs. (The figures he gives for wages and savings are always so precise that one wonders if, through the decades, he had kept physical notes of them or whether it was simply that these hard-won sums were engraved on his memory as they apparently were on the memory of his unlettered father.)

'I was proud of this result and very happy to be seeing my wife again . . . I was going to be able to prove to her and her mother that she had not joined her fate to that of a good-for-nothing who would consume her dowry and get chased out by the bailiffs, as so many people had said.'

According to Nadaud's account of this return, he arrived at La Martinèche to find that his wife had gone to see her father, who was seriously ill. In spite of the journey he had just made on foot from Paris, Nadaud continued on at once to Monteil, only to hear the church bell tolling on his arrival: Jean Aupetit was dead.

'The day after [the funeral] my wife and I set off back to La Martinèche. On the way she told me that her father had spoken of wanting to lend me 1,000 francs to pay off a certain Gadoux, who had a claim against our own property.'

It had been the Gadoux family who had particularly jeered at the Nadauds and their debts, making threats to gain possession of La Martinèche and turn them out. (They were near neighbours. Clearly, local relationships were sometimes uglier than one would suppose from the nostalgic reminiscences of winter *veillées*.) Nadaud was much gratified to know that he had won his father-in-law's confidence, but was able to tell Julie that the claim would now be paid off anyway.

There is one thing wrong with this account: according to the Death Registers of the Commune of Monteil, Jean Aupetit of La Chaux did not die in late 1839 but at the end of 1842.

Whatever the chronological vagueness, it is no doubt true, as Nadaud says, that in the winter following Aupetit's death he and his wife could not indulge in the usual round of dances and weddings as they were in mourning. In the evenings, he seized the opportunity to teach her to read 'as I had already done for my older sister and for two other girls in the hamlet'.

Among the haphazard accumulation of letters that Nadaud sent and received, those that have survived the vicissitudes of the last hundred-odd years and to which we are now drawing near in this account, there is no letter from Julie. One early letter to his father mentions that she has 'written' to him, but this probably means she had dictated a letter for him to someone else. I expect she mastered her own signature by then, but it does not seem as if her husband's help with literacy extended as far as the writing of a whole letter. A pity. It might have been possible to glean from some brief message of her own a further inkling of this person, who remains so shadowy. Her potential destiny was not, as Nadaud thought when he married her, to endure years of separation with peasant stoicism, but to become the companion of a man of ambition living in a quite other world. Could she, in the long future, have risen to this challenge? He remarks much later, in a letter, that they read the Fables of La Fontaine together. Probably he also used as a reading primer with her the book he mentions elsewhere using with his builder pupils: *Paroles d'un Croyant*, by the renegade Abbé de Lamennais, which he succinctly describes as a daring book written to encourage people to hate kings. Was he hoping to teach Julie eventually not only to communicate about cows and repairs to the roof, but to share in his dreams? In the event, the future was not long at all, but the image of the young mason instructing his wife in the firelight remains fixed: a promise of many might-have-beens.

Nadaud appears to have stayed in Paris from the spring of 1840 till late in '42, embarked on a marathon of work that was to reap its reward. Now a master mason, he took on several piecework jobs at a set fee, employing his own band of men whose wages he settled out of the profits, with all the attendant risks and anxieties. Knowing how to motivate his men and working alongside them, he several times turned jobs into contests against the clock with a promise of a celebratory supper at the end of it – 'up on the scaffolding we went, under a driving rain, with the boys who had agreed to this contest bringing up fresh mortar in relays the moment we needed it. We had been careful to take off our shirts, working only in smocks, so as to have something dry to put on afterwards. Towards evening, the rain changed into snow, but no one gave up . . .

'That night we went up to the town gates at Clichy [a place for late-night fun]. Roby and I paid for supper. Needless to say, we drank a good deal. Everyone spoke of our endurance at work, and I don't believe I ever spent a gayer, livelier or happier evening. B— and D— were the heroes of the celebration, as both of them had kept at it, singing songs out loud, throughout that gruelling day, although we were all wet to the bone.'

Eventually he and Roby were to decide that the risks of subcontracting from sometimes under-capitalised employers were not worth the trouble, but meanwhile satisfying amounts of money had been made.

The most probable reason, therefore, that Nadaud, in his account displaced the death of his father-in-law to his earlier return, is that he wanted to present the triumphal home-coming of 1842 in its full colours, without distraction. Quarried out by more than one social historian as a nugget of unreconstructed peasant life, it seems almost to belong to the Middle Ages rather than to the decade when the railway lines were working their way south from Paris to Orléans and on to Issoudun, and as he recounted it long afterwards Nadaud seems to have thought so too. For me, it has something of the aura of a fairy-story; the exactly remembered details strike one as authentic, but there is a dream-come-true quality about the event. I feel that Nadaud both planned it in

advance and often contemplated it with satisfaction afterwards, and in memory the money that figures in it shines like
fairy wealth – which, fortunately, it was not.

'I was such a novice at money matters that I did not even
think to change my 100-sou [20-franc] coins into gold or
bank-notes. I stuffed the lot into four bags, which I put in the
bottom of my trunk, and set off by stage-coach to Châteauroux.' (This journey of 250 kilometres then took three days.)
'Another coach carried us on to La Châtre' – both road and
coach in that direction were a new, modern amenity – 'and
then to Guéret. In that town were to be found wagons, which
were laid on at periods of the masons' travels, to make the
journey on to Pontarion. From there, one of my cousins
helped me to carry the trunk to my house.' This was a good 2
kilometres more, on a steeply rising track.

'As you might imagine, when the migrant comes home,
especially when he is regarded as the principal support and
bread-winner of the rest, it isn't so much joy that runs
through the family as delirium, for instead of laughing
everyone cries.'

The laughs came later, after soup made with milk, sitting
by a good fire, when news was exchanged all round and
everyone present was sworn to secrecy on the financial results
of the campaign.

'My unopened trunk was put on the large kitchen table.
First I brought out a fine dress for my wife, two others for my
two sisters, a little winter shawl for my mother and a pound
of snuff for my father.' Léonard Nadaud must have been a
prodigious snuff-taker!

'Then I brought out one bag of 1,000 francs, then another.
At that, father, mother, wife and sisters could not contain
their delight and began to jump about and hug one another.

'A moment afterwards, I said to my wife, "Look in another
corner. There might be something else." She fetched out
another, saying as she did, "I think there's one more as well."
She put the two further bags alongside the first two. We all
gazed at each other with lumps in our throats too big to be
able to speak . . . "You've gone ahead of me, Martin [*tu m'a*

surpassé]," said my father. "I've worked a great deal, but I never made my fortune like this." We began emptying out the bags and putting the contents into 100-franc piles.

'The table was half covered as if with a silver cloth of dazzling whiteness. It was past two in the morning when we had finished gazing at what we all called 'a beautiful picture'.

I am reminded of some sentences written later in the century by Guy de Maupassant, an infinitely more cynical man than Nadaud but one who yet appreciated the almost immeasurable value to a poor family of such a sight: 'that small change slowly hoarded, coming in franc by franc, sou by sou, that good, everyday money, silver or copper, worn by hands, purses, pockets, café tables and the deep drawers of old cupboards, that money that is the jingling record of so many efforts, anxieties, wearinesses and labours, that money so dear to the heart, the eyes and the fingers of the peasant' (*Mont-Oriol*).

In the days that followed, other satisfactions were in store. Word had inevitably got around and everyone was congratulating Nadaud. The family reputation was from then on secure. A substantial part of the money went to settle the debt to François Thaury. We are told that Julie's face fell when she saw the basket containing it disappear down the road on her husband's back, but Thaury gratifyingly said he'd always had faith in Martin Nadaud's future ever since the latter had been a boy-mason, and that now he confidently expected to see him come home one day as a successful entrepreneur.

Martin Nadaud and Julie went to visit her mother, who was duly impressed by this gentlemanly figure in a frock-coat (*une longue redingote à la propriétaire*). Julie told her mother the good news. More kisses and exclamations. 'Madame Aupetit adored her daughter, and included her son-in-law in her affections.'

There were Sunday outings to neighbouring villages, with Julie in her fine new dress, where the couple met 'the liveliest and the best turned-out masons [*les plus fringants*] of Paris and Lyon . . . You had to keep up with the fashion, and get sisters and wives to follow suit. In fact it was by wearing lovely dresses from the big towns that our peasant girls made something of themselves well before the girls of other neighbouring *départements*; they distinguished themselves by their manner, their outfits and particularly by their ability to hold a conversation.'

Evidently the lessons at the fireside, and perhaps letters from Paris too, had paid off. But Nadaud remarks a page or two later, when writing of the city, that the young men, too, were better educated and a little more particular in their manners and dress than those he had accompanied to Paris for the first time twelve years before. France was still decades behind England in the equivocal amenities of an industrial civilisation, but the future was at last beginning to arrive.

'The month of March recalled me to Paris. Whether I wanted to or not, I had to live again through those scenes of tender emotion that take place in united families when the moment to separate comes. It was time to pack bags and be off.'

Although there is no mention of it in his Memoirs, when he left, Julie was pregnant.

7

In Which Life Advances in Various Ways

I am not attempting any detailed examination of Nadaud's political activities. To him, this might have seemed perverse, a wounding disregard for what he saw as his life's work. But many other people have written on the events of Louis-Philippe's reign, the growing dissatisfaction that erupted into the revolution of 1848, and the establishment of the Second Republic which was to turn, by 1852, into Louis-Napoleon's oppressive eighteen-year empire. Nadaud himself devotes many pages of his Memoirs to his perceptions of the period running up to the events of 1848–9. But he writes anecdotally, weaving back and forth in time, telling the stories he retold to himself, sometimes making factual mistakes or conflating political events or ideas that, in reality, were separate. He was writing long after the events and for an audience whose general assumptions had shifted and evolved over the years even as his own had done. To decode and amplify all this would be for me to write another kind of book. So if I summarize only briefly his public life in the 1840s, that is because it is the private individual I am pursuing – whose scent, from this time on, becomes lighter and more elusive, certainly more patchy, and yet with moments of intensity that even the Memoirs do not provide.

The would-be reasonable, constitutional monarchy of Louis-Philippe came to disappoint by its mediocrity. It was so extremely and cravenly reasonable that it seemed to lack any particular aim, let alone a vision. Famously incarnated in Prime Minister Guizot's urging the people '*Enrichissez-vous*' ('Go on – get rich') it began to disgust even the upper bourgeoisie who benefited by it. To a nation reared on the blood and idealism of the Revolution, nurtured on Napoleonic dreams of grandeur, glory and an orderliness like the *pax romana* imposed across Europe and North Africa by French civilization, life under Louis-Philippe eventually became an embarrassment, not in spite of its material advances but because of them. 'Who does not recall', wrote the republican Duvergier de Hauranne in fine, sarcastic mode, 'the tempests unchained by sesame on the most pacific benches of the chamber, and the agitated, tumultuous, almost revolutionary appearance of the *salle des pas perdus* on the day that saw the great fight of beetroots and colonial sugar. Who can have forgotten the burst of patriotic enthusiasm evoked from the galleries by the branch line to F—? These are the triumphs and defeats, the joys and griefs, of our time. These are the causes that have taken the place of those for which our fathers shed their blood on the scaffold or the field of battle!'

There is a certain irony that Nadaud himself, supposedly a Red republican, was much preoccupied all through the 1840s with the triumphs and defeats of his own monetary affairs, and that the 'branch line to F—' (in his case Bourganeuf) was eventually to become one of his long-running preoccupations. In addition, his most enduring political statement, made in 1849 and recalled in reference books wherever his biography is sketched, was '*Lorsque le bâtiment va, tout va*' – 'when the building trade is going well, all is going well' – a remark which, on the face of it, would seem to have more to do with crude capitalism and a simple admiration of material progress than with any more utopian and socialist vision. But perhaps this is unfair: when he made his much-quoted remark his mind was fixed on the precarious lives of the building labourers he knew so well, and on his realistic perception that their well-being was a barometer for the situation of the working classes in general. In sweeping away all guilds, closed shops, corporations and other restrictions in the name of free competition, the Revolution had effectively made it impossible for the working classes to protect themselves against the harshest effects of market forces. Add to this the industrialisation now belatedly changing for ever the old, home-based manufacturing ways, destroying traditional livelihoods, cutting costs and driving down wages, and one sees why Nadaud was obsessed with the anarchic inhumanity of the system under which he found himself living.

Another national crisis in 1840 brought a further slump. Once again the hungry, ill-clad men gathered hopefully in the street in front of the few building sites where work was currently proceeding; wages were forced down further. Eventually a general building trade strike was proposed – the first ever – and Nadaud was one of the strike committee that met in secret at a wine shop on the left bank rue du Bac. A large demonstration was organised on the Plaine de Bondy which, like nearby Villemomble, is now covered in industrial and suburban development, but was then a great open space well outside Paris. Six or seven thousand men marched, under the slogan borrowed from the Lyon silk weavers: 'Let us live working or die fighting'. The army arrived to disperse the demonstrators who, on this occasion, went quietly. But this event, which the government and the ruling classes imagined to be a victory for themselves, was in fact the turning point of Louis-Philippe's reign. Attempts to placate the moderate left had failed, and now the king and Guizot embraced a stultifying policy of 'prudence'. From then on the road led inexorably to the débâcle of 1848. As for the masons, from the collapsed strike was born a builders' mutual aid society which existed from then on, even though the mass of migrant masons did not turn out to be particularly clubbable. Much later in life, Nadaud was to become its president.

It was in the early 1840s that Nadaud began to meet, in one left-wing organisation or another, men such as Edgar Quinet, François Vincent Raspail, Alexandre Ledru-Rollin, Louis Blanc and others who were to be the republican leaders of the mid-century. Because of the laws preventing public gatherings, these meetings used to take place in the homes of members, whichever was the most comfortable and spacious apartment available. This enabled Nadaud to observe polite society at close quarters and adjust his manner and style of speech accordingly. 'I left in these meetings many of the uncouth habits that weigh like a leaden cloak on the spirit of the body of most working men.' At this time he also met Etienne Cabet – the man whose paper, *Le Populaire*, founded in 1834, he had used to read aloud in a wine shop. Cabet is a rather strange figure among the fauna of eighteenth- and nineteenth-century French idealists, and even stranger perhaps is the fact that Nadaud was so taken with him, in view of Nadaud's own essentially modest, pragmatic opinions and his down-to-earth experiences. But then Cabet is said by all who knew him to be the most gentle and friendly of men, with an open-hearted simplicity that particularly appealed to Nadaud. (Nadaud was to warm temporarily even to Louis-Philippe after seeing him, umbrella in hand, thanking the workmen for his visit to the site.) Years later the moderate and deeply humane Louis Blanc, rather than Ledru-Rollin or Lamartine, became Nadaud's particular mentor and friend for the same reason, and later again, after 1870, Nadaud hitched his wagon to the star of the charismatic but sometimes slippery Gambetta.

It is worth dwelling for a moment on Cabet, partly because his utopian vision represented a gulf into which Nadaud narrowly escaped falling and partly because Madame Cabet became a confidante to whom Nadaud wrote letters in the early days of his exile in bleak, strange, black London. Of an older generation than Nadaud, Cabet had already been a leading figure in the revolution of 1830 and was subsequently a Member of Parliament. His writings in the *Le Populaire* and elsewhere – among other things, he asserted that Christ had been a communist – so annoyed the government, however, that they managed to have him prosecuted. Preferring exile to prison, he made off to England, that great, benignly uncaring place of safety for Frenchmen of a whole range of political colours at different times from 1789 for the next 150 years. (The future Emperor Louis-Napoleon himself was to sojourn there in the later 1840s shortly before his elevation to power, living as a country gentleman in Chislehurst, Kent.) Cabet was back in France by 1840 and two years later published his lightly fictionalised *Voyage en Icarie*. This describes a utopian, agrarian commune run on visionary, if regimented, lines, drawing on Christianity, on Plato and on the eighteenth-century philosophers. Other political idealists had had similar ideas before him, but in essence all these dreams seem now to have belonged more to the pre-Revolutionary, pre-industrial world of Rousseau's noble savage, than to the world of burgeoning urbanisation, railways and labour relations which Cabet, Louis Blanc, Nadaud and all the others actually inhabited. However, Cabet's dream of founding a new world in the literal New World chimed with the persistent French republican belief that revolution could bring about instant social change, establishing a new country of the spirit. America, too, bred such ideas. When, in 1847, Cabet published his manifesto *Allons en Icarie* ('Let us go to Icarus') there was no lack of people interested in joining him – including Nadaud.

In January 1848 the first contingent set off, though Nadaud, hard at work building Paris as usual, was not among them. They were supposed to take possession of an idyllic site on the suitably named Red River Valley in Texas, but, predictably, problems dogged the venture from the first and members of the community almost at once began to quarrel with each other. Cabet joined them at the end of the year, by which time many members had already either died or left in disgust, and he and the rump finally made a harrowing journey to an abandoned Mormon township far away in the harsher territory of Illinois. In the course of the following year of unremitting physical labours and set-backs reminiscent of the Pilgrim Fathers of two hundred years before, Cabet found himself accused by his supporters of fraud. By that time he was back in Paris participating in the new revolution, but he rushed back to Icarus before he could stand trial there, for Icarus never managed to survive without the constant infusions of financial support that only he could raise. Strife, rain, snow, drought, wild beasts, fires, plagues of grasshoppers and the disappointment of ideals continued through the 1850s. News of some of this in Cabet's own letters, lightly veiled in unquenchable optimism, reached Nadaud, who was by then in exile in England. In 1855 Cabet demanded to be put in sole and autocratic charge of his 'egalitarian' community in order to save it. Following a similarly well-worn French tradition he was deposed the following year, and later made his way back south to St Louis, where some of the fractured community eventually trickled down to join him. He died there of a stroke not long afterwards.

It is lucky that Nadaud was too deeply committed in Paris in 1848–9 to fulfil his original intentions towards Cabet, and that he did not turn to America as a place of exile himself in 1852. Had some slightly different turn of fortune's wheel led him across the Atlantic, he would no doubt have made valiant efforts to keep Icarus going. His practical resourcefulness, his ability to build and his peasant knowledge of farming, would have been of great value to the community. But he might well in that case have sunk without trace into oblivion, just another anonymous part of the immigrant ancestry of twentieth-century America.

Throughout the 1840s, Nadaud's two lives – that of hardworking mason and that of increasingly prominent figure in republican circles – ran in tandem, with his third occupation, that of evening teacher to other masons, as a bridge between them. It was an extraordinarily busy, dynamic existence, and it is perhaps not surprising that the Memoirs to these years contain scarcely a reference to his personal and private life:

he could hardly have fitted much that was personal or private into his over-filled days. Nevertheless, other events did occur; other expeditions back to the Creuse were obviously made after the famous triumphal return with four bags of money. What is remarkable, and frustrating to those who have followed his life story this far in the human detail of his own words, is that, from 1843 onwards, the private man quietly vacates the stage. The public figure is in the ascendancy, and though for a few years more the individual is vividly present in the Memoirs at certain moments – being acclaimed by his peers, hearing that he has become a *député*, being arrested at dawn – references to family matters, even to important landmarks of birth and death, virtually disappear.

It may be that, once Léonard Nadaud had retired definitively back to the Creuse in December 1840, having passed responsibility as head of the family on to his son, the ever-present link that bound even this exceptional young mason to his peasant identity was subtly broken, and that *le pays* was no longer daily in his thoughts in the same way as before. Of course he went on fulfilling his duties, sending money home, concerning himself with debts and land purchase and with his sisters' welfare. It was the Creuse he was elected to represent in 1849 and its Préfecture to which he triumphantly returned from exile in 1870. But however conscientiously loyal he was, he was not really, for most of his life, a man of rural central France, but a Parisian. Since the age of fourteen it was Paris that had been his natural habitat, not the countryside, and it was Paris that had turned him from the shy *patois*-speaking child into the ebullient and notable man that he had, by his mid-twenties, become. Throughout his public life the causes he tended to adopt were to do with urban and working-class life rather than with rural matters. Unlike some other commentators of the period who were interested in central France, men such as Louis Bandy de Nalèche and Léonce de Lavergne, he did not concern himself with agricultural reform. During his long years in England he was impressed not by the advanced English farming practices of the period (which he doesn't seem to have noticed) but by the sheer scale of British industrialisation, by the docks of Liverpool and by the shipyards of the Clyde.

There are other possible reasons as to why Nadaud, originally so open about the events of family life, good and bad, later becomes discreet to a fault. But for the moment it is time for a personal detour of my own.

If you set to work to explore the life and times of a known person out of the past, you soon notice two or three names that figure and repeat themselves at the foot of articles in reference books or specialised journals. You realise that Dr Y or Professor Z have done work of their own on your particular person or on the world in which he moved: you begin to want to meet Y or Z to talk about your mutual interest, but at the same time you are wary of appearing to be invading their territory. You feel it would be outrageous of you to pick their brains for facts that they themselves have quarried out only after years of primary research. However, there is no point in each researcher making his or her own way absolutely without guidance over the same territory, and in any case once the original research has been distilled into an informative article it has become part of a corpus of public knowledge: that, after all, is the point of publication. So you find yourself having circumspect conversations with third parties –

'So X was your supervisor when you did your doctorate? How lucky for you! . . . Is he nice?'

'Oh yes, he's a decent old thing . . . Why don't you write him a letter?'

'You don't think he'd mind or think it impertinent? After all, I am a foreigner . . .'

'Oh, I should think he'd be pleased to hear you're interested. Anyway he loves talking about the travelling workmen . . .'

It was with encouragement of this kind that I first wrote to a contributor to a Dictionary of Biography, saying in essence: 'You seem to know some facts about Nadaud's life that I don't. Could you give me some indications as to where to start looking for them?'

And so it was that I found myself invited to lunch in a Creusois home on one of the coldest winter days in that region for several decades. With the efficiency born of a lifetime in school teaching, my host had also invited someone whom he knew (but I had not known until then) that it was essential for me to meet. This man, also a teacher and a researcher, was the son of a peasant farming family and was reared in a remote hamlet just like La Martinèche. It is largely to him that I owe access to many of the letters that I shall cite in the rest of this book and without which the traces of Nadaud, the private man, would, for certain periods, have become almost too faint for me to follow. I have met my benefactor several times since, but that first lunch has created an enduring image for me. Beyond the windows of the small house the sun hung red in a sky milky with snow as yet too high up and too cold to fall. The hilly fields swept away to the black woods that were petrified under a thick white frost that had not lifted all day. ('*That winter was cruelly hard . . . our sheep stayed in the byre, fed on leaves and bracken.*') I sat opposite my fellow guest, and as we passionately discussed Nadaud's life and adventures, all the while I felt I could see in his face and build, as in Nadaud's, the countless lives of unremitting labour on the land that lay behind him. His was the first generation in his family to escape from the fields, the sheep, the cows, the mud, the heat of summer and the cold of winter, into the realm of books and ideas and ambitions.

Understandably, the idea of pursuing any kind of manual activity himself, even as a hobby, was entirely antipathetic to this man. And yet certain ineradicable traits from his childhood had remained. At lunch, he ate the cured and dried saucisson of the hors d'oeuvre with good appetite, but refused the rare roast lamb that followed it. He had never, he said, really taken to butcher's meat. ('*I did not like meat . . . at home my mother had brought us all up on soup, bread, pancakes, potatoes and dairy products.*')

That same winter I had the good fortune to make another

new friend. On an early visit to a certain archive collection, I felt for a while discouraged. Highly codified French systems have their advantages, and at least in France once records are deemed sufficiently ancient to be in the public domain they may be consulted free – which does not always apply under the esoterically confused British system. However, the bureaucratic structure of a French archive does not lend itself readily to those friendly, informed contacts between staff and researchers that sometimes produce crucial pieces of information. I was sitting one afternoon on my numbered chair at a crowded table, having already been reprimanded for trying to move myself and my papers to the unoccupied spaces of an adjoining table. I was grumpily leafing through the very few copies of a local newspaper of 1871 that I was being permitted to consult at any one time. Suddenly I became aware of a diminutive figure at my side, who was murmuring something to me. This good fairy from the back regions of the archives, who managed to seem both mouselike and exotic at the same moment, whispered that it had happened to notice from the slips I had handed in that I must be working on Martin Nadaud. The fairy wondered – just wondered, it was so sorry to disturb me – if I might be interested to know that there were boxes and boxes of uncatalogued Nadaud papers lying in the basement below us? It might be possible for me to get permission to have a look at them . . .

As may be imagined, I devoted considerable time and energy over the succeeding weeks to composing letters designed to convince functionaries and lawyers that while on the one hand I was essentially harmless, on the other I might nevertheless cause ongoing difficulties if my request was refused. To my relief and delight, this mixed message eventually produced a satisfactory result. I was allowed to get at the boxes of papers.

In March 1843 Nadaud left the Creuse and Julie once more to make his way back to Paris. The earliest letters that survive between him and his family date from this period. His own level of literacy still led him then to make mistakes in grammar and spelling, and at that time too he continued to follow the French peasant custom of referring to other family members by relationship rather than by names: thus Julie is always 'my wife', except in moments of extreme emotion. In fact when he does mention people near to him by name in his Memoirs, there is often no consistency of spelling, even though the Memoirs were written long after he had perfected his education. His elder sister appears haphazardly both as Magdelaine and Madelaine, and the spelling of local hamlets is similarly nonchalant.

To his father in the high summer of 1843, Martin Nadaud wrote:

'I was very pleased to hear my wife was in good health. I do beg you to take into consideration the condition [*la position*] of a young woman who has not been without her share of troubles. I don't want her to exhaust herself working, and particularly not for her to lift even small loads ... Don't let her go out harvesting, or do any work that could go against her condition. I would rather pay someone else to take her place for the time being ... Don't hesitate to let me know of everything that happens in our house.'

It seems clear that Julie was expecting a child, and also that she had already had one or more false alarms or miscarriages [*des ennuies*]. Alas, Nadaud's next letter, postmarked 23 August of the same year, indicates in almost illegible scrawl the turn events must have taken. Or rather, it expresses Martin Nadaud's anguished assumption as to what had probably happened, following a letter from home which has not survived.

'My dear father, what can we have done that our family has so much misfortune? Oh, the pain [*douleur*]. So I have not been allowed to keep for any longer the person I loved so much.

'You haven't dared tell me straight out. You've just hinted for now, hoping that way to let me down gently –

'My poor Julie is no longer on earth. But tell me at once if she is still here for me. Death must not hide itself. I would have been so happy with her. So she had to die. Ah, if it were just the poor child that would seem like good fortune. I feel that the Nadaud family is fated to ill luck.

'If she is really still as the letter says, do everything possible to save her. Have the doctors along every day, within the week you'll be getting 200 francs from me. Write to me every three days, don't miss a day, send the letters to rue de l'Oratoire des Champs Elysées . . .'

But Jeanne-Julie Aupetit was not dead. She recovered, and two years later, on 11 November 1845, a daughter was born to them. The child must have been conceived during the previous winter's homecoming. The only surviving letter from Nadaud to his wife that I have found dates from this pregnancy. It was written at the end of June, by which time Julie would have been between five and six months pregnant, assuming the baby arrived more or less at term. Perhaps the father-to-be felt reasonably confident by then that this time all was going well: at any rate there is only a veiled allusion to her *situation* – her 'condition'.

The first page is mainly apologies for not having written sooner – 'But it's been more than three weeks now that the young man who's going down to the country ought to have left.' Evidently the masons were still, at this date, inclined to send non-urgent letters home via friends. The pre-paid, flat-rate stamp system, copied from the English, was not introduced in France until 1849; before then letters sent on the mail-coaches had to be paid for by the recipient.

'In his last letter my father said I should write to you more often. If I haven't done so, don't hold it against me . . . I enjoy writing to you, but I would enjoy seeing you still more.

'I'm working a lot, which is to say I am very busy but don't do much actual labouring . . . I know you've received the very small present [*le minime cadot*] that I sent you for the time being. I also said that I would pay for whatever you asked. Everything that you want I'll send you, unless I can't. You haven't yet let me know if your arm is really better or if it still pains you. I would like to know. And tell me all about your condition.'

There follow messages from her brothers and enquiries about neighbours and country news. And has father taken out the insurance we agreed on yet?

'As for me, I can tell you that if you saw me you wouldn't recognise me, for I haven't been shaved since I left you. I'm in good health, couldn't be better, and I hope very much that you may be the same.

'Tell father that the carpenters' strike is hampering workers a lot this year . . .'

In his Memoirs Martin Nadaud does not mention receiving the happy news of this baby's birth – a marked shift away from the complete and detailed accounts of family life in the earlier pages. Still more disconcertingly, the Memoirs only ever mention the existence of this daughter once, in passing, years later. She was, however, destined to be his only child, and one must assume, from what had gone before and the half-dozen years that had passed since their marriage, that she was much wanted. They named her Désirée.

'*It was an odd fate that befell the women who married masons. Today, some of them bring their young wives with them to Paris, but at that time this practice did not exist.*'

So Nadaud wrote in his Memoirs immediately after the description of his marriage. He invoked the theme again after the triumphal return of 1842. 'That abominable habit of marrying and then not living with your wife was more or less general. What was the reason? The fear of not having enough to live on as a couple on the limited working man's wages of my young days.'

Nadaud, true to his political convictions, neatly turned his separation from his wife into a complaint about wage-rates. But in reality monetary constraints seem to have been only one part of a complex syndrome, which included the determination of most parents of masons to keep the daughters-in-law with them, both as docile workers and to bring the sons back home. Their down-to-earth perceptions were all too correct. For when, by the late 1850s, the spread of railway travel, the increasing urbanisation and modernisation of Paris and a general rise in wages had emboldened far more masons to have their wives join them – then seasonal migration began to turn inevitably into depopulation. Louis Bandy de Nalèche, writing in 1859, lamented:

'In the past, the mason left at twenty and returned at forty; he reappeared every other year at least and found his home waiting for him. Today he leaves at fifteen and returns at sixty. He reappears once in five years, sometimes only once in ten. His wife follows him to the city, and this in itself provides him with a good reason for putting off his return, for she works there a seamstress or a laundress, that is to say at occupations which thrive particularly in the winter.'

Quite right too, one is inclined to think. Much better for a grown man to be sharing a lodging with his own usefully occupied wife than with a troop of drinking companions, even though the children of the marriage were not often included permanently in this new idyll, but were sent back to the extended family *au pays*. The Census returns for Paris for much of the nineteenth century show a marked lack of young children in comparison with other age groups.

Such was the way of life presently adopted by Martin and Julie Nadaud, a good ten years earlier than most of their kind. Nadaud's work had been going increasingly well; he had recently completed the rue de Pontoise job and was now offered another job also on the left bank. Up the hill, facing the Panthéon, a majestic new *mairie* was to be built for what was then the Twelfth Arrondissement. On the strength of his acquired skill in architectural measurement and calculation, Nadaud was taken on as foreman.

'I was so happily placed that I wrote to my wife that her hard times were over and that she should prepare herself to come to join me . . .

'Her joy was great. We had been separated, more or less, for seven years; and she had been patient as were all the wives like her.'

'Seven years' suggests a date of late 1846 or early '47. The railway line to Paris then ran only from Issoudun. Probably Julie made the first part of her journey on a series of coaches, in company with a brother or cousin.

'I rented a small room in the rue Saint-Jacques, at the back of a courtyard almost on the corner of the rue Sufflot. As my worksite was on the place du Panthéon, I had all my meals at home. Our happiness was complete.'

I assume, from this, that Désirée was left in the care of her grandparents. She would have been fully old enough to be weaned, even by the rather lengthy breast-feeding standards of those days. Years later, when the child was rising nine, Nadaud was to write sadly: 'I have never spent even one whole week in her company', and he surely would not have expressed himself like this if she had been part of the little Parisian household?

It does not appear either that Julie sought work herself in Paris, in the way suggested by Bandy de Nalèche, in spite of Nadaud's earlier remarks about the Creusois women working still harder after marriage than before. In fact that paragraph in the Memoirs continues – 'See [the women] in our factories, see them at home busy earning a pittance doing pieceworks for the big stores and other institutions and tell me if such hard and tiring labours ought to be the lot of those destined to nurture human life in a civilised society. Philanthropists have trumpeted the opening of day nurseries and boarding establishments. Yet has the result not been to drive the wife out of her home and to force her to hand over the care of her child to paid workers?'

Of course this was written many years later, when Nadaud's own views on the domestic idyll had been formed by the poignant lack in his own life of this very thing. Indeed, in England he became sentimental about the large families that were commonplace there, and was fiercely opposed to the secret practice of birth control that was much in evidence in France. But probably in youth, too, the hope of further children was there. It would have been one reason among several for wanting Julie in Paris with him, and he was no doubt concerned, as before, that she should not overtire herself. Maybe he thought as well that she would be better off in Paris with no farm work expected of her.

'From time to time her brothers went out with her in the evening, while I was busy with my pupils.'

Presumably it was in Jean Roby's big room in the Ile Saint-Louis that Nadaud continued to run his classes. 'For fifteen years we were room-mates and I don't believe that two men ever lived together in more complete understanding.' It is curious to think that this, rather than his marriage, was Nadaud's defining relationship for so many years, but in this he was typical of his kind.

I have an image of Julie, that 'tall and beautiful girl', her dark hair bundled up in the usual white Creusois cap, her eyes wide at the sights and sounds, sites and smells of Paris as her husband's had been fifteen years before. I imagine that for the first few weeks she stayed in their small room much of the time, washing the old red floor tiles across which so many other lives had passed, tending the fire of wood over which she hung their cooking pot, perhaps mending all her husband's linen, perhaps making him a new smock, gradually accustoming herself for the first time in her life to hours on end in her own company. But I think she also spent long periods with her elbows on the window-sill, gazing down past other windows, past potted plants and washing strings, at the procession of people who came and went in the courtyard several storeys below – the numerous inhabitants of the house, the water-carrier with his barrel on his back, the sellers of charcoal and fish and song-birds and lavender and pans, each crying his wares in voices that echoed off the old walls. The endless, diverting parade of strangers, there and in the streets beyond, was the oddest thing to someone who had lived her life till then almost entirely among people she knew and who knew her. Till she became used to it, she must have had to gather her courage each time she took up her blue cloak, her basket brought from the Creuse and a few coins in her fist and went down into those streets. There, iron-bound cart-wheels grated on the cobbles, and the scent of fresh white bread from the town bakeries vied with the unfamiliar reek of the butchers' meat her husband had learned to like and with the pervasive odour of the Parisian gutters.

But life on these airy heights near the Panthéon and the Sorbonne was quieter for the country girl than it would have been in the old Hôtel de Ville quarter – which had in any case suffered substantial demolitions. The rue de la Mortellerie was a truncated fragment of its former self and further destruction was planned so as to extend the arcaded rue de Rivoli, the embodiment of mid-nineteenth-century chic. The left bank was more peaceful since, for the time being, it lagged behind in the various urban modernisation programmes. The rue Saint-Jacques, which ran to the southern gate of Paris and was the start of the ancient pilgrim way across France for Santiago de Compostela in northern Spain, was still its principal street. Neither the boulevard Saint-Michel nor the boulevard Saint-Germain, the two main arteries of the present-day left bank, yet existed; nor did the rue des Ecoles. But Nadaud's job, working on the monolithic new Mairie by the Panthéon that was designed to form a pair with a new School of Law opposite, was a sign of things to come.

By and by the young couple moved from the rue Saint-Jacques onto the place du Panthéon itself. In the mid-1840s, the town proper still ended only a block or two from there, petering out into builders' yards, workmen's shacks, market gardens, cow-byres, drying yards, garden-cafés, convents, schools and hospitals and a new gas-works. An extensive sapling orchard lay uphill of the Luxembourg Gardens, where the avénue de l'Observatoire now runs. The River Bièvre still wound under the open sky, in what Balzac described as 'a deep hollow populated by countrified workshops intersected by patches of greenery'. The smell from the Bièvre tanneries mingled with that of lilacs and hawthorn, the creak of wheels and the cry of hawkers vied with the crowing of cockerels and the song of larks. Here, the village streets of Pontarion or Saint-Hilaire would not have seemed so far after all.

Some of the new road schemes that were to eviscerate Paris a decade later were already on various visionary drawing-boards. But the most significant event on the ground in the 1840s was the building of the so-called 'fortifications of Thiers' – the new ring of walls much further out from the centre than any previous one. Why a great city should equip itself with fresh fortifications in an era when there was no perceived military threat, and when a general demolition of town walls was beginning to happen almost everywhere else, was never properly explained. It seems in retrospect to have been an expansionist move by the then Préfet, Rambuteau, that was worthy of the future Préfet Haussmann himself. The new barrier included, in a great, high-handed sweep, not only the Paris that already existed but much of its surrounding semi-tamed countryside. Abruptly, villages such as Vaugir-ard, Grenelle, Passy, Montmartre and Belleville found them-selves administratively part of the urban conurbation, and other rural communes such as Gentilly, Montrouge and La Villette were cut in half.

Needless to say, the very existence of the wall ensured that the town would soon reach out to fill the vacant spaces between it and the existing built-up area. This, indeed, had happened by the time the political exiles of the Second Empire – Victor Hugo, Louis Blanc, Nadaud himself – returned in 1870, rubbing their eyes like so many Rip van Winkles:

> *Le vieux Paris n'est plus; la forme d'une ville*
> *Change plus vite, hélas, que le coeur d'un mortel.*

> (Old Paris is no more: the lineaments of a town
> Change more quickly, alas, than does the mortal,
>   human heart.)

· 8 ·

A Triumph and a Tragedy

By the later 1840s, Nadaud's personal Glorious Days were approaching. A temporary halt on work on the Mairie of the Twelfth sent him off to an interim job in the old rue de la Grenelle, near Saint-Germain des Prés, with a difficult employer who at first treated his team as a gang of drunken ruffians for wanting to observe the usual drink-buying rituals before starting work. But while this problem was diplomatically resolved, one drunken ruffian's mind was elsewhere, going to meetings, helping to publish papers, getting up petitions, distributing hand-bills and generally becoming known. He often visited Cabet, then living, perhaps appropriately, in the rue Jean-Jacques Rousseau, in the heart of Paris, between the Halles markets and the Palais Royale. He visited Louis Blanc, then a neighbour in semi-rural Montparnasse, a place of laundresses and windmills; and also saw Pierre Leroux, a philosopher, a publisher of clandestine tracts and a Creusois like himself. He met Pierre Proudhon, another visionary in the mould of Cabet, and reported that he was living in the narrow rue Mazarine in the Latin quarter – 'in a rather dark little ground-floor room from which one only saw daylight through a window on to a narrow courtyard . . . In his manner and his slightly bloated face he appeared like an amiable peasant who had just come back from making a satisfactory sale at the local market.' In fact, Prudhon is mainly remembered today for having coined the phrase 'property is theft', which has had a seductive appeal to subsequent generations of revolutionaries ever since. Indeed the slogan echoed round his own Latin quarter streets again during the highly ritualised revolutionary psycho-drama now known as the Events of May 1968.

Nadaud met and was initially impressed by the barrister Ledru-Rollin, an accomplished if pompous republican, whose fame as a Red was to filter through to the more reactionary and fantasy-prone peasantry as *Le Dru Rollin* (Terrible Rollin); he was rumoured among them to have two mistresses called La Marie and La Martine (Marie was another lawyer, who defended Cabet; Lamartine was a diplomat and a romantic writer who, for a brief period, made common cause with the left).

George Sand heard of Nadaud and wanted to meet him and Agricole Perdiguier, another republican of working-class origin. Nadaud was impressed at being approached by the famous and aristocratic writer, and kept her letter to him inviting him to her play, although that meeting does not seem to have come off. It was inevitable, perhaps, given Nadaud's origins, that, though he valued his working-class counterparts, the republicans who most impressed and influenced him were all from a higher social class. Rustic sincerity was, to him, no novelty. Some ten years later, he was to visit Sand at her country house in Nohant, the place he had passed as a tramping mason. She found him then, as she wrote to Louis Blanc, *si bon, si doux, si sage*, terms which, even if they do not quite carry the connotations of the English 'good, gentle and well-behaved' nevertheless convey that Nadaud was, by Sand's standards, unworldly. If he knew that several of his republican associates, including Pierre Leroux, were among Sand's one-time lovers, that is the sort of thing he would have preferred to ignore, and George Sand must have sensed the fact. At all events, he was not added to her collection.

A neat intersection between Nadaud's now separate but parallel worlds of work and politics occurred when he was returning to the place du Panthéon site. The employer of rue de Grenelle, having finally recognised his qualities as a master mason, told him that he was thinking of giving up the building trade and would make Nadaud a present of his ladders. The implication was that this would help Nadaud to set up finally as an entrepreneur in his own right – 'But just over a year later, my good boss was to hear that I had been elected to represent the people. He asked me to visit him at home in the rue de Clichy. I found him sick in bed. He congratulated me very warmly, but there was no more talk of him giving me his ladders.'

In the end, the reign of Louis-Philippe collapsed more swiftly than even its sworn enemies could have predicted. Foreign policy was going badly, Louis-Philippe was not respected and there had been several attempts on his life, but what really precipitated his fall was an economic crisis of a new, complex kind. An exceptionally bad harvest in 1846 led to a rise in the price of bread, local shortages and age-old fears of famine, accompanied in the following year by assaults on bakeries and grain riots in some country areas. Such natural disasters had been happening for centuries, and this one, in fact, was almost the last of its kind in France, as road and railway networks spread and the traditional dependency on purely local food sources declined. But at the same time a new kind of slump occurred, relating to industrial and business cycles, which affected the whole of Europe. In France there were massive lay-offs in railway construction work, in coal-mining and in the newly developed iron and textile industries. Once again in Paris many building sites fell silent. A couple of financial scandals among ministers (*'Enrichissez-vous'*) made the government look still less impressive.

Even so, the opposition was much divided and there was no concerted call for revolution: Guizot and Louis-Philippe hung on. In the end, events were precipitated by the highly French 'affair of the banquets'. Prevented by law from holding public meetings or even private gatherings of their own members, reformist and republican groups had taken to staging celebration meals – ostensibly purely social occasions – as a cover for political debate. This device was justified but there is some irony in the fact that one of the things the middle-class diners were debating, over the pâté, oysters and beef, was the presence of unemployed working men, gaunt with hunger, who clustered round the coffee stalls and potato sellers on the quais, trying to eke out their last few sous. In February 1848, when a banquet planned in the Twelfth Arrondissement was banned, the parliamentary opposition decided to call the government's bluff by attending it. The row escalated: a torch-lit procession was proposed. A few barricades were raised in the Latin quarter; the government called out the National Guard, but most of this essentially middle-class citizens' militia chose to stay at home. Shocked by their defection, the king finally dismissed Guizot. But the gesture came too late. On the night of 23 February there was a demonstration on the boulevard des Capucines. Someone fired a pistol, the regular army responded with a volley; twenty demonstrators died. But the army were unprepared for a full-scale battle, the National Guard impeded them and many of them defected to the cause of the demonstrators, now parading their dead bodies by torchlight in a cart. The frightened government ordered the troops to avoid further confrontations with the Paris mob, and from that moment the kingdom was lost.

Louis-Philippe and his family slipped out of Paris in the night, headed for Saint-Cloud – in a hired cab, according to one story – and eventually for England, the usual destination. For a few hours there had been a suggestion that his widowed daughter-in-law might become regent for her ten-year-old son, but republican *députés* led by Ledru-Rollin and Lamartine blocked this move. The Chamber was invaded by a Parisian mob, said to have been led by that traditional bogeyman of the French right, a butcher in his blood-stained overalls. By the following day the Provisional Government of republican politicians and journalists had been proclaimed. Many of them were known personally to Nadaud.

He, as it happened, had his own close but limited view of all that passed, for the final banquet that brought down a king was to have been held in the Mairie of the Twelfth – not the new Mairie, which was still under construction, but the old one, a building further up the rue Saint-Jacques. Back at work on the place du Panthéon site, preoccupied with the

delicate and dangerous job of lifting huge blocks of stone up
to the top of the façade, Nadaud and his companions were
only spectators to the growing unrest that began to manifest
itself among the students of that quarter. Indeed, on the day
on which the news of the king's abdication broke, the
building team, having received no orders to stop work, were
at it as usual. They found themselves prisoners on their site
for several hours, with the army drawn up on one side of the
square and the National Guard on the other. Later that day,
however, Nadaud got together with a retired colonel who
lived in a house near by, 'an energetic man of revolutionary
temperament'. The two of them, along with three or four
hundred others, marched up the rue Saint-Jacques and took
formal possession of the Mairie – 'not that we had to do
anything very much, for all the doors were standing open'.
Later that evening he was present in the huge but relatively
peaceful crowd that, in time-honoured fashion, invaded first
the Tuileries Palace and then the Hôtel de Ville.

The Provisional Government had no real powers to decide
the form the future administration of France should take, but
in practice they found themselves more or less compelled by
popular acclaim to announce a Republic, followed by a
declaration of universal (male) suffrage. The right of workers
to associate together was proclaimed, and the government
also incautiously promised 'work for all'. So the National
Workshops were at once set up, in theory to keep unemployed workers under control, though in practice this led,
within a few months, to large mobs of dissatisfied men, for
whom there was no real work, queuing up for welfare hand-
outs to the disgust of the tax-paying classes. The red flag did
not replace the tricolour and the death penalty was abolished
for political offences. Those newly in power, mainly the
liberal bourgeoisie, were at pains to show that 1848 was not
1790: no new Terror was about to begin. For a while at least
the spirit of optimism, fraternity and pacifism prevailed.
Everyone congratulated themselves and each other that all
had passed off so relatively well: even priests and aristocrats
helped to plant trees of liberty. Of this halcyon spring,

Nadaud wrote in his Memoirs: 'By the proclamation of the Republic the dream of my youth had been realised. I went back to my building site happy just to be an observer of the efforts of the Provisional Government.'

In reality, it was not as simple as that. The Provisional Government had immediately set up what was called the Commission to sit in the Palais de Luxembourg, near the Sorbonne. Its ambitiously wide brief was to examine social problems and propose reforms; it was headed by Nadaud's friend and mentor Louis Blanc. As well as other members of the government, such as Ledru-Rollin, Marie, Lamartine and the old survivor from the original French Revolution, Dupont de L'Eure, it was to include workers' delegates: Nadaud was put forward to represent the builders. 'The first meeting took place on 1 March 1848. About two hundred working men, of whom I was one, took their places at nine in the morning in the seats that had previously been occupied by the lords of France.

'At the first sight of that hall with gilding on the walls, on the ceiling and on each of the chairs we were about to occupy, I was so strangely struck that I hardly knew where to look: all this sumptuousness took my breath away.'

This, incidentally, is one of the last times in the Memoirs that we see the young mason frankly amazed by an exotic world beyond his previous experience. By the time we next hear of him in public office, as a Member of Parliament the following year, the shift of identity from labourer to political leader had taken place, and the memories accordingly are filtered through a different and less vivid perspective.

For the moment, however, the shift had not yet come and Nadaud soon ceased to attend the Commission meetings, for a reason that is revealing. The 'enthusiasm and compassion' which were noted years later by an old comrade as the outstanding characteristics of his political thinking, here seemed to be at odds with each other, the personal compassion acting as a brake on the political enthusiasm.

'I was a master builder then, and as the meetings were held at nine in the morning I could only go to them if I abandoned my building site. I knew that my boss would be forced to put someone else in my place and that that someone might well, according to long-established practice, bring in a new team. So all the workmen I had been responsible for hiring might find themselves out of work, at a time when there was a severe building crisis.'

He was replaced on the Commission by a fellow official from the Builders' Association, Bouyer, a man he esteemed but whom, years later, in the loneliness of his English exile, he came to regard as a traitor to the cause. Forever after in his life, it seems, Nadaud was to look back on this relatively brief period after the Revolution of February and before the rise of Louis-Napoleon as a kind of gold standard in the way things should be.

For this reason the Memoirs covering the period 1848 to '49 are an unreliable guide to what actually went on. Writing so long afterwards, when the virtual dictatorship of the Second Empire had risen, flourished and then collapsed again, and the Third Republic was firmly ensconced, Nadaud was at pains to suggest that he had been opposed to Louis-Napoleon's elevation to power from the beginning. He has rueful or occasionally unkind things to say about fellow masons who were 'fooled' by him. However, it would be fairer to say that in late 1848, when Louis-Napoleon Bonaparte was elected President of the new Republic, he still appeared to many as a liberal-minded intellectual with a sincere interest in the poor and in trade unions.

What is probably more accurately portrayed is the distaste Nadaud felt, even at the time, for the extreme revolutionism that was to erupt only four months after the uprising of February. These were the bloody Days of June, which left thousands dead. He had come a long way from the adolescent who had responded with simple and strong emotion to the powder-stained heroes of the last completed revolution, that of 1830. He had also changed from the pugnacious young man of ten years before, who had got into street fights with rival gangs. 'One fact that struck me very much in the days immediately following the Revolution of

1848 ... was the sudden transformation in the behaviour and the reasoning of both the masses and the better educated ... Those among the workers who had always made an issue of their rights and freedoms suddenly became so demanding that nothing the Provisional Government could have done would have satisfied them.

'I must say, I heard many vehement speeches to which I was by nature quite unsympathetic. My own tastes had always drawn me towards questions of work; it seemed to me that I was not fulfilling my duty towards my work-mates when I was not occupying myself directly with things that concerned us and from which the masses of workers could benefit. In a word, I came to feel that the world of revolutionaries pure and simple did not bring me the satisfaction I sought.'

As for the events of June, when the spectre of Red Terror was abruptly revived, there is only the briefest reference to 'the terrible combat ... which for seven days made French blood run in the gutters of Paris'. Then Nadaud diverges into a personal story of having, two days earlier, gone to fetch some of his gang of men out of the wine shop and finding them drunk and aggressively toasting Louis-Napoleon. He remarks (twice) that one of them, a very strong immigrant German worker – possibly Alsatian? – whom he had often employed, was later guillotined for the murder of General Bréa at the south-eastern gate of Paris.

Although the place du Panthéon, where the National Workshop men gathered to collect their pay, was in the heart of Red land, I do not think that Nadaud was to be found on top of a barricade during that week. Just what he did we do not know. Maybe, long afterwards, he felt some need to excuse his failure to play any sort of heroic role. His suggestion that the whole insurrection formed part of a Bonapartist conspiracy to overthrow the infant republic seems rather far from the truth.

Meanwhile came the exciting development that Nadaud was to recall as a great moment all his life long, though he gives slightly different accounts of it in different places.

According to his Memoirs, it arose more or less by chance. His boss at the Panthéon site was having a small country villa built for himself out at Porte Maillot on the western edge of Paris, where, today, the Conference Centre and the air terminals stand – 'I used to go there for several hours each day to oversee the work.' Porte Maillot is a long way from the Panthéon: I hardly think Nadaud could have walked there and back daily, in the time-honoured masons' way, merely to put in 'several hours'. Probably he took one of the buses, still shaped like light-weight coaches, that were then proliferating in the city.

It was at Porte Maillot, while Nadaud was having a drink with a painter for whom he had fixed up a job, that this man picked up a newspaper lying on the counter. The two learnt from it that that very evening a meeting of Creusois in Paris was being held at the Sorbonne. The paper added that the list of candidates who should represent the Creuse in the National Assembly (at the forthcoming general elections) was going to be drawn up.

Did Nadaud really know nothing of this already? Given his contacts, it seems unlikely. But at all events, he went to the Sorbonne 'without wasting time – without going home first to change out of my working clothes. I found the amphitheatre packed, up to the highest levels, where I found standing room.'

Confusion reigned: until the proclamation of Votes for All two months before, voting had been the preserve of a tiny segment of the population, the property-owning bourgeoisie – as it was to become again under the Second Empire. For the moment, large numbers of apparently well-educated young men wanted to present themselves as candidates to a new and as yet unknown Creusois electorate of 70,000. According to Nadaud, these would-be Members were mostly Bonapartists, and he listened to them with growing annoyance – 'till, carried away by anger or by my heart's impulse, and without really knowing what I was going to say – for I had never before spoken in public – I demanded to be heard'.

After a second interruption and further confusion, he was

Martin Nadaud as the young *député* of 1849

The house in La Martinèche where
Nadaud was born, with a detail of the
upside-down door-lintel (p. 10)

The masons leaving for Paris.
The man in front carries a local
musical instrument.

Rue de la Mortellerie in the 1860s – until then, no one had thought it worth depicting

Two packed floors from the interior of a *garni* (p. 66)

Masons at work –
the 'boy' carries up a
heavy head-load of
mortar (p. 59)

Masons waiting for work in the place de la Grève.
Entrepreneurs hiring them are in frock-coats on the far right and left.

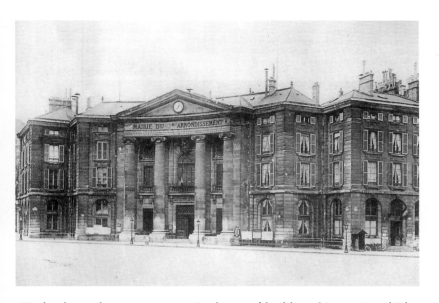

Nadaud was the master-mason in charge of building this *mairie*, which stands across from the Panthéon

'Lamartine Rejects the Red Flag in 1848' (*detail*): in spite of the corpse, the message is that this was to be a peace-loving revolution.

Louis-Philippe

Louis Blanc

Etienne Cabet

John Malcolm Ludlow

The only known likeness of Léonard Nadaud. One can imagine the Guéret photographer of the 1860s deciding to make a feature of the old man's knotty stick.

Probably by the same photographer, on one of Nadaud's unofficial visits to France in his forties (p. 239)

No. 10 Gerrard Street today

Wimbledon School in the late 1860s

Nadaud's public image
late in life still had him fixed
in the building trade

The house at La Martinèche
where Nadaud spent his last years.
The old house lies immediately to
the left and behind it.

In the garden
in old age

finally located up among the crowd of smock-wearing workmen and hustled down to the platform. There, by his own account, he gave a radical speech, defending the infant Republic, denouncing the sitting Member of Parliament for Bourganeuf in particular (a swashbuckling figure called de Giradin) and all the other aspirants in general (*Applause*). As he returned to his place a 'tall and handsome young man' got up and declared, 'Citizens, the meeting has heard many would-be candidates already. I now offer you one more – the speaker who has just left the platform. That one knows the People, he speaks their language, he understands their needs; your hopes are his, and he can only want what you want for yourselves.'

And so, after several more noisy meetings, Nadaud was adopted.

That, at least, is the story. And, by the time Nadaud was an old man in a frock-coat, the image of the young, strong man in workman's clothes standing up entirely on the spur of the moment to denounce bourgeois *arrivisme* was so well established that Nadaud himself had probably come to believe that had been exactly how it was. Certainly, when he did get elected – not that spring, as it turned out, but the following one – the press made the most of the first-ever *député en blouse* – Member of Parliament in a plasterer's smock. He had, in the space of one year, become rather famous.

In April 1848 Nadaud, nervous, knowing few republicans at home in the Creuse and with little money in his pocket, travelled from Paris to Guéret. Anti-republican tales that he was a drunken pimp and a town hooligan [*voyou de barrière*] had travelled ahead of him, and at first even the local republicans cold-shouldered him. No doubt, too, he still looked and sounded more like a street-fighter than a Member of Parliament. However, he managed, thanks to one Parisian contact in particular, to make himself accepted:

'My affirmation of allegiance and my election papers were

printed at public cost; my name was to be spread into even the smallest hamlets. I failed to get elected but earned a very respectable number of votes [*une belle minorité*].' This is true: he only narrowly missed getting in.

An obituarist 50 years later recalled him in an election meeting at that date 'in his vigorous prime . . . the meeting took place in the house of a grocer, and freedom was so unfamiliar at that time that people hid themselves as they slipped in to hear Citizen Nadaud.

'Monsieur Nadaud was then a physically powerful man who held his head high. With a healthy complexion, his face was ornamented by a handsome black beard and illuminated by his lively and frank expression . . . His generous soul was pained by the disdain which the bourgeoisie then openly expressed for the ignorant working man.'

In the following spring, 1849, the chance came again. This time the election was for a more permanent Legislative Assembly, and this time Nadaud was successful. The pages of the Memoirs that deal with this are a litany of gratitude and faithful remembrance for those who helped him, many of whom were later to take their own road into political exile. At the last minute the opposition tried to confuse the electorate by launching a candidate of their own also called Nadaud – a fairly common name in the centre of France. An energetic republican on the spot 'at once roused seven of our friends who set off on horseback to the most distant corners, as far as Aubusson, while he himself went to Guéret . . . Thus it was repeated from one canton to another that the first name "Martin" must be added before "Nadaud".'

Yet he himself was not there. On this occasion he had stayed in Paris, following the election campaign in the newspapers and finishing off the edifice by the Panthéon.

'One morning, when I was busy lending a hand to the men at plastering the huge ceiling of the wedding chamber of the Mairie, Antoine, my boy-mason, appeared with something in his hand. It was a letter that my wife had just handed to him at the foot of the scaffolding, for him to bring up to me. He was laughing out loud. The envelope read *Citoyen Nadaud*,

Représentant du Peuple [Citizen Nadaud, People's Representative]. Bouyer . . . snatched it from him and read it aloud, while I went on plastering my bit of ceiling.

'Great was the delight shown by all the masons, the stone-cutters, the roofers and carpenters. Five minutes later we were all in the wine shop, and, needless to say, we drank deep. In the days that followed people came from all over the place to congratulate me, for it seemed so extraordinary then to see a plain mason get to the Parliament Chamber.' But why had Nadaud not been in the Creuse at his moment of triumph? In this very convoluted part of his Memoirs, in which much that is told seems altered by hindsight and one feels the presence of things untold lurking behind the text, we have already, several pages before, been given a practical, hurried explanation for this:

'During that election campaign I decided not to go back this time to the Creuse. The expenses of the previous year had sickened me.' He mentions too that 'as a faithful friend of Cabet, I had promised to leave for Icarus with the second cohort, and I really meant to keep my word.' This does not quite make sense. Cabet had already left for America to join his supporters at the end of 1848 and no further reinforcements from France followed. Anyway, if Nadaud had seriously intended to throw in his lot with Cabet, Icarus and the New World he would hardly have stood for election a second time.

What is surely the real explanation for his unwillingness to leave Paris in 1849 is slipped into a line and a half without any full stop between election expenses and Cabet, as if it were almost incidental: 'The expenses of the previous year had sickened me; the long and cruel illness which was, this year, to lead my wife to the grave, had not allowed me to make any savings at all, and then, as a faithful friend of Cabet . . .'

So, when Julie makes her fleeting but telling appearance at the foot of the scaffolding, having come from their lodging at the corner of the square to hand over the exciting letter right away, we know already that within a few months she will be dead. The back-to-front and hasty method of imparting to the reader such a significant fact tells its own tale.

Six years before, when he believed Julie to be dying or dead from a miscarriage, he had written in an agonised scrawl: 'Oh, the pain. So I have not been allowed to keep for any longer the person I loved so much.' Subsequently, and in defiance of prevailing custom, he brought Julie to Paris so that they could be together; clearly this love had continued. One concludes that the private pain of his loss, coming at the time when his public life was expanding unprecedentedly, was so great that he was unable to express it even forty years later.

His wife is never even mentioned again in his Memoirs, nor is his state as a widower. But this omnipresent fact must have affected his attitude to everything that happened in the packed years of change and movement that immediately followed his bereavement. In an undated letter to his father that seems to have been written the next spring, and which deals mainly with his new political life, he wrote, 'My health is good; I am not very happy [*je m'ennuit un peu*], if only I could forget the mother of poor little, little Désirée.' Another letter, which has been wrongly dated at a later time but which must, from internal evidence, have been written soon after, is addressed to 'the workmen of the Creuse' and strikes a more doom-laden note. Predicting 'an imminent and terrible revolution' he goes on to envisage his own likely death from a bullet within a secret prison. He exhorts 'the few genuine republicans that remain' to be of good faith, says that he has always tried to do his duty; he mentions anxiously 'small debts' he has been able to pay off and those he has not. He commends to the care of the Republican Party 'an old father, an old mother and a poor little orphan of four and a half years, my dear little Désirée who, at the age of just four, has had the misfortune to lose the most gentle and good of mothers'. The whole letter reads like a last Will and Testament: one's impression is of a man too traumatised and depressed to take anything but the most pessimistic view. Yet this was also the man who was fighting his corner in

Parliament in every way: by a happy chance he occupied seat number 2, on the extreme left-hand side of the Chamber. He made frequent speeches on reforms dear to his heart while robustly ignoring Members who jeered at his grammatical or sartorial mistakes. 'My friends told me that people had laughed at my air of embarrassment, and at my red-check waistcoat which was not, it seemed, the proper thing to wear.' He also took early morning lessons to fill in some of the gaps in his education.

Three years later, when the long-feared disaster had happened, and he had had to draw on further reserves of energy and courage to cope with a complete reversal of fortune and an ignominious new status as a refugee, he was still fighting. But another republican exile, the journalist Victor Schoelcher who was his companion on the boat to England, wrote long afterwards that at this time Nadaud seemed to him 'still heartbroken [*l'âme brisé*] from the death of his young wife' and, in the same sentence, that in London he 'waited for justice to return'. Schoelcher seems to have perceived that Nadaud's distress at his political defeat and exile was not wholly distinct from his distress at the fate that had robbed him of the person who should, in all circumstances, have been his life's companion.

Nadaud may also have felt that he himself carried some blame for Julie's death. Once I had established that she had died in 1849, I supposed, for a while, that her death had taken place back at home in the Creuse – perhaps in attempting to give birth to another child, the very scenario dreaded by Nadaud some years earlier. But a better-informed friend finally guided me to the Paris records for her death entry. Or rather, not to the original records, which were consumed in the firing of the Hôtel de Ville during the Commune of 1871, but to the records which were painstakingly reconstructed subsequently from other copies:

'*L'an mil huit cents quarante-neuf, le vingt et un Octobre, est décédée à Paris, rue Sufflot, douzième arrondissement, Jeanne Julie Aupetit, âgée de trente ans, née à La Chaux*

(Creuse), mariée à Martin Nadaud, Le Membre de la Commission.'

The funeral service for Julie was held at Saint-Etienne du Mont, near to where the Nadauds had been living. Where she was buried, I do not know. It is very likely to have been in the new Cimitière du Sud, today's Montparnasse Cemetery, the resting place since then of an enormous number of Parisians, both obscure and famous.

The year 1849 was another in which cholera reappeared all over Europe. But by late October the epidemic in Paris had waned, and in any case the fugitive reference in Nadaud's Memoirs to 'a long and cruel illness' (*une longue et cruelle maladie*) suggests, not the sudden blow of cholera, but an even more classic nineteenth-century scourge: tuberculosis.

Although, as the century went on, TB became common in the countryside too, it was widely perceived as a sickness of the city. It seemed like an outward and dramatic demonstration of a whole range of more nebulous urban evils that were deemed to lie in wait for the unwary country dweller tempted by the bright lights: thus moral and physical nemesis were neatly combined. On a more prosaic level, tuberculosis was believed to lurk dormant in buildings for years on end, particularly in damp or dark corners, and thus to be literally part of the fabric of the town. Dr Villard of the Creuse, that indefatigable hygienist and opponent of migration, wrote about this later in the century, when many more wives were joining their husbands. His apocalyptic vision was of Paris as a vast engine breathing out foul airs from domestic chimneys, furnaces, steam trains, sewers, gas mantles and the like, plus the 'exhalation of two million chests'. (Paris had something over a million people by 1849, and close to two million thirty years later, by which time the villages round the fortifications had been annexed as well.) Here is Dr Villard in a fine peroration on the plight of accompanying wives who, since they could not fairly be accused of succumbing to city Temptations, like unaccompanied laundresses and nurse-maids, appear to have wilted from their very respectability:

'The couple rent a small room somewhere, buy a few essential items of furniture. The wife usually does sewing work for the clothing trade and gets the meal ready for her husband each evening. She thus leads a toilsome, very sedentary life, shut up almost all day and all of each night in a restricted space that is often ill ventilated . . . impregnated with the vapour of cooking and of burning coal. In such a situation, often ill nourished and working all day and into the night, she soon finds her strength diminishing and her health becomes precarious. How many young wives have I seen, leaving our airy mountains robust, with colour in their cheeks and every appearance of a flourishing constitution, only to return to the homelands, after several years, pale, languishing, thin, harbouring the germ and often the clear signs of mortal illness?'

A somewhat exaggerated view, one might feel. After all, part of the complaint of Villard and other Creusois is that increasingly couples settled in Paris and did indeed flourish there. But then there is Julie Nadaud, dead less than three years after her happy arrival in the city her husband had made his own. If being with her husband led to another pregnancy, this in itself would have exacerbated a tubercular condition wherever its true origins lay. Bitter, secret, unassu-ageable regret – at having brought his wife to Paris at all, and having deprived their one existing child of a mother she would not even remember – must have been part of Nadaud's mourning, and contributed to the cloud of discretion which, from this point in his Memoirs, descends.

The story he was telling himself and his readers was one of long endeavour rewarded, trials and set-backs overcome, justice at last triumphing and dreams coming true. It was to be read as a secular pilgrim's progress on both the political and the personal front: for this opponent of the Catholic Church, the long-awaited achievement and resolution had to come in this life, for there was no other. In this inspiring fable, the pain of irreparable loss and defeat simply could not find a place.

Downfall

After 1851 Nadaud had good reason to hate Louis-Napoleon Bonaparte (*ce misérable gredin*) and the heavily policed Empire he built. Yet there is a certain irony in the fact that this was the man who came to incarnate, during Nadaud's long years of exile, all that he most disliked, for Nadaud and the Emperor had more than one thing in common. Louis-Napoleon, Bonaparte's nephew, spent virtually all his adult life in exile, in Geneva, London or America, until he came back to Paris in 1848 and offered himself as a popular choice for Prince-President. He had written a treatise on poverty and another on trade unions. He had twice tried to overturn Louis-Philippe, and the second time he had been imprisoned for it, supposedly for life. What's more, when he managed, after more than five years, to escape from the fortress where he was being kept, it was by disguising himself in a mason's smock. Works were being done on the fortress at the time, and a Bonapartist mason gave his hero his clothes. Just as Louis-Napoleon had stepped outside the walls, he was accosted by another mason who, thinking he was a new workman, greeted him with the time-honoured question '*Quand est-ce que?*' ('When will you buy us a drink?'). With a private irony, Louis-Napoleon replied '*Ce sera pour quand je reviendrai*' ('That'll be when I come back') and went rapidly on his way.

The disguise was appropriate, for Louis-Napoleon fancied himself as a builder. As soon as he was ensconced as President of the Second Republic, he began following in the footsteps of those who had already drawn up ambitious plans for the reconstruction of Paris. The transformations of the next two decades are commonly considered the work of his Préfet, Haussmann, but it was Louis-Napoleon who appointed Haussmann and he also contributed ideas of his own. After his life abroad, Paris was a new city to him and therefore perhaps all the more tempting. He was often found by his advisers and ministers busy covering its map in pencil lines, pursuing and revising his ideas of exactly where new cross-routes would open up the old place to light, air, traffic circulation, a nicer class of tenant and easier access for the forces of Law and Order. The notion that the straight, wide Haussmann avenues were constructed to allow Imperial troops to fire down them has passed into mythology. However, there is plenty of evidence that the transformation of Paris in the 1850s and '60s was just the most notable example of a much wider contemporary concern with hygiene, communications and civic pride. These preoccupations appeared at the same era in other major cities as diverse as London, Vienna and Bombay that did not have the same tradition of militant uprisings. More specifically, Louis-Napoleon saw that, with the arrival of railways, the old *barrières d'octroi*, the customs barriers round Paris, were becoming obsolete, and that it was the railway termini that would be the new gates of Paris. He had seen the newly opened Euston station, with its famous portico – 'Gateway to the North' – while he was still in England. The first grand Parisian station of this kind, the Gare de l'Est, was being built by 1850, and the Gare Saint-Lazare soon after.

Those on the idealistic wing of the government felt that a brave, new, cleaner world might emerge from the demolition of medieval streets, while pragmatists thought that plentiful building sites would provide much needed employment for the honest working man ('Always honest', according to Flaubert, 'as long as he is not rioting'). Neatly conflating both views, Balzac remarked: 'The mortar trowel is, in Paris, a more civilising tool than you might suppose.' Nadaud, with his acquired horror of both unemployment and street violence, and his desire for social improvement, was unlikely to be displeased. From its early days in 1848, the Provisional Government rushed through plans for the Paris municipality to acquire compulsorily all the properties it would need for the projected new avenues. There was no money in the coffers at that point to fulfil this dream, but the government voted to finish off the Louvre at last and to prolong the rue de Rivoli as far as the rue Saint-Antoine, eradicating in its route the Marché Saint-Jean and the rue de la Tissanderie where Nadaud had lodged as a teenager. Covered market buildings, the long-planned Halles, were soon begun in the new ironwork now being produced in the Paris region. The next couple of years saw the rudimentary beginnings of sanitary regulations regarding the inside of houses. It also brought an end to the practice of nightsoil men depositing barrow-loads of untreated faeces in a dump at Montfaucon, in the northeast, on the site of a one-time gibbet.

By August 1851, the traditional French public prejudice against loans and credit seems to have been on the wane; the Paris municipality was allowed by Parliament to borrow fifty million francs, against which it issued public bonds. In this manner, the famous or notorious Haussmann transformation scene, attended by years of lucrative speculation in real estate, first got under way. Parisians, indeed, rushed to lend, believing that they would eventually get back much more. The 'golden rain', satirised Zola, was about to fall.

Eventually *les comptes fantastiques de Haussmann* were to become one of the major scandals of the Second Empire. But between 1849 and 1851, while Nadaud was in Parliament, the new plans for Paris seemed a most decent public-spirited initiative, in the best traditions of republicanism. Indeed, it would probably be true to say that even if the Second Empire had not come, in the next two decades Paris would have been transformed in any case. Martin Nadaud's first speeches in Parliament were made in favour of the changes. This was when he claimed, in his one unfortunately immortal phrase, 'A Paris, lorsque le bâtiment va, tout va.' Much later, he recalled: 'In 1848 by chance I had in my hands the plan for the boulevard Sebastapol well before Monsieur Haussmann appeared, and I said that this substantial route absolutely must be opened up.' He never did quite sort out his ideological view on Haussmann's Paris, which his belief in progress led him to admire rather than to condemn. At one point in his Memoirs, in the space of two pages, he treats his old companions such as Bouyer as traitors for having remained in Paris working as building entrepreneurs under the Empire, while yet praising what they constructed. 'Our friends were sub-contractors on the important Gare d'Orléans [the Gare d'Austerlitz], then on the official residences for Louis-Napoleon's ministers, who had risen to power as swiftly as their master and by much the same means. They [the ministers] built for themselves superb houses in various parts of Paris, particularly round the place de l'Europe.'

The eventual verdict of liberal republicans on this new Paris was to be more condemnatory. George Sand, alone among them, liked the sense of freedom in the new, wide streets, around which she walked at night when in her Bohemian trousered mood. But Victor Hugo, who was Nadaud's colleague and close associate in Parliament in 1849–51, wrote:

> *Ce vieux Paris n'est plus qu'une rue éternelle*
> *Qui s'étire, élégante et belle comme l'I,*
> *En disant: 'Rivoli! Rivoli! Rivoli! –'*

('Old Paris is nothing but an everlasting street, which stretches ahead as elegant and straight as the letter "I", saying: "Rivoli! Rivoli! Rivoli! –"') The Goncourt brothers, summing the matter up in the 1860s, complained that the spacious new quarters 'no longer have the scent of Balzac's Paris, but make one think of some American Babylon of the future'.

The real problems, indeed, were created not by what was built but by what was destroyed, which was much more than the atmosphere of Balzac. Nadaud himself, in the enduring tradition of left-wing politicians, seems to have been largely devoid of nostalgia for the past. He had known too well what life was like in the crowded, medieval houses of the Cité and the Hôtel de Ville quarter to want to see them preserved. But he also seems to have failed to realise – as, in fairness, did his colleagues in 1850 – that by demolishing an old street in the interests of social progress you create a new social problem of displaced people. All in all, during the 1850s and 1860s, some 25,000 houses in Paris and the suburbs were demolished. Hundreds of streets were removed, wholly or partly, and most of these were in the traditional working-class quarters of central Paris.

Already, in the 1840s, the Hôtel de Ville area had been the target of 'improvements'. By the time the rue de Rivoli was finished and boulevard Sebastapol, the north–south cross route, completed in 1858, 2,000 houses had been pulled down in that district alone, driving 25,000 people to look for homes elsewhere. The Ile de la Cité was similarly eviscerated. In the early 1830s it had had about 12,000 inhabitants: by the time first Rambuteau and then Haussmann had finished with it thirty-odd years later, filling it with huge institutional and governmental piles, it had only a few hundred. But long before that thoughtful Parisians, including many who had originally welcomed the idea of cleaning and beautifying the city, began to express disquiet. By the mid-1850s it was beginning to be realised that new rent levels were the big drawback to the demolition schemes. Lodgers had no right to be re-housed and received no compensation – unlike the leaseholders and owners of the demolished houses, who were fully recompensed. It was noted that workers who, in 1849, had still been able to find lodgings in the rue de la Tissanderie for 110 francs a year, when their streets were pulled down had taken refuge further out. When they returned to the centre after the dust had settled, they found that the new houses were much more expensive than the old ones, and that even in the old houses rents had risen. The building works themselves had attracted to Paris a new influx of labourers, all of them wanting accommodation. Like property developers the world over, those who financed the building of the new Paris optimistically built houses and flats for the middle classes regardless of whether that was what was needed. The few schemes for workers' dwellings on the London model (Louis-Napoleon was an admirer of Prince Albert) were also too costly in rent, and hedged about by too many regulations for popular taste.

The dispossessed working classes therefore settled in the territory between the customs barrier and the new fortifications, where taxes were lower. They colonised Montmartre, Batignolles, La Grenelle and Vaugirard, and especially the north-east districts of La Villette, Menilmontant and the misleadingly named Belleville. This area was still semi-rural; the rather disreputable cafés and dance-halls of Belleville, where Nadaud had encountered 'loose women', were prettily set among market gardens. However, parts of Belleville had long been blighted by the memory of the Montfaucon gibbet and the subsequent spreading rubbish dumps, by debris from slaughter-yards and by quarries. Often the newcomers accommodated themselves on these wastelands in home-built shanties that were inferior to and less convenient than the 'insalubrious streets' they had been forced to leave. It was pointed out that a mason living in Belleville had to get up at four in the morning in order to arrive on foot at his work-site in one of the smart, expanding western suburbs by six. Omnibuses were still beyond the budget of such men, who earned from 3 to 6 francs a day. The suburban ring-railway, La Petite Ceinture, on which future generations of Parisian workers based their daily lives, was not built until the 1860s.

So the slums of the poor were simply displaced. By 1860 the Menilmontant quarter, like a number of other outlying districts, was annexed to Paris: it became the Twentieth Arrondissement, new style. By then it had 60,000 inhabitants. The neighbouring area of La Villette had 30,000, and a great deal of the new industry – forges, distilleries, candle and soap works, etc. – that was replacing the smaller-scale workshop culture of the rue Saint-Antoine. The 'dangerous classes', with their reputation for Red violence and for tuberculosis (both ills associated with bloodstains) had shifted here from the old centre of the city. The quarries at the Buttes Chaumont, in the north of Belleville, were to be a revolutionary bastion during the Commune in 1871, and many of the Communards met their death by the wall of Père Lachaise cemetery in the south.

Once the immediate trauma of the Commune had passed, Nadaud was elected to represent the Twentieth Arrondissement on the municipal council of Paris and did so for five years. Today the arrondissement and its neighbouring ones are sprinkled with streets named after people who were his friends in life – Gambetta, Louis Blanc, Ledru-Rollin – or who followed after him in the same tradition – the socialist Jean Jaurès and 'Colonel Fabien' of the Resistance. This section of Paris was to retain its working-class character for the next hundred years. The 'accent of Belleville' was a phrase used until recently to denote a vulgar Parisian intonation, and the French Communist Party has long had its headquarters there. Jewish immigrants settled in Belleville between the two world wars; Arab ones afterwards. But in the 1960s and 1970s another convulsion of urban rebuilding transported the poor further out again – to the desolate, utopian tower blocks of the modern *zone*.

Well before the social drawbacks to urban improvement made themselves apparent in the mid-1850s, Nadaud, along with Victor Hugo and a number of others, had been removed from the government and from France.

Louis Blanc had been in exile from late 1848, a fate which Nadaud, having not yet risen to national prominence at that point, and not having been implicated in the Days of June, had avoided. Ledru-Rollin, too, was in England from 1849, after further republican protest and another round of arrests. Nadaud himself and several others were arrested at a demonstration and taken to a guard-post, but escaped by climbing through a window and running off. 'I took a circuitous route across Paris and reached, on foot, the customs barrier at the Etoile, where in a nearby street Madame Cabet was living. Three days later I came back to my seat in the Chamber. Either I hadn't been recognised or, having run off, I had managed to avoid being banned.'

Because Nadaud's time in this brief Parliament of the Second Republic is viewed retrospectively in the light – or rather the darkness – of the defeat that followed, it is not always easy to know what his true feelings were at the time. At one point he admits that some of his colleagues disappointed and shocked him and 'I felt sadness take hold of me. This trouble in my spirits came near to destroying my competence, in spite of the love of work which had been rooted in me in my evening classes for young labourers.' But when one considers that this was in the same period as the death of his wife, his sense of depression and disorientation seems neither surprising nor wholly due to political circumstances.

He refers at one point to that era as 'the most shameful and humiliating to be found in the annals of an enlightened and civilised people such as we purport to be'. But whatever the machinations of Bonapartists and monarchists during those difficult two years, and the signs of creeping repression, it is hard to believe that Nadaud himself went round for all that time in a state of moral indignation. It seems more likely that, punch drunk with events both public and personal, he was nevertheless learning fast. As the first-ever working-class Member, with his personal warmth, his strong orator's voice and his occasional lapses in grammar, he was a notable figure and, one suspects, something of a mascot. Many of the original leaders of the Republican Party were now missing, and the sturdy figure who was always portrayed in a voluminous smock, trowel in hand, mortar-trough on shoulder, became a staple of mainly affectionate cartoons. Nadaud remarks ingenuously in his Memoirs: 'I do admit at this point, without either ostentation or pride, that I had some success in Parliament . . . I often held the floor for hours on end, and found myself congratulated by men such as Jules Favre and Michel de Bourges.' These men, like Victor Hugo and Nadaud himself, belong to the democratic socialist tendency which had adopted the old name 'La Montagne' –

The Mountain – in a conscious harking back to the days of the first French Revolution.

We are spared, in the Memoirs, the text of these lengthy speeches. This is partly because Nadaud had, by that time, published many of them elsewhere (complete with '*Applause*' and '*Bravos*') and partly because his own scrapbooks were to be seized by the police.

'At the moment when I went into exile, I gave the key to my rooms to a relative of mine, Martin Julian, a person of heroic courage and sacrifice. One day he found his own small room had been ransacked by the police and the collection of cuttings, which meant a lot to me, were stolen by them.

'Why not admit it – I derived a real satisfaction from reading and re-reading the views of those newspapers who reported on my speeches in Parliament or in the public gatherings to which I was often invited.'

Faithful to his background and to what he felt he had been elected to do, Nadaud agitated for the abolition of the much disliked *livret*, the worker's police papers, and made speeches on poverty. One day when his adversaries were baiting him and 'uttering peacock cries', he was protected by the Speaker and encouraged to continue.

'"Will you still deny", I repeated, "that in France we have between one hundred and eighty and two hundred thousand workers whose wages are inadequate to keep them and their families alive?" Continuing in this mode for almost two hours, in the midst of repeated and violent interruptions, I was able, by showing myself to be tenacious and resolute, to stand up to the enemies of the Republic.'

Heady stuff it must have been, for the man who had once been a tongue-tied teenager, not even speaking proper French. One of the few other speeches that he quotes verbatim from this period relates to his opposition to new regulations regarding drink shops – hardly, you might think, a particularly noble cause. However, in this too Nadaud was showing himself faithful to his origins. The ceremonial buying of drinks for each other, and the almost universal masons' habit of having a glass of white wine every morning before even starting work to settle the stomach (literally 'to kill off the worm'), had been part of his own culture for twenty years. But in fact there was more in the drink shop question than immediately appears. The majority of the right wing in the government, also known as 'the party of order', wanted an excuse to shut down cafés and drink shops that they suspected of being used to hold subversive meetings. But since there were far more cafés in Paris and in other towns than there had been in the 1830s, they were able to cloak their real motive under a concern for public morals, citing cafés as places of drunkenness and working-class debauchery. Since Nadaud himself had been slandered two years earlier, during his republican campaign, as a 'drunken pimp' and 'town hooligan', it is not surprising he was infuriated by this piece of humbug.

'Once again, I rose to speak. As I began, I was so stirred that I raised my voice too loud. A burst of sardonic laughter greeted my words, and the Speaker interrupted to tell me to speak more quietly.

'"Since the question of public morality is preoccupying you so much," I said to them, "let us once and for all be clear on this matter, seriously and categorically. It is our belief that a man who is not honest in his private life cannot be so in his political life, (*Indications of approval from all sides*). Gentlemen, when one has the honour of representing a country such as France, one must above all things, in both public and private life, set an example." ("*Very good, very good.*")

'*Voice on the right*. "That's why we must regulate the drink shops."

'*Nadaud*. "And France will be disturbed and suffer from pains until the day she finds a government which sets an example in private virtues –"'

And so on. Many of the later pages too of the Memoirs, dealing with the period after 1870, are taken up with this kind of thing. Exactly why this man, who was regarded by everyone who encountered him over the years as profoundly good-hearted, honest and modest, should have needed in old age to blow ancient trumpets in this way, is something one can only decide for oneself, in relation to the unforeseen paths his life was to take.

It should also be added that the 'private virtues' on which Nadaud insisted were not at that date likely to have been sexual – that is a preoccupation of our own times and an Anglo-Saxon one anyway. Victor Hugo, one of Nadaud's main allies in Parliament, was anything but a model of marital fidelity: he had been embarrassingly arrested *in flagrante delicto* by the Police of Morals some years earlier, under Louis-Philippe. Nadaud probably had in mind more general forms of integrity, consistency and the keeping of promises. The way so many people, in 1850–1, seemed to renege on the republican ideal that they had briefly embraced and that was so dear to him, was a source of constant pain. All his life, he never quite reconciled himself to the idea that when circumstances change, minds may, in good faith, change too. This tenacity was both his strength and his weakness.

One more accolade awaited Nadaud in public life at this period. When Louis-Napoleon had been voted in as President in late 1848 this was meant to be for a set term to expire in 1852 and he was not supposed to be re-electable. He subsequently sought to have this overthrown and at the same time, amid dispute about who should or should not be allowed to vote, several more presidential candidates were proposed. Each faction was wary of the others, and among the republicans the main and realistic anxiety was that too much power was becoming concentrated in one man. They favoured someone who might be less authoritarian and more symbolic: a man of the people – and who better, in this case, than the honest working man Martin Nadaud?

The suggestion was at first made provocatively and not entirely seriously, but it gathered weight. Its originator was none other than Emile de Giradin, who had been the member for Bourganeuf, Creuse, before Nadaud had unseated him, but had found another constituency. De Giradin was a complex figure of considerable looks and charm; he was the illegitimate son of an aristocrat, but was responsible for launching in France the first newspaper cheap enough for the working man to buy. His wife had a Parisian reputation as a beauty and a poetess, and when her husband decided to acquire a property in Bourganeuf and cultivate personally its hundred and fifty electors she wrote regular newspaper articles on the 'untouched romantic beauty' of the spot. Nadaud's own view of de Giradin varied. He did not fundamentally trust this essentially self-interested celebrity with a flair for money-making and publicity. However, he felt that at least the de Giradins, with their popular news-sheet that included Parisian stories and their firework parties and dances for the gratified citizens of Bourganeuf, had helped to raise that little town out of its traditional political lethargy. An operator like de Giradin seemed to him on the whole preferable to the entrenched local notables, with their bucolic ignorance and their sneers about drunken Parisian pimps; also, de Giradin now often voted with the democratic socialists. In any case Nadaud would hardly have been human had he not warmed to the man who had proposed elevating him to the giddy heights of President of the Republic!

But a quite other fate awaited Nadaud and most of his supporters. No presidential elections took place in 1852. Instead, Louis-Napoleon staged a *coup d'état*. This move was not unexpected but, as a contemporary remarked afterwards, they'd been waiting for it for so long they had almost stopped believing in it.

On the evening of 1 December 1851, Nadaud had been dining with associates in the east of Paris, near the place de la Bastille. According to him, the talk at table was, even then, of whether armed resistance might be feasible if Louis-Napoleon should move against them.

He was then living in bachelor quarters at No. 9 rue de Seine, near Proudhon's back room, and round the corner from the alley where Balzac had had his printing press. (No. 9 has disappeared today, one of several houses that were badly damaged in the Great Flood of 1911; a small public garden behind the Institute now covers the spot.)

Leaving the Bastille area, Nadaud followed the rue Saint-Antoine to the Hôtel de Ville, one of the familiar routes of his youth that was soon to be swept away by a new street layout. He continued his walk westwards along the still unembanked quais of the river, as far as the Louvre, crossed the Pont des Arts, continued further along the left bank and then retraced his steps to his lodgings. It is rare, by this stage of his Memoirs, that he gives such circumstantial detail: presumably, in the long afterwards, his circuitous night walk appeared to him as an unconscious farewell to Paris and to an epoch.

'Every district through which I passed was calm and peaceful. Yet, three or four hours later the population was awakened by the movement of troops due to occupy all parts of Paris in readiness to crush our people, who were unarmed and defenceless.

'It was almost one in the morning when I got to my lodgings. I had hardly fallen asleep when I felt myself being woken up by my concierge. He had given the key of my flat to a police inspector, Langrange. Opening my eyes, I saw that I was surrounded, for this policeman was with four strapping constables. I did not know what they wanted; the chief made a sign to his men to leave my bedroom, and they went to sit in the adjoining room. "I've been ordered", he said to me, "to search through your papers, the warrant says that you are accused of harbouring prohibited arms. But you can get dressed. Since we're neighbours, in a manner of speaking [he came from the Haute-Vienne], and I don't like causing trouble to fellow citizens, I suggest you come along to my place. There, we'll do together the interview I have to submit to the Préfet. Here, with my men around, I can't pretend to be asking you questions when I'm not."'

Nadaud did not entirely believe in the good faith of this Limousin 'neighbour' (a spiritual ancestor, it would seem, of the police of German-occupied France ninety years later), but he did what he was told.

'Crossing the courtyard and then the alley which led to the street, I practically bumped into a carriage that was waiting for me on the edge of the pavement. I got in, along with the inspector and one constable. Almost at once we turned into the rue Mazarine, then the chief suddenly stopped the carriage beneath a street lamp; the dawn had hardly begun to break. Pretending to read through his order papers again, he said, "I've made a mistake. I'm supposed to take you straight to Mazas."'

Mazas was a large, new prison, built in the 1840s, on an open site now mainly occupied by the Gare de Lyon.

'"I didn't make any mistake about you, M'sieur, but I am within my rights in telling you you are a deceitful liar." After that, I remained obstinately silent, consumed by a suffocating anger.'

That is how Nadaud recalled his arrest forty years later. The account he gave his parents a month after it, in a letter written from prison, is the same in outline but rather different in detail and feeling. The letter begins with some heroic reflections on its being an honour to be imprisoned in such circumstances, then continues:

'I was fast asleep . . . it was the police inspector who woke me . . . At once, numerous police officers grabbed me by the arms and legs, and there were other officers on the stairs, in the courtyard and at the gateway. In face of all this, I could offer no resistance, I had to go with them and get into a cab. No one would tell me where I was going, I thought I was going to be shot and had already reconciled my mind to it. My only sorrow was for all of you, because I knew I would be leaving you so badly off. However, the police chief, who was essentially very polite, admitted by and by that he was taking me to Mazas.'

In both this letter and in the account in his Memoirs, Nadaud goes on to say that, among many familiar faces in the crowd in the admissions hall of Mazas (clearly the prison was having an unprecedentedly busy night) he encountered Adolphe Thiers. Thiers had been Louis-Philippe's contentious Foreign Minister, and until that moment Nadaud had not realised that the monarchists too had been swept up in the same net as the democratic socialists. Evidently the man who was about to proclaim himself Napoleon III was not going to allow any opinion to rule but his own. Nadaud did not like Thiers, who had opposed universal suffrage with a sneering remark in Parliament about 'the vile multitude'. But he was shocked when he noticed that the clerk of the admissions desk – 'a pallid, slippery little fellow with dead eyes' – was sniggering as he wrote down Thiers' particulars.

'All at once, I elbowed aside the two policemen I was seated between, and went and made to punch the man in the face – "Show some respect for the age and the name of the man who has been a figure of French Government and has always served your cause, you cowardly and vile reactionary."'

That, at any rate, is what is described in his Memoirs, although to his father he just mentions having said something to Thiers himself. He also remarks that, when he eventually got out of prison, one of Thiers' associates said, 'Monsieur Thiers was very touched when you defended him against those insults.'

Upon this, Nadaud was seized by several policemen and carried off to solitary confinement for between two and three weeks. This was not a particular punishment reserved for him, though at the time, being given no information at all, he felt as if it was. Mazas was a new-style prison, built on the model of Pentonville, in London, which it resembled. Inmates never encountered one another; even when they were sent to exercise on a treadmill, they were separated by a complex system of barriers and partitions. Designed to remove the evils attendant upon the older, crowded jails, with their lack of privacy and their high rates of infection and mortality, prisons such as Mazas evidently introduced another range of ills.

'Never, no never, has any man spent heavier and sadder hours than I spent in my cell. My heart was torn in two and it seemed to me that I had been buried alive.'

In one account Nadaud says that he saw nothing but 'the

hand of the warder who passed me my meals through a little grille'. But he was moved after a few days to a different and larger cell where 'it did seem to me that the jailer who came with my food looked at me sympathetically and kindly. He couldn't talk to me, but he moved his head in such a way as to give me to understand that things were not going well for us.'

Much later, in a third account that he wrote when campaigning with Victor Hugo against the isolation-system, Nadaud adds: '[My warder], like all the others, was in prison just as we were.' Here he goes on to give more details on the unhealthy cold of the cells – he considered, with his mason's eye, that Mazas had been badly built – and the desolating sense of having dropped out of the human race and knowing absolutely nothing of what was happening outside the walls. The larger cell had a small window of frosted glass high up on the wall, which, once reached, could be propped open about a dozen centimetres:

'By pushing my table underneath this small aperture and putting the chair on top of it, I could squint sideways at several houses opposite. These were lived in by working men, I could tell that from catching a glimpse of their smocks. All through the Tuesday and Wednesday of that week they were at home, leaning over the railings of their balconies . . . The voices of these men, as they chatted quietly to their wives, together with the songs and cries of the little sweeps in the street below, overwhelmed me with sadness. But I did not hear a single sound of cannon or gunshot, nothing suggested fighting in the streets. The presence of Monsieur Thiers in prison had made me fairly sure that all my colleagues had been arrested – but what of all those other young men, those ardent revolutionaries among whom I had lived for twenty years? They must have been put behind bars too . . .'

However, after the first bad days, Nadaud did not languish totally without occupation. In the Memoirs, he says that he asked for, and managed to obtain, reading matter, including a copy of Guizot's *History of Civilisation*, of which he had heard, and that that book laid the foundation for his later studies in England. In his letter to his father, though he says much the same about his solitary confinement, adding in addition that he only had 35 sous (7 francs) on him when he was arrested, he continues in a different vein:

'I will never forget that time, but I was not at all bored. I occupied myself by writing about the life of a child of poor origins who worked on the buildings and came to represent his people, giving speeches and knowing, willy-nilly, how to make himself heard by prominent people. I am telling in outline the story of our family. One day, it will be interesting to read.'

So does all the early part of the Memoirs substantially date from this prison sentence? Did Nadaud manage to bring the manuscript out with him, keep it through the years, and use it as the basis for his writings in old age? It does not seem very likely – and yet this simple fact might explain the difference between the limpid recall of childhood and youth and the relative flatness of the account of the middle and later years. If, essentially, the Memoirs were written in two stages, separated by half a lifetime, no wonder the vivid recall is missing after a certain moment and the vantage point changes.

The long and relatively cheerful letter to his parents does not seem to have been finished; it may be a rough draft that was never sent in that form. It was written from Sainte-Pélagie, the other prison, to which Nadaud was moved by and by. Sainte-Pélagie was an old-style building near the Panthéon. Once a convent and a home for fallen women, it had been turned into a jail at the Revolution. It was often used for political prisoners – Nadaud's early republican friend, Laurence Luquet, had been sent there in 1834 – and was considered damp and unhealthy. However, Nadaud was much happier there than in Mazas: now he had the shared accommodation and constant company to which almost all his life hitherto had accustomed him. It was the *garni* all over again.

'There was nothing to distress us there, save only the death of the Republic. All the arrested Members of Parliament were put together in the left wing . . . Our days were passed in as peaceful and pleasant a way as possible. Friends came to see us and sent in provisions – wine and things to eat, even more than we needed.'

In letters to others he mentions the imprisoned Members of Parliament walking up and down together and singing to keep their spirits up, though he also says that not many of their erstwhile friends visited them. In the first, edgy weeks of the new regime many people, no doubt, were mainly concerned not to call attention to themselves. However, to his family at that moment he was determinedly optimistic. 'There's a rumour going round that tomorrow we will be set free.' (The letter is dated 1 January 1852.) 'As far as I am concerned, I am doubtful, I don't think we will be out before the end of January, although I don't at all understand our detention. As soon as I am free I will busy myself about our friend in Saint-Hilaire. Will you ask after Françoise? Console her, and tell her that her husband will soon be free.'

This seems to be a veiled reference to Françoise Roby, the wife of Nadaud's faithful room-mate on the Ile Saint-Louis all the years of the evening classes. (Veiled, in case the letter, which was probably slipped out through a friendly visitor, fell into unfriendly hands.) Nadaud always maintained that Roby had never interested himself in politics, but after the *coup d'état* the presiding lawyer in the Court of Limoges denounced a large-scale conspiracy 'against the security of the State' extending throughout the Haute-Vienne and the Creuse. Seventy-two people of known liberal sympathies in the area were targeted and condemned to various penalties, among them Roby, who suffered banishment and internment in Angoulême and then Besançon. Thirty years later, when Roby was an old man, and kept the inn in Pontarion, Nadaud was instrumental in getting a state pension for him and others by way of reparation.

On the last page of his letter Nadaud asked his parents not to let themselves be distressed by any ill tales (*calomnies*) they might hear about him. 'As for me, as soon as I am free, I shall get back to work and will soon have sorted out our affairs. I'll find some money if necessary, all I need.'

However, his confidence was not to be rewarded.

The lithograph of him at this period of his life is annotated in his hand 'St Pélagie, 16 January 1852' and dedicated to his father and mother. Looking younger, if anything, than his thirty-six years, he gazes out over his ruff of beard, high collar and *député*'s ribbon at the uncertain future. The likeness was evidently sent as a keepsake for the long years that lay ahead. As it turned out, Marie Nadaud was never to see her son again. Léonard Nadaud next set eyes on him in 1860.

In his Memoirs Nadaud describes the blow thus:

'One morning we received news that put an end to our comfortable prison life. It came to us by *L'Officiel* [the Government Gazette]. This published a decree of the President, the saviour of law and order, as they called that evil-doer then inhabiting the Elysée Palace.

'We were exiled in perpetuity.'

· 10 ·

His Own Resources

It could have been worse; he could have been sent to North Africa, or to the prison island of Cayenne off the coast of French Guiana, from which few ever returned. That, at least, was what he told his parents in a letter sent care of the Mayor of Soubrebost, a republican and a friend, adding: 'You should know that the reputation of your son will grow from day to day, and that though I shall be far from my native land there are many people who would be glad to be in my shoes and be assured of having, like me, a little place in the history of their country.' In another letter written from prison within the same few days, urging on his parents 'your usual courage', he emphasised: 'I have a trade [*un état*], I will always find work, and you will be able to receive money saved by me abroad. I shall be free, and I shall make haste to get myself fixed up on the railway works, either in England or in Belgium ... Keep yourselves in good health for my dear Désirée, as soon as I'm settled I will find a means for you to be able to come and see me ... A man like me can always find work, and I'll be so good and quiet and obedient with a new boss that I'll stand out from the crowd ... Believe me, I have many friends and I will never abandon you ... It'll really be no different from my being away in Paris or Lyon.'

It was all true, in its way. But it was also true that almost everything that Nadaud had achieved in the twenty-two years since he had first arrived on foot in Paris had been taken away from him, and he was going to have to start all over again in a strange country. Long ago, in Parisian eyes, he had been a despised chestnut eater, a speaker of halting, rustic

French, fit only for the communal lodging house – but in those days he had always worked, slept and woken among friends and compatriots. Now, abruptly denuded of status, power and acclaim, he was about to find himself once again an insignificant outsider in an alien city, with another language to learn, another form of literacy to master, daily bread to earn, a career to be made. The difference was that, this time, he would be essentially on his own. Having no previous experience of this, save in his solitary cell at Mazas, it is doubtful if he fully realised what it would mean.

Once released from prison, Nadaud was required to leave the country immediately. Belgium, which had been a French province under Napoleon I, was the obvious place of refuge: a number of other *proscrits*, men forbidden residence in France after the upheavals of 1848 and '49, were already there. Nadaud travelled to Brussels by train that same day, cheered by an encounter with a friendly passport official at the Belgian Embassy in Paris who, knowing he was a mason, offered him an introduction to an architect. On arrival in Brussels he and Agricole Perdiguier, the republican carpenter, agreed to share lodgings together:

'Perdiguier was more used than I was to domestic life, for I had lived mainly out of Parisian *gargotes*. So he prepared our meals himself, and our expenses barely reached one franc a day for each of us, which was not the case for our friends who went to eat in restaurants.

'The look of Brussels, the dress, manner and language of its inhabitants all brought to my mind a traditional French provincial town.'

Nadaud would have been thinking of Guéret, and of the other staging posts on the mason's route between central France and Paris, such as Issoudun and Orléans, for his experience at that time contained no other models. Had he stayed in Belgium, able to treat the place simply as an extension of his native land, his years of exile would probably have been more comfortable but they would not have transformed his life and developed his thinking as they did.

As things turned out, his time in Brussels was brief. Belgian workers wanted to organise a welcome reception for the new French arrivals, and this was enough to give Nadaud unwelcome prominence in the eyes of the Brussels police. The Burgomaster summoned him and indicated that he must leave the town, together with two other exiles, Victor Schoelcher and Pierre Malardier. The three men were sent by train to Antwerp, and here it was that the second great departure of Nadaud's life, the second adventure into the unknown, really began.

For the first time, at the age of thirty-six, he was in a port city, on an estuary with the smell of the sea, large ocean-going ships, and sailors of all different nations, dress and tongues. He was grateful for the more worldly company of Schoelcher, who was a fellow republican *député* from a wealthy liberal family of china manufacturers. Schoelcher had made a valiant attempt to organise resistance to the *coup d'état* in the Saint-Antoine quarter, and was lucky to have escaped a worse fate than banishment. He was a traveller by nature and a lover of art. He seized the opportunity to buy several Flemish paintings, and took his two companions to look at Antwerp's great cathedral. Nadaud was impressed, almost in spite of himself, by the 120-metre-high perpendicular spire and its pealing bells, but his own sights were fixed elsewhere; he could not look through Schoelcher's privileged eyes:

'A man out of work, feeling that his pockets are empty, has no taste for other things . . . The streets of high, gothic houses with their dormer windows were not what I looked at most. What I had my eye out for was new houses being built, building sites where I might get myself taken on.'

But he had already discovered that wages were low in Belgium compared with Paris, and there were the exciting ships, some plying regularly between Antwerp and London. There also, in Nadaud's pocket, was a letter, from Louis

Blanc, who had been ensconced in that city, with his wife and family, for the last three and a half years:

'My dear friend,

'If I haven't replied at once to your letter, it is because I wanted before I did to have something to tell you. I have made some rapid enquiries. Better still, I have tried to find out if it might be possible for work to be found for you immediately on your arrival, and I am hopeful of this. Mr Pickard, the head of the builders' association here, has promised me an answer to this, and I do not expect to wait long.

'The wages for a day's work in London in your line are acceptable, not less than 5 shillings (6 francs 25) and I believe they may go higher than that . . .'

So London was to be Nadaud's destiny.

Nadaud, Schoelcher and Malardier embarked from Antwerp on 8 February 1852, to dock in the Thames the following afternoon, on a ship called (prophetically, in the Frenchmen's case) the *Soho*. In the Port of London registers, Nadaud filled in the particulars for himself and his companions, styling himself 'ex-Representative, native of France'. On the trips made by the *Soho* in the preceding weeks of the year there had been, among the seamen, workmen, merchants, nuns, clerks, governesses, servants and gentlemen of assorted European nationalities that made up her staple passenger list, a distinct sprinkling of French names and various designations – 'ex-*Député*', 'ex-functionary', 'professor', '*homme de lettres*' or, simply, 'refugee'. Running my finger down the sheets that today have come to rest in the Public Record Office, I chanced upon the name of Nadaud's old opponent and prison companion Adolphe Thiers ('ex-Deputy'), but he travelled with his butler and he knew England well already.

Rain was falling in torrents as Nadaud and his companions embarked in Antwerp, and the sea was rough for the whole journey. In his Memoirs, he writes:

'Once on board the ship, I lunched with a healthy appetite,

but I soon regretted this. Gripped by sea-sickness, I suffered horribly. At one point I was so completely laid out, I did not reply to anything the ship's crew said to me.'

He says nothing of the River Thames up which he passed, or of the Pool of London. Tower Bridge did not then exist, and the entire waterway below London Bridge was alive with the wharves and shipping of one of the busiest ports in the world: presumably he was in no state to appreciate the scene. Later he became ardently interested in the Thames and its proliferating docks. As an elderly politician back in his own country, the desirability of developing deep-water docks and shipyards off the Seine at Paris became one of his favourite themes.

'At last we reached London. A *"cab"* carried Schoelcher, Malardier and me to the door of a small hotel in Gerrard Street, Soho Square, where I fell into a deep sleep.'

In fact it was not so much a hotel, in the English sense, as a house tenanted by French people who let rooms to compatriots and performed other services for them, such as receiving mail. In later years, Nadaud used 10 Gerrard Street as a forwarding address, and the Census of 1861 shows it to have been occupied by a French family named Courtault. Today, like most of the buildings in the street, No. 10 houses a Chinese restaurant. We would not now be inclined to locate Gerrard Street in reference to Soho Square, but that is because, since Nadaud's day, both Shaftesbury Avenue and the Charing Cross Road have been carved through what was earlier a mass of narrow streets, with Soho Square as the only obvious landmark. It had been an airy aristocratic quarter in the early eighteenth century. Its social status had declined as the spreading town enveloped it, but, unlike the adjoining Seven Dials district to the east, it remained a more or less respectable address. It had been popular with the French since the arrival of the Huguenots a hundred and fifty years before, and later with refugees from the Revolution of 1791. Indeed, in the 1850s, almost the only proper restaurants in London were located in Soho, run by and largely for this expatriate population. Otherwise, before the big railway hotels began to be built in the 1860s, there were few places to eat in the metropolis except the exclusive gentlemen's clubs in St James's, or the grubby, noisy and equally male chop-houses in the city, modelled on the dining rooms of coaching inns. This lack of pleasant or respectable places to eat outside private homes was one of the many things which discomforted visitors to England.

Soho still represented, until the mid-nineteenth century, a traditional if declining way of London living. Becky Sharp and her improvident father live there in *Vanity Fair*, the faintly sinister lawyer Jaggers in *Great Expectations* has his private rooms in one of the brown-stained Georgian houses of Gerrard Street itself, and lodgings are found for young Nicholas Nickleby a few blocks away, 'where thick black smoke poured forth night and day from a large brewery hard by . . . There is a bygone, faded, tumble down street, with two irregular roads of tall, meagre houses, which seem to have stared each other out of countenance years ago . . . To judge from the size of the houses, they have been at one time tenanted by persons of better condition than that of their present occupants, but they are now let off by the week in floors or rooms, and every door has almost as many plates or bell-handles as there are apartments within.'

Dickens has the better-off tenants occupying the lower floors and the poorest the attics – the same system as pertained in the old houses of Paris. Nadaud continued to visit the French world of the Gerrard Street house, and another French home in Newman Street just north of Soho, throughout most of his years in London, though his life, in many respects, moved into quite other settings.

The sheer immensity of nineteenth-century London amazed and baffled foreign visitors. In his first letter home Nadaud told his family London was 'four times the size of Paris': in fact its population, then at something over two million, was about double that of Paris, but it was growing much faster – it was to increase sixfold between 1800 and 1870. The real difference, however, was that London covered a much greater tract of land than any other city in the world.

It had been spreading for several centuries already, unrestrained by the kind of local strife that kept the capitals of mainland Europe penned inside defensive walls, but once the nineteenth century was under way the pace of London's growth increased exponentially. Louis Simond's observation of 1812 – 'London is stretching out her great arms on all sides . . . the centre has become a trading counter, a place of business. Instead the people live more spaciously in the suburbs' – was more than ever true forty years later. The 1820s, '30s and '40s had been the first great era of the speculative building venture. Estates of land all around London were judged 'ripe' for development and fields which had hitherto produced hay, milk and vegetables for the humming city near at hand now sprouted terrace after terrace of two- and three-storey houses – a vastly more profitable crop for the fortunate ground landlords. If the drama of Paris in the 1850s was that of demolition in the heart of the city and the replacement of the old, irregular townscape by a classical one, the drama of London was the wholesale transformation of adjacent countryside into bricks and mortar in ever-widening rings.

There were, of course, some changes within London proper: new, heavyweight public buildings appeared, a few new, wide roads, even the occasional grand plan on the continental model: Trafalgar Square was endlessly under construction in the mid-century. But the great change brought by the nineteenth century to the English capital was the rise of the suburb as the norm for middle- and lower-class living – characteristically, one family per house plus a servant or two. Nowhere else in the world did such large numbers of supposedly urban families occupy individually constructed dwellings with their own private gardens. Understandably, continental visitors became confused as to the social status of these people living in stucco-fronted villas like miniature castles in the spacious districts that now spread out on all sides beyond the city proper. This confusion led to a persistent mythology of the ubiquitous rich and possibly aristocratic Englishman – *le milord anglais* – a fantasy which had, however, a grain of truth of a more general kind. The United Kingdom, having industrialised much earlier and more completely than its continental neighbours, was at that time the richest country in the world. The profits of this industry did not directly enrich the labouring masses, but they created a comfortable existence for unprecedented numbers of people slightly higher up the social scale.

The Great Exhibition, which was designed to place all this wealth and technical ingenuity and industriousness on public display, had been occupying Paxton's huge glass palace in Kensington in 1851, a few months before Martin Nadaud's arrival in England. The following summer the central pavilion was re-erected out at Sydenham – which responded by becoming yet another suburb of the town. Nadaud was among the further hordes of people who visited it with wonder and appreciation.

The great retreat to the suburbs clearly owed a lot to the large, intricately graded class distinctions that this prosperous nation had the leisure to cultivate. It owed much, too, to the long-standing British desire for *rus in urbe*. The private patch of grass, the cottage garden flowers and the mock gothic country-style parish church, all within half an hour by horse-omnibus of 'enormous smoking London', exemplified a very British dream, just as much as the grand, classical vistas of Haussmann's Paris came to define a French one. But the smoke of London provided a compelling reason for its more comfortably-off citizens to live outside the centre of town, for by the mid-Victorian era London had become famously and uniquely dirty. Wordsworth's dawn River Thames 'open unto the fields and to the sky/All bright and glittering in the smokeless air' dates from before 1800, but already the implication was that the skies for most of the day would be less clear. London had always burnt the brownish sea-coal whose particles mingled with the river mists and left their taint. But soon Wordsworth's 'ships, towers, domes, theatres and temples' were to lie less close to fields, and with more industrial chimneys among them, and the river was to turn from green to a slimier tint. As early as 1812 Louis Simond was at pains to convey to his French readers the peculiar nature of London's self-created climate: 'it is difficult to imagine the type of daylight that the town of London enjoys in the middle of winter. The smoke from coal fires creates above it an atmosphere which is visible from several miles away, like a large round cloud attached to the earth . . . the air is positively loaded with small flakes of soot in suspension . . . the black snow attaches itself to clothes, to shirts, to one's face.'

Ironically, in trying to escape the worst of the smoke in the Thames basin, suburb-dwellers steadily created more and yet more square miles of smoky townscape, as each new green retreat in turn became tainted by the hearths of its own growing population and hemmed in by a newer suburb beyond.

Another continental visitor, thirty years after Simond, Max Schlesinger, commented memorably that 'English houses are like chimneys turned inside out; on the outside all is soot and dirt, on the inside everything clean and bright'. This theme of the dank, inhospitable unpleasantness of central London's public spaces in comparison with the comfort and even sumptuousness of her private interiors for those with access to them, persisted in the reports of resentful or admiring foreigners for the rest of the nineteenth century and well into the twentieth, as long as the smoke-induced fog persisted. The 'brown, rich, dim, vague' London admired by the American Henry James was an acquired taste. The French historian and philosopher Hippolyte Taine, visiting in the 1860s for less than three months, took a resolutely unfavourable view:

'A wet Sunday in London: shops closed, streets almost empty; the aspect of a vast and well-kept graveyard. The few people in this desert of squares and streets, hurrying beneath their umbrellas, look like unquiet ghosts; it is horrible. A thick yellow fog fills the air . . . After an hour's walking one can understand suicide.' In the same decade his compatriot Jules Vallès, who was a republican activist and, like Nadaud, a target for the police of the Second Empire, made his first visit to London and condemned it absolutely. It was so *triste*, silent, dirty, muddy, foggy, terrifying, rude, cold and drunken; there were no pretty women, such women as there were were immodest (they kissed too readily on park benches) yet also hypocritical and not adequately warm or lively ... But then, to Vallès (who had had a wretched childhood and proceeded to make enemies and express hatreds throughout his adult life) the whole of England was 'the country of ill-living, where one is ill-lodged, ill-fed, ill-seated and badly slept'.

Nadaud was made of very different stuff from Vallès. He accepted his new life in London bravely, for he felt he had no choice but to do so. How did he fare?

In general, the descriptions in his Memoirs of his struggles to establish himself are brief, and he puts a good face on things. Various letters he wrote, however, to his family, to Madame Cabet or others, give a subtly different picture.

He was determined to get to work at once in his old trade: it was a matter of principle with him. Already, on emerging from Sainte-Pélagie, he had refused a hand-out from a well-wisher, and within his first few months in London he was to decline a subscription got up for him by the stone-masons' union. He asked for it to be donated to the general, charitable fund for the French *proscrits*, which paid those without other means a minimal dole. He had to have a job.

'The morning after [his arrival in Gerrard Street] one of those French women who have a lively and relaxed manner came to wake me to tell me two Englishmen were there waiting to talk to me.' One of the two turned out to be Pickard, the secretary of the builders' association whom Louis Blanc had mentioned in his letter. The very next day found Nadaud setting off for a building site, which he locates in Islington but which was more exactly in Copenhagen Fields towards Kentish Town, north of King's Cross, where the huge new Metropolitan Meat Market was just beginning to be constructed. Until then, the animals had been walked in

from the country round and slaughtered at Smithfield in the
heart of the City; in London as in Paris new ideas of hygiene
and order were beginning to prevail.

'Since I didn't know a single word of English, Louis Blanc
asked if he might accompany me . . . to the site. In a still more
friendly gesture, he had got hold of a boy of thirteen or
fourteen who would be able to act as my interpreter . . . It
was a pouring wet day; the tracks across the site had been
churned up by the coming and going of heavy carts of brick
and sand, and were almost impassable on foot. My distinguished friend, who was a slight man, walked at my side and
got submerged in mud half-way up his legs. I didn't know
whether to laugh or to tell him to go back home, for when he
extricated himself from one pot-hole it was only to fall into
another one. I had often before seen Louis Blanc in his high
seat as President [of the Commission of the Luxembourg],
and the memory of him then, linked to the present sight of
him, has remained with me as a combined image of both
grandeur and misery.'

Nadaud refrained from adding that his own situation, as
he splashed through the liquefied London clay, bag of tools in
hand, anxious to create a good impression with English
labourers, was a far cry from that of a one-time candidate for
the Presidency of France.

He took to the foreman, liking his manner and his 'open,
good-humoured face', and, once installed, he politely offered
to pay for a round of drinks for his new companions in the
usual French way. He does not say how this offer was
received. After that, Louis Blanc left to make his way home
through the mud and Nadaud was on his own.

'It remained to me to show my goodwill through my work.
In less than a month my qualities as a workman had made me
some good friends, who tried to be nice to me. But as I didn't
even know the names of my tools, I could hardly chat to the
men and so I worked without any breaks.'

He was cheered by two Irish labourers, whom he noticed
crossed themselves and smiled at him each time they carried
him up fresh supplies of mortar. He realised that they had

assumed, from his French nationality, that he must be a Roman Catholic and therefore a spiritual brother. It was an ironic basis for friendship for the anti-Catholic republican, but Nadaud was grateful for their kindness.

'At dinner time, they used to go and buy my meat and potatoes and cook them in a shack made of planks where we came to eat our meals. The *gargote* doesn't exist as it does in Paris and each person cooks what he wants for himself.'

Nadaud was probably more grateful to these Irishmen than he admits, for though he is silent on the subject of English prejudice against foreign labour, it is unlikely that he did not encounter it. In fact he admitted later to a friend that he had had said to him, at this period, 'French dog, you've come here to eat our bread.'

His letter to his parents strikes a bleaker note than the Memoirs:

'The days are well paid but the living is expensive, especially lodgings, which cost me no less than 75 centimes to 1 franc per day. In addition each Sunday is a day off. All the same, I will earn enough not only for myself but to look after our family affairs. My daily rate will be 5 shillings (that's 6 francs in money) . . . I don't want to give the satisfaction to my political enemies of hearing that I am in a low state [*tombé dans un abattement moral*]. I feel I am setting a good example by getting to work and becoming an apprentice all over again at the age of thirty-seven. I say "apprentice" because I only know how to work in plaster and here there isn't so much as a handful of the stuff. Cement is what they use.

'In the workplace I am with a large number of men, who stare at me but aren't on terms with me because they can't understand me. I can tell you, it's not much fun, but I've made up my mind, it is my duty –' Here follow a few uplifting thoughts on people and democracy.

The *Illustrated London News* for 1854 published plans and an architect's view of the Meat Market. It showed the large, four-square public houses at each of the four corners of the site, one of which is still there on North Road, and the ornamental clock tower in the centre of the huge yards, which has also survived and stands today amid the irrelevant high-rise blocks and grass of a 1960s council estate. The plans sketched in a railway line designed to plunge down into London, linking the site with Smithfield. This, in common with a large number of the new lines that were proposed in the heady railway era of the 1850s and 1860s, was never actually built. But Copenhagen Fields had already, in 1852, been recently crossed by two lines, one a branch from the London and North West at Camden Town running round London to the East and West India Docks, and the other, the Great Northern line, into the new station at King's Cross which was then being built. The surrounding area, known as Battle Bridge, had lost the chalybeate-spring-and-tea-garden quality it had had in the previous century, and had acquired a smallpox hospital, brick-kilns, and the huge dust heaps that were immortalised by Dickens in *Our Mutual Friend*. The fields immediately to the north still had their quiet and pretty corners and their flocks of sheep, but the detritus of the growing town was eroding them, and they were said to be unsafe at night. Copenhagen House, an old country seat, still just figures on the large, illustrated map that was issued for the Great Exhibition year, but it was by then situated uncomfortably near to brickfields and equidistant between two model prisons – Pentonville, in the Caledonian Road, and the still newer jail at Holloway that would later become the women's prison.

It was off the Caledonian Road, near the half-built station, that Nadaud found digs for himself, within a short walk of his mud-churned work site. His Memoirs are silent on this, as on much of his life over the next two years. I only know his early address in London because it was there, at Upper Winchester Street, that in April his father sent a letter to him. '*Mon très cher enfant*, your long silence is becoming too worrying for us. Since you've been in London we have only had one letter from you . . .'

To this Nadaud replied with a long letter pointing out that, in the past he'd often been an irregular correspondent: they

were not to imagine anything had happened to him. On the
contrary, he was 'neither unhappy nor ill' – in fact less tired
and in better health than he'd been during his two and a half
years in Parliament. (In a subsequent letter, he complained of
constant tiredness 'which weighs me down'.) The first letter,
heavily freighted with reflections on history, democracy,
tyranny, honour and his own modest place in the scheme of
things, is determinedly upbeat. Only obliquely do his struggles become apparent. He was having great difficulty with
English; he ought really to take four months off to study it
but could not afford to. However, he was happy in his
lodgings, well looked after by his landlord – 'and particularly
by his wife, who spends part of the evening keeping me
company and makes great efforts to teach me . . . She really
takes an interest in me, looks after my clothes, makes my
dinner in the evening, and all this with a willingness which
almost hurts me.' The widowed Nadaud does not explain
this further, but one senses what he means.

'About a week ago, I was rash enough to confide in her
that I was sad [*ennuié*]. In fact, when I think of Roby I cry.'
(Roby, too, was exiled from home and Nadaud felt this was
his fault – that Roby had been condemned simply by
association with him.)

'The next evening she made me come downstairs to her
part of the house, and meet several ladies and gentlemen, one
of whom spoke French. I had to promise her never again to
use the word "sad".'

Nadaud indeed had good fortune in landing in such a
sympathetic and relatively genteel environment in what seem,
in other respects, to have been classic London lodgings. The
situation was essentially different from that in Paris, where
the large collective *garni* was kept by a professional in the
trade, and higher-class accommodation (such as Nadaud had
occupied in the rue de Seine) normally had only a concierge
on the premises, whose role was midway between that of
servant and spy. In London, informal sub-letting became a
whole way of life and it has been reckoned that by the mid-
century as many as three quarters of the entire population

were either lodgers themselves or kept lodgings. The terraced town houses of the period had more floors than real spaciousness and were memorably described by Louis Simond as resembling bird cages, with the inhabitants continually hopping up and down the perches. Typically, the principal tenants occupied the ground floor and the basement if there was one, furnished the whole place, and then let one or more of the upstairs rooms, frequently with 'service' – laundry, jugs of hot water for washing, breakfast, often other meals as well in view of the scarcity of restaurants or coffee shops at that time. Sometimes the lodger (or lodgers) was of roughly the same background as the family and became a friend; sometimes he was of a higher social standing and was 'the young gentleman in the top floor front', an object of respect and pride.

No. 3 Upper Winchester Street fits this picture. The terrace itself has now disappeared, in common with many of the others in that district, but, judging from a few nearby survivors, it was a standard brick house, high but narrow, with a semi-basement, steps going up to the front door from a scrap of garden, a yard at the back, and two rooms on each floor – six rooms in all. Since 1851 was a Census year, I have been able to establish the occupancy of the house only a few months before Nadaud's arrival there. On the Census return are listed two brothers, John and Philip Deedy, ten years apart in age, both 'general dealers' (a term as vague as 'director of a company' is today, but clearly neither lumpen working nor professional class) and also Philip's wife Charlotte, aged thirty. No children appear, and the other occupant, who is eighteen years old, is listed as 'visitor, single gentleman' – i.e. a young man of education and private means. Almost certainly he was a lodger, since Nadaud apparently replaced him early the following year.

From the handful of letters that exist for 1852, it would seem that Nadaud was in London for most of that year, cut off in several different ways from almost all the things that had made up his life before. 'I am not in touch', he wrote to his father at one point, 'with anyone from our Département, no more than if I were already in my grave.' He asked if the family had got back from Paris Julie's rings and a lock of hair? Their retrieval had apparently been entrusted to the unreliable brother-in-law. In a subsequent letter he indicated that the kindness he received in Winchester Street during those months had been an important factor in his emotional survival. He had always been apt at finding 'treasures ... within women's hearts'. In this new, posthumous life of vulnerability and strangeness, did his relationship with Charlotte Deedy become *so* good, one cannot help wondering, that eventually it caused domestic tension and Nadaud had to move? There is no word of the Deedy family in his Memoirs, though one might have expected them to figure, along with the two Roman Catholic Irishmen.

I see Charlotte Deedy in the front parlour that would only be used on Sundays or for social occasions such as the evening when visitors were invited to meet her exotic lodger. There is a coal fire in the round iron grate, a round table with a chenille cloth and spoon-backed chairs padded with horsehair. An oval mirror hangs at an angle over the chimney-breast. Thick curtains, lace and then plush, occlude the murk of a dirty London evening. Brass 'Benares ware', made in Birmingham, gleams softly. It is a more comfortable room, in its own cramped way, than any French family of similar income would have. Everything is covered, rounded, muffled. Charlotte, with a neat centre-parting and side-ringlets, is muffled too – padded on the hips herself with horsehair to make the voluminous skirts stand out. The new, airy crinoline swinging free on a steel frame, as worn by the Empress of France, would not become general among ordinary Englishwomen till later in the decade. Charlotte, who would do the cooking and dusting herself, but who probably has a teenage skivvy in daily to attend to the floors, the doorstep and the black-leading of the grates, has an air of resolute ladylikeness. She sits mending a shirt. Martin Nadaud's?

But some months later Nadaud had left the Deedys. There is a brief reference to time spent at Foots Cray, in Kent, then a completely rural area where he enjoyed Sunday walks and evenings in the local pubs to which work-mates introduced him. However, no dates are given, and I rather think this relates to the year after. Later, too, we learn that he spent time on a building site near Wimbledon, but this is not described directly. At all events, by early in 1853, we find him still (or again) in the King's Cross area but at a different address only a couple of streets away.

In any case, some considerable time before this point, the Nadaud of the Memoirs and the one glimpsed intermittently but more closely in letters have begun to diverge. One gets increasingly the impression, as the years go by, that the matters that touched him most closely were simply not recorded. Apart from the briefest passing reference, we would not even know from the Memoirs that he had a daughter. Yet it is evident from his letters that she was frequently in his mind. The classic situation of the itinerant mason far from home, trying to direct his children's upbringing at long range, now replicated itself in his own particular situation, first as a widower in Paris, then as an exile. Within a few months of Julie's death, we find him writing to his parents: 'A big kiss to my little Désirée, does she need me to send her anything? I would like her to be kept nicely, though without getting her used to fancy things [*sans l'habituer à la coqueterie*].' From Mazas prison he wrote: 'Take great care of her, don't let her run wild, you know how boisterous she is', and when he was sentenced to exile and urged courage on his parents, he begged, 'Look after yourselves for my dear Désirée's sake too.'

In London, she seems to have become, if anything, more present to him. Now that he could no longer even visit the Creuse, he must have been afraid that she would forget him: 'Ask my Désirée if she remembers that day when I found her shivering, icy cold in our chestnut grove. She was crying and I had to carry her into the house and warm her bed up before putting her into it.' Following on the passage where he speaks of his landlady and his 'sadness', he writes:

'I am always happy when you write to me of my daughter.

The poor girl is almost an orphan: she has lost a loving mother. Her father does not know and cannot know what he can do to bring her up, to lead her in the right way . . . Well, I don't know why, but I really can't write concerning this child. It is as if my pen won't do it. I am glad you have settled her in G. Don't let her come and go from there unaccompanied.'

'G' was Guéret, for Désirée, by then six and a half, had been placed as a border with a Madame Baillet, a schoolmistress. Nadaud refers to this in his Memoirs solely in the context of its being 'an additional expense of 400 to 500 francs a year'. The editor of the Memoirs comments at this point:

'The sending of the daughter to board in Guéret is a sign that the family were then adopting a *petit bourgeois* way of life: peasants would have placed the orphan child with other farming relations.' Indeed, although Nadaud did sometimes have immediate money worries during his early years in England, and borrowed more than once from Louis Blanc, one senses that the problem was partly because he had committed himself to keeping the family in the Creuse in modest comfort. In any case, the small-holding there had been enlarged and improved by old Léonard's efforts. In general, the whole situation of the Nadauds had changed from the hand-to-mouth existence of the days when Martin Nadaud's mother, on learning that her teenage son had come home without savings, had burst into tears because she hardly knew what to put on the family's plates.

That mother, Désirée's grandmother and the child's chief carer, was very soon to die: she was sixty-two, not young by the standards of that time and society, but not old either. Her husband was to outlive her by sixteen years. Perhaps the apprehension that the grandmother's end might be approaching was one of the reasons that the little girl was sent away to board. The loss of his mother within four months of his own exile is yet another blow over which the Memoirs pass in silence. But the letter Martin Nadaud wrote to Léonard as soon as he received the news in mid-June makes poignant reading, calling up again the still recent loss of Julie:

'There are misfortunes so great, pains so cruel and poignant and dreadful, that nothing can soften them.' He counsels 'the strength of reason', but 'I know how difficult it is; I who am writing to you like this cannot manage to write, nor speak the name of the mother of the orphan who you have under your eyes without experiencing a shiver in my body that I cannot explain . . . My mother had been unwell for some time, she was more than double the age of my Julie.' But he worries how his father will manage on his own; what will he do with his time? The sisters were both married, and living away from La Martinèche; Magdelaine at Saint-Hilaire and Françoise in Paris, where her unsatisfactory husband Bouteille kept a *garni*. 'It seems to me you are free to do as you like until February or March, when you could come and join me, bringing with you my Désirée, from whom I hope to be no longer separated.' At the same time, however, he wrote to Françoise suggesting she and her husband should come back to live at La Martinèche, where Bouteille might be subdued into working.

But the plan, several times mooted, of Léonard Nadaud coming to England never materialised. Evidently the old man had other ideas. Nor did he want Bouteille in his house either. I was pleased to discover in a dusty box, mixed up with unrelated papers, a long communication which is clearly from Léonard (though the signature and the last sentence have been eaten away by mice) and which dates from exactly this period. Illiterate Léonard Nadaud may have been, and forced to dictate, but his way with words is eloquent and exact. His son shouldn't worry, he said, about his father's strength of reason; he had known too much sadness and too much happiness mixed together – 'and I can never be entirely healed, but I'll find enough courage to bear with firmness the hard lot that is to be mine. I only have one wish, but that wish is dear to my heart, and unfortunately its accomplishment does not depend on me. It is that you remain for ever as you are, always the same brave and steady man, despising vice and all its miseries.

'As for my dear little Désirée, don't worry about her, she is extremely well. This dear child is my great consolation, and if you send for her to join you as you mean to, that will be a fresh blow for me from which I will comfort myself only with difficulty.'

He had his life as a widower on his own worked out. 'Bouteille likes to drink; he has often come to this house drunk out of his mind . . . and if I say the least thing to him off he goes. So I know very well that we could never live together.' Daughter Magdelaine had found him a good servant who would care for Désirée too when she was at home. 'I've had all the linen washed and tidied up the house. Everything is in its place, and I renewed the insurance for you as you wanted –' (Here the mice have been at work.)

He added in a postscript that in future he wouldn't stamp his letters to England, since 'you'll see when they come from me by this sign I'll put after your name'. Evidently he had not yet caught up with the flat-rate postal system.

It is hard to imagine this elderly peasant stone-mason, with his views formed under the first Napoleon, transferring to a London lodging house. In addition, Nadaud himself was becoming depressed with England as the year wore on, and felt isolated in his political convictions. His English was improving, but that did not necessarily help. 'Apart from a small number of Socialists belonging to the school of Robert Owen, and some Chartists, the rest of the population [of Britain] is much less advanced than the French, from the political point of view and especially the moral, idealistic one.' This, he concluded, was where freedom under a series of constitutional monarchs had led. 'Less advanced' means, I think, that Nadaud had found the English simply did not understand liberal republicanism and the ideological package it represented. He would also have been aware that the Chartists, who were the most confrontational group and whose People's Charter demanded radical political reform, had failed ignominiously in their attempt to get a mass movement going in 1848 on the model of what was then happening abroad.

To anyone familiar with the historically different development of the United Kingdom this failure does not seem surprising. Nadaud himself eventually became well informed about the evolution of English institutions and admiring of them in many ways. However, he initially attributed the English lack of political awareness to 'the isolation in which they live, since each family exists almost alone in its own small house. There, the head of the family does not teach the children a scrap of history, even though in general everyone knows how to read and more or less write.' He was evidently recalling his father's and uncle's tales of the Napoleonic campaigns, and the ever-present background awareness of the French Revolution twenty years earlier on which all his generation had been brought up.

The same criticisms of English society, and its lack of anything recognisable as a homogenous culture, are still levelled by the French a hundred and fifty years later. However, it must also be said that Nadaud, on his limited experience to date, seems to have formed a rather one-sided view. Of course all English families did not, in the 1850s, live in separate houses. There was a vast labouring and casual working class living hand-to-mouth, mainly in the older central quarters in conditions of squalor and overcrowding very much like their Parisian counterparts. With new concerns about public health, led by the sanitary reformer Edwin Chadwick, these 'dangerous classes' were becoming increasingly visible to the better-educated citizens. Dickens wrote of them; Henry Mayhew began publishing his revelatory survey *London Labour and the London Poor* the year before Nadaud arrived, and went on doing so for the next eleven years. The note he struck was taken up by others and continued to be repeated, in tones of increasing humanitarian fervour, to the end of the century and beyond. Yet almost all of this, it seems, passed Nadaud by, not only in his early days in London but many years later, when he was planning his book on the working classes in England. The picture presented in that is almost entirely based on the regularly employed or skilled – that is to say, on the upper end of the working-class spectrum: those who joined unions and sought to improve their lot by being, among other things, extremely respectable. His book is all valid comment, but it is hardly a balanced picture of the English labouring masses of that era.

He had already learnt so much about life and come so far, and the self-taught feel a particular need to protect the intellectual structures they have so laboriously erected for themselves. It is as if, faced with the looking-glass world across the Channel, where nothing quite corresponded with his assumptions based on previous experience, he was only able to make sense of it by focusing selectively. He seized on those aspects of English life which seemed meaningful in terms of his existing preoccupations. In this way, no doubt, he maintained a precarious sense of coherence and continuity – at the cost of some perception.

11

A Frenchman on His Travels Again

But, you may say, Nadaud surely had a ready-made world of comfort and support in the company of the other French exiles and their British sympathisers? Certainly his earliest letters from England give that impression.

'A large number of English democrats have come recently to pay me visits, inviting me to come to their big meetings. Last Sunday, I went to a dinner ... We celebrated the centenary of Robespierre.' Louis Blanc and Cabet (briefly back from his American utopia to try to settle a lawsuit in France) were also there. Nadaud was invited to make a little speech in French, which was then translated: 'My language difficulties will, I'm afraid, hold me back all this year.'

Among these 'English democrats' of Nadaud's slightly inappropriate phrase was John Malcolm Ludlow, the founder of Mutual Aid Societies and of the Working Men's College in Camden Town, who was to be a good friend to Nadaud later when they were both living in Wimbledon. Ludlow had the great advantage, from Nadaud's point of view, of being bilingual, since much of his childhood had been spent in Paris. He had also visited Paris during the Revolution of 1848, to which he was sympathetic. But he and his particular associates – Frederick Denison Maurice, Charles Mansfield, Charles Kingsley, Thomas Hughes – were Christian Socialists, the products of the Whig tradition and of Victorian Anglican principles; as such, they occupied a very different mental world from the one that Nadaud had carried with him across the Channel.

Late in life, Ludlow was to write, with a fine British

combination of conceit and humility, 'I believe now, as I believed then, that if the French Revolution of 1848 had been, if I may use the term, taken in hand by earnest Christian men, able to understand and grapple with the social questions, it might have regenerated France and Europe.' In time, Nadaud's own views were to be modified, for keeps, by contact with men of Ludlow's stamp and with what is generally known as the Protestant ethic. But in the early 1850s he was still at the stage of expecting to find in England a mirror-image of the mass radical, revolutionary spirit in which the whole of his young manhood had been passed. Of course he did not find it, and this gave rise to his disappointed remarks about the lack of political awareness or idealism among the English.

But once the first flurry of welcome was over, the French *proscrits* themselves do not seem to have offered much to Nadaud in the way of emotional sustenance. Just as, in Paris, most prominent republicans apart from Nadaud had been of liberal bourgeois origins, so now most of his fellow exiles belonged in that category: the life they led in London was, simply, different from his own. In his Memoirs, he expresses this in a positive way, but behind his brave stance lies a tissue of problems.

'From the first day I arrived in London, I became submerged among English people and on building sites. I was very fortunate in that I did not have to share the lot of many of my companions in exile and confront the grinding poverty that faced the majority of them. Manual work saved me; it was my insurance for earning my bread, and this was a great comfort to me. It was even possible for me to contribute my own regular mite to the fund for those living in exile.'

The pride and self-respect ingrained in the young workman who managed to pay off his father's debts were not going to be eradicated by misfortune. He saw himself as a giver not as a receiver, and he did not want to be patronised. When money was collected for him, probably on the initiative of Pickard, at a union meeting in the Craven Head, Drury Lane, he refused to take it for himself. He also did well to stay outside the foetid and inward-turning world of the more needy refugees who, with no other occupation, were soon quarrelling about who should have how much of the meagre funds available.

But the more comfortably established *proscrits* with sources of private income, people such as Louis Blanc, Victor Schoelcher and Ledru-Rollin, were not his natural companions either; they never had been. Louis Blanc was unfailingly kind to him with advice and occasional loans; later, when Nadaud's own social status had changed again, one gets the impression that they became more genuinely close, and during one summer holiday in the 1860s Nadaud was to occupy the Blancs' house in St John's Wood while the family were away in the Isle of Wight. But in the early years the Blancs were already living in bourgeois comfort in the area round Portman Square, while Nadaud was renting single rooms near the new railway yards or in still more obscure and transitory addresses in old, working-class Lambeth or near the docks at Greenwich.

Other divisions in French refugee circles soon became apparent, mainly because these had existed already on the other side of the Channel. Nadaud expresses this circumspectly, as is usual with him when admitting that brotherly solidarity between people with the same political aims could break down, but the general message is clear:

'The exiles who met each other in a few public meetings soon split into groups, some under the leadership of Ledru-Rollin, others under Félix Pyat, and others again under Louis Blanc.' Ledru-Rollin's coterie were only moderate republicans, hostile to socialism, and were therefore despised by Pyat's men. Louis Blanc's group, which included Cabet while he was in England, Pierre Leroux (the Creusois publisher) and Nadaud himself, were more eclectic, and possibly more tolerant. However, even this humane coalition broke down when – as Louis Blanc complained in a letter to Nadaud – Leroux failed to pay the printer for a large number of political pamphlets that he had ordered. Louis Blanc had to foot the bill for 7 guineas, a not inconsiderable sum, and therefore felt that the remaining members of the group should produce 10 shillings apiece to cover it – 'But a number of members have left London. It is partly Bourra's fault; he was supposed to attend to these things.'

This picture of petty intrigues and squabbles is familiar from refugee circles in any time and place. These disparate people were bound together by nothing but their dislike of Napoleon III and their mistrust of religion as they knew it in France – a mistrust irrelevant to English society, as Nadaud was later to discover. They didn't want to be in England, and there was nothing they could actually *do* there to unseat Napoleon III but write pamphlets for each other to read and ferment resentments. In his Memoirs, Nadaud remarks soothingly that the quarrels 'did not, I do sincerely believe, become really bitter and there was no very pronounced violence'. What less pronounced violence took place, he does not say! In fact there was a notorious incident in the autumn of 1852, when one *proscrit*, Emmanuel Barthélémy, a veteran of the Paris barricades since 1830, killed another Frenchman, Cournet, in a duel about who had insulted or slandered whom. The incident took place at dawn in Windsor Great Park, and although Nadaud does not mention it he can hardly have failed to hear about it.

This passage in the Memoirs simply continues: 'Luckily, I avoided these discussions [among refugees], which ended up by becoming painful and often noisy, since I had to live and work all these years among the English.'

It was not entirely true. A letter he received from Madame Cabet in 1857 makes it clear that Nadaud *was* sometimes drawn into emotional disputes, as one might expect. But with a verbal sleight of hand that is his usual way of avoiding a painful topic, he passes straight on to reflections on human nature, beneath national differences in style, being the same the world over, and hence to how he got on with his English associates. He came, he says, to appreciate the English working man, in spite of an exterior that was, by French standards, rather dour and taciturn. He adds disarmingly: 'Often I got quite angry at one or another of my work-mates;

but on thinking things over I nearly always realised I was wrong.'

Because so many of Nadaud's French colleagues figure in his Memoirs with the aura of Great Men, it is instructive to read what John Malcolm Ludlow, in his own *Autobiography*, has to say about some of them. Although Ludlow was far more cosmopolitan than most upper-middle-class Englishmen of his time, the down-to-earth, reductive note of his comments is instantly recognisable as the Anglo-Saxon voice consciously refusing to be impressed by French talk of *gloire*. He liked the errant Pierre Leroux best – 'Of all the leading French socialists, he was the one with by far the most cultivated mind . . . and was to the last a religious – I do not say really a Christian – socialist.'

He did not like the handsome Ledru-Rollin, whom he met in Paris in 1848: 'It seemed to me impossible not to measure Ledru-Rollin's mediocrity at a glance. Portly and pompous, wearing his tri-colour scarf round his waist with anything but dignity, you could see at once that no one was more astonished than himself, to find himself where he was.' He was also wary at first of Louis Blanc, of whom he had heard as a 'wild revolutionist'. However – 'Carlyle's description of him as a "harmless little man" was much nearer the truth . . . he spoke at one at least of our meetings or conferences, and I met him a few times besides . . . He lived in this country a quiet, honourable life, maintaining himself by his pen, took pains (as Ledru-Rollin did not) to understand England, learned English thoroughly . . . But indeed, though friendly, I never grew intimate with him, as he seemed to me shut up, if not in himself, yet in a certain narrow circle of ideas which have become himself.' Louis Blanc also delivered at a dinner table an elegant French-style eulogy on the virtues of the potato: this irritated Ludlow, who proceeded to lecture him in turn on the horrors of the Irish potato disease and subsequent famine.

Poor Cabet too, according to Ludlow, was 'a man of second-rate abilities . . . but thoroughly sincere and well meaning', who had adopted communism through intellectual limitation. 'Loved by his family, by all working men who came across him, he was anything but a vulgar demagogue. He never flattered the working man as such. Nadaud . . . told me that Cabet always corrected among his working-class friends any roughness of speech or manner, and took pains to teach them proper and polite behaviour, giving them lessons on how to enter or leave a room; or in pronunciation or in spelling, when their speech or their letters showed them to require it.'

It is not hard to see why Nadaud, whose own beloved father could offer no such help or advice, had come to adopt Cabet as a substitute father-figure. He was also, at Cabet's request, a loyal son-figure to Madame Cabet, concerning himself about her when she was in straitened circumstances in Paris during Cabet's years of absence, and getting up a subscription for her after his death.

It comes as a relief to find that the rather arrogant Ludlow did approve of Nadaud. 'He was fairly generally educated for a French working man of those days . . . [he] joined one of our builders' associations as a plasterer, and maintained himself for some years by his work, though labouring under the disadvantage that the French method of plastering is different from our own, so that, as I was told by the manager of the Association in which he worked, he could never have earned the highest rate of English wages. He was, however, thoroughly steady and dependable, and was always liked by his English comrades.'

Ludlow further comments that almost all the French refugees he encountered were essentially 'honourable men. And yet, instead of being received with honour in a free country as the opponents of despotism, as men who preferred exile to dishonour, they were abused and calumniated by more than half the [English] press, and by the great bulk of "society" so-called . . . Men who were struggling to maintain themselves by their labour, often undergoing the greatest privations, were too often treated as a set of lazy, good-for-nothing revolutionaries.'

That, in a nutshell, was the situation. In France, Nadaud

and his kind had been people of stature, looked on as a serious political threat: Louis-Napoleon would hardly have bothered to imprison or banish a set of politicians and journalists he regarded as without significance. In England, however, their significance, their identity as dangerous radicals seemed simply to have evaporated in mid-Channel. It must have been at first hard to grasp, then highly disconcerting and wounding.

A sense of this cultural dislocation of view still persists today. While I was researching this book, two separate French academics commented on my good fortune in being better placed to locate and read British archives than they were: neither of them doubted that I would unearth British police records on Nadaud and his associates comparable with those kept by the police of Louis-Philippe and Napoleon III. I found myself in some difficulty trying to explain that I had been able to find no such thing, and that in any case I was extremely doubtful if anything like coherent police dossiers on individual French subjects had ever existed. There was considerable British opposition to what was rumoured of policing methods on the other side of the Channel. The apparatus of identity papers, domiciliary visits and organised spying was (and is) seen as offensive to British concepts of freedom. But in any case the bald fact is that the tolerant but chauvinistic English, police force included, were inclined to regard this latest wave of French incomers just as one more contingent come to swell the already large community of 'Continentals' in London. True, there was a surge of anxiety when an Italian national, Orsini, made a failed assassination attempt on Napoleon III and it was discovered that the bomb had been manufactured in London, but this did not occur till 1858. Earlier in the decade, the British attitude to foreign nationals was one of largely benign indifference.

Provided they did not seem to pose any threat to society in general (kept away, that is, from the Irish Fenian cause) the French, like the Italians and the Germans, were left in peace variously to run restaurants, bake bread, make ice-cream, mend clocks, frame pictures, polish tables, dress hair, give lessons in dancing, music or their native languages, and provide comic relief in theatres and in the novels of Charles Dickens. Whether they had originally fled from monarchy, Republic, revolution or Empire, was immaterial: Continentals were notorious for melodramatic changes of government, and in England *no one cared*. As one of Dickens's commercial travellers put it: 'They are a revolutionary lot – always at it.' When Barthélémy killed Cournet, the duel was widely reported since duelling was by then illegal in England – renegade English aristocrats wishing to settle a matter of honour normally slipped over to Calais or Ostend for the purpose. There was a certain amount of huffing and puffing about the need to charge Barthélémy and the two seconds with murder. However, in the six weeks that elapsed between the committal proceedings in front of the local Justices in Windsor and the appearance of the three defendants in the Assize Court, British phlegm prevailed, and it was decided that, since this was a matter of foreign hotheads shooting at each other, perhaps British justice could take a relaxed view. The Frenchmen served only brief prison sentences.

It was a different matter two years later, when Barthélémy shot an English soda-water manufacturer in a house in Soho, apparently in an argument about money. He was subsequently tried at the Old Bailey and hanged.

All in all, it seems unsurprising that over his years of exile, while Nadaud remained loyal to certain French friends and to the tenets of his republican faith, he eventually fashioned a new life for himself and another identity in a very different sphere.

To reconstruct Nadaud's life between 1853 and 1858 is like doing a jigsaw in which many of the pieces are lost and some of those that survive may not actually belong in that frame. The Memoirs give an extremely sketchy and artificially simplified picture; with the exception of one or two brief paragraphs there is hardly a hint of what he actually thought or felt during these years. The gaps can be partially and haphazardly filled by the letters, both those he received and those he wrote. Some of the latter appear to be rough first drafts, which is why they have survived among his own papers, and one does not know whether they were actually sent. Others seem to be incomplete. He no doubt destroyed some letters himself, perhaps whole categories of them, and others again must have been lost over the last hundred years through time and chance. There is, for instance, only a handful of letters between him and his family members between 1853 and 1855. Obviously it did not help ease of communication that he knew the police in the Creuse, directed from the Préfecture in Guéret, were opening anything he sent.

A few letters between himself and other correspondents, notably Cabet and Madame Cabet, have survived from this period, and these I have quarried out of the unorganised mass of papers in the cardboard boxes that spent many years shut up in the empty house at La Martinèche. As you handle them, a fine, grey dust – the pollen and moths' wings of unimaginably distant summers, the ash from long extinguished wood fires – comes off on your fingers. Tiny, friable brown crumbs scatter all around you from the eroded edges of the paper: the sheets look as if they have been scorched, but it is probably just the repeated effects of damp and drought succeeding each other over the years in central France. Woodworms and mice have also played their part. In addition, where the wads of paper have been disturbed and sorted in recent years by other hands, some letters have been summarily assigned to what may be the wrong period or even the wrong correspondent. Many people's handwriting at that time varied a good deal according to the kind of nib they were using, the quality of the ink and how much of a hurry they were in. In the world before typewriters, people who wrote a lot often had two different hands, one for rough notes for their own eyes and those of close friends and another, more elegant one for formal communications.

Nadaud's own writing, having been acquired late, varies so much with time and circumstances that one cannot always reliably recognise it.

Trying to piece together the patchy evidence, the picture I offer is therefore tentative. But it is my belief that Nadaud managed to keep his spirits up, mainly by the familiar context of manual labour, through 1852 and '3, and that a crisis that was partly within himself and partly in external circumstances began to catch up with him in 1854. That was staved off by a long and inspiring journey round the British Isles, but trouble set in again the following winter. Through 1855 until '7 or '8 his emotional state was precarious and often wretched, even though he was also taking active steps during that time to change his way of life – eventually with some success.

At the end of 1853 Nadaud must have sent traditional French New Year greetings to Louis Blanc, since the latter replied on 4 January 1854: 'In exchange for your kind wishes, you have mine in return. I have done my duty, as you have done yours: between two high-minded people [*deux âmes élevées*] this is a strong bond.

'I am so pleased you are giving me the opportunity to come and see you, and I would very much like to meet the pleasant lady you have talked about so much. But if her absence is to be prolonged, I could still come and pay a visit to you and also to citizen Barrère.' (Barrère was a fellow *proscrit*, a teacher by profession. His son, Camille, who was a little boy in this London period, was to become Nadaud's secretary in the Préfecture in Guéret when the triumphant republican return to power eventually took place: later he was an ambassador for France.)

It seems clear from this careful letter that Louis Blanc and Nadaud had not seen each other for a while – that there had been some kind of disagreement which both *âmes élevées* were now anxious to repair. As to the reference to the lady, it is tempting to read much into this. Couched like that, it is unlikely to refer to the kind Charlotte Deedy, intriguing as it

would be to imagine her still conducting a discreet relationship with Nadaud a year after he had ceased to be her lodger.
Nadaud would hardly have talked so much to Louis Blanc
about someone else's wife, and anyway Louis Blanc was of a
different class from the Deedys. But here, as so often during
Nadaud's long years in England, one comes up against a set
of incontrovertible but enigmatic facts: Nadaud was a strong,
healthy man in the prime of life, who had been accustomed,
at least for several years, to the comforts of marriage. He was
emotional and warm-hearted, had always liked the company
of women, and clearly many of them had a soft spot for him.
True, mid-nineteenth-century London was notorious for the
number and variety of women visibly available on the streets
(I think a shocked reference in a letter home to English
'depravity' refers to this) but all the evidence we have
suggests that prostitutes, even pathetic part-timers, would not
have fulfilled his needs at all: he wanted tenderness, a
sympathetic ear.

Even if he had decided, French style, not to marry again (to
keep the family property intact, to conserve everything for
Désirée) it is hard to believe that he did not have at least one
serious, intimate relationship while in London, and perhaps
several. In Louis Blanc's letter is a faint trace of one. Another
trace may be picked up in a passing, derogatory reference in a
letter of 1857 from Madame Cabet: 'Your letter of June came
as a great relief to me, hearing that you're not thinking any
longer about English women. I should so have hated to know
you were unhappy' – but then Madame Cabet had her own
agenda. She apparently hoped for a while that Nadaud
would marry her daughter, who had been widowed while
still young. Perhaps Nadaud actually did entertain the
thought at one time, or perhaps Madame Cabet (whose
meandering, ill-spelt letters are full of complaints about
people letting her down) optimistically mistook his filial
attentions to her as a sign that he might become her son-in-
law. At all events, in May 1858, Nadaud received a rather
stiff letter, forwarded by Louis Blanc, from a mutual friend in
France who suggested that Nadaud was not treating

Madame Cabet and her daughter correctly. This was apparently one of those periods, recurrent during the 1850s, when Nadaud had simply ceased to communicate.

In March of 1854, the outbreak of the Crimean War brought about an abrupt slump in the London building trade. Concerned that his precarious security would be lost, and that he would not be able to keep up the payments for Désirée's board in Guéret, Nadaud enlisted the help of Louis Blanc and other contacts. A job was found for him in the north, in a suburb of Manchester, then a rapidly growing industrial mecca.

This new sortie into the unknown started as a voyage of necessity but, thanks to a timely loan from Schoelcher, it became a four-month excursion round the British Isles, and one of the most instructive experiences of his adult life. He claims in his Memoirs that he felt 'a new man' at the end of it, and though the evidence of his letters suggests that this cheerful state was only temporary, he did, as he says, encounter large-scale manufacturing for the first time. Until then, his personal world had been largely pre-industrial. Builders built as they had done for centuries – and as they still do on many sites today – at their own rhythm and with their own skills, not as cogs in a great machine.

'Father, it is such a surprise to see from far-off the mass of great chimneys, 50 to 60 metres high . . . You would seek in vain, in Europe, such organised and mechanised works.'

A small mystery attends Nadaud's presence in Manchester. He says in his Memoirs that he was met on arrival by 'a friend, called Frederick, an Alsatian', who had arranged a building job for him through contact with the site-owner. The editor of the Memoirs speculates inconclusively on which French exile this might have been, suggesting the name of a workman from the Vosges. However, I think it was Friedrich Engels.

Engels, five years younger than Nadaud, was born in the Rhineland, adjacent to Alsace, and spoke fluent French from making trips to Paris and Brussels on behalf of communist associates. His family owned textile works in Manchester and by the early 1850s he was there himself, attending to the family business. In 1848 he had been in Paris during the revolution, had subsequently been embroiled in the similar events in Germany and, with a warrant out for his arrest, had had to flee to England. In 1849 and '50 (that is, during Louis Blanc's first years there) he had lived in Soho, near Karl Marx, the life of a poverty-stricken socialist refugee, but then he struck a bargain with his disapproving family and returned to working life on a comfortable income.

When I began to consider this, it seemed to me extremely likely that Louis Blanc knew Engels, or knew of him, and that it would have been natural for him to call on this contact to help Nadaud. In fact it would have been odd if, while in Manchester, Nadaud had *not* encountered Engels. He admits in his Memoirs to having met Ernest Jones, who was also the friend of Marx and the organiser of the Chartist 'Workers' Parliament'. Nadaud was invited to attend one of their meetings that was being held then in Manchester, and it was proposed that he and Louis Blanc should become honorary members.

And yet Nadaud never once mentions Marx or, overtly, Engels – a fact which has led one unwary French academic to conclude, in a doctoral thesis, that 'even the name of Karl Marx appears to have been unknown to Nadaud'. The First Workers' International was launched by Marx in 1864 while Nadaud was still in England. Nadaud was keenly interested in workers' movements, whatever his personal view of the International, and Marx was keen on raising support from all likely quarters. It seemed to me on reflection that Nadaud and Marx could not possibly have been unaware of each other's existence, even if they never actually sat down together to make common cause, and I was gratified when a friend capable of reading Marx's unabridged letters to Engels in the original German confirmed my guess. For in March 1854, Marx was writing to Engels: 'I have received an invitation from the Labour Parliament to be present in Manchester as an honorary delegate, Nadaud and Louis Blanc too –'

But why then, you may ask, does Nadaud not write of Engels? Why should he disguise him as a German-speaking French subject with an ambiguous name?

The answer to this is relevent to much of what is evasive about Nadaud's published account of his time in England and his subsequent career. The puzzling absence of a name which ought logically to crop up in an account carries its own significance.

My conclusion is that, in the 1850s, when Nadaud was still finding his feet in England and learning what this leading industrial nation was like, he encountered potential associates whom he was later to avoid. Essentially, the whole idea of a class 'struggle', and hence of the fellow citizens of the same country pitted against one another, was antipathetic to him. His own hero was Gladstone, whose decent liberalism was to bring in many reforms during Nadaud's English years, without changing society in any more fundamental way. Later, back in France and in positions of power in the 1870s and '80s, Nadaud was a follower of Gambetta, one of those who lay low during the excesses of the 1871 Commune, and Nadaud's later career is that of a middle-of-the-road republican. It was not so much that he moved to the right with advancing age as that the left moved away from him. It is understandable that, by the time he was writing his Memoirs near the end of his life, he was wary of seeming to have been allied in any way with the likes of Marx and Engels.

He comments in his Memoirs that at first the Manchester workmen 'were rather cold towards me'. (No doubt they felt, with reason, that this foreign plasterer had been imposed on them by the management.) He also says that they drank vast quantities of beer on site. In general it is clear from one or two letters that he found the citizens of the north a loutish lot. However, being Nadaud, he managed to make friends. He found himself lodged in a factory district surrounded by Lancashire mill-hands and mill-girls, but remarks that the apparent promiscuity and looseness of talk was superficial and that really these youngsters were good-hearted. This world of rough-and-ready sexual equality was, of course, a far cry from the old-fashioned male standards of the masons of the Creuse. He was taken several times to a public-house-cum-music-hall called The Shakespeare, where he enjoyed, rather wide-eyed, a series of comic turns featuring female jealousy and fat drunken ladies looking for fleas before getting into bed.

His next stop was Preston, to which 'Frederick' took him, also to Sheffield and Leeds. (This confirms one's impression that Nadaud's mentor was not a fellow impoverished refugee but a man of some leisure and means. Indeed Nadaud remarks later that Frederick had helped him several times with travelling expenses.) Preston was then in the grip of the first major cotton-weavers' strike: it is the Coketown of Dickens's *Hard Times*, which describes the strike and was published later that same year.

'It was a town of unnatural red and black like the painted face of a savage. It was a town of machinery and tall chimneys, out of which interminable serpents of smoke trailed themselves for ever and ever, and never got uncoiled. It had a black canal in it, and a river that ran purple with ill-smelling dye, and vast piles of building full of windows where there was a rattling and a trembling all day long, and where the piston of the steam-engine worked monotonously up and down, like the head of an elephant in a state of melancholy madness.'

Nadaud did not encounter a Bounderby, declaring that the factory hands all wanted to be fed 'turtle soup and venison from a gold spoon'. Nor, with his basic faith in material progress, was he repelled at the very nature of a great industrial city, as his compatriot Hippolyte Taine was a few years later, shrinking before 'the anonymous roar of labour'. Nadaud, with a left-wing optimism that has not been uncommon in the twentieth century either, was inclined to think that mechanisation ought to be a Good Thing for the working man, since it made his labour less dependent on sheer physical strength – the literal earning of bread by the sweat of his brow. Nadaud, unlike Dickens, was eager to know how a cotton mill actually worked. The scribbled notes he took on Watt and Arkwright, on 'warps', 'wefts', 'spinning jennys' and the like, each word entered with its approximate French equivalent, are still there among his papers.

But he was impressed by the strike: 'The unselfishness and the courage displayed in this situation by so many starving families showed the strength and tenacity of the English workman.' He was right about that; according to an article written by Louis Blanc for a French paper, the strike lasted twenty-six weeks, a full half year, during which mill-hands who usually earned 20 shillings a week got 4 shillings instead. Nadaud was struck by the orderly public distribution of the strike dole, which he ascribed to the moral power of free trade unionism. He was presumably recalling the disaffected mobs of the National Workshops in 1848.

I wonder if the sacks of shillings and sixpences, which he described being emptied out onto tables, recalled to him the far-off day when he had returned to the Creuse with his own sacks of silver?

In these northern towns he also met Co-operative Society leaders to whom he had introductions from Ludlow and from Thomas Hughes. In Wigan – spelt 'Wigam': his grasp of English place-names remained approximate even when he came to know English well – he was taken down a coal-mine. He enjoyed showing the miners that he knew how to use their pick-axes. Then he made his way by train to Liverpool.

'Liverpool, *mon cher*,' he wrote to a friend in the Creuse, 'is not a town but a whole universe which meets at the great spring of the ocean.' To his father he wrote: 'There, the world of Christopher Columbus is all before you.' Did he regret, momentarily, having decided against Icarus and the New World? He visited the docks and was elated by the sense of Britain's vast commerce overseas and the quantities of people that were continually shipped there. He became convinced that France must acquire a Far Eastern empire of her own. Was this, too, not progress and, so, good for the working man? He was far from being the only man of the left to think in this way. The notion that, in the next century, the mills of

Manchester, like those of Lille and Lyon, would fail in the face of competition from ex-colonies on the other side of the world was then unthinkable. The colonialist dream remained with him for the rest of his life.

From Liverpool he went to Dublin by steamer. He had been attracted by the place because the Irish were a Celtic people and therefore, in his idiosyncratic view of ancient history, brothers to his own race of central France – '*nous autres gallois*'. He had hoped to look for work in Dublin where he had a contact, a fellow republican who had escaped, after the upheaval of 1834, from Sainte-Pélagie prison. However, he was shocked at the obvious poverty and apparent degradation of the Irish labouring classes, thinking, rightly, that he could not live and work among them – 'Workmen are so despised in the streets they can only talk to one another; one sees them in troops of a hundred or more, their clothes all in rags . . . I even saw some who had their trousers patched with newspaper.' This oppression of the common people he ascribed, rather arbitrarily, to Papistry. The curse, he felt, would disappear only if Gladstone had his wish and gave Ireland Home Rule, a viewpoint which seems neatly to turn reality on its head. Like Louis Blanc, he does not seem at that point to have been aware of the recent devastation of the potato famine, though later during his years in England he became far better read and more knowledgeable.

The next lap of his journey was to Greenock by boat and up the Clyde to Glasgow, then also in rapid expansion since the dredging and canalisation of the river had made it accessible to the sea. By happy chance, he ran into two more Frenchmen, who were working there, and they took him to see the new furnaces and shipyards. These delighted him – he never ceased to speak of them in later life when trying to convince his fellow Members of Parliament to canalise the Seine. Perhaps because of the general prosperity of Glasgow then, Nadaud, in spite of spotting street-dwellers 'below the level of brutes or savages', seems to have found the Celts of Scotland more impressive than those of Ireland. 'The race is one of the handsomest in Europe, and as education goes it probably has no equal.'

His friends also took him on a trip to see what he refers to as '*lac* Lhomond', which must have been the only time he glimpsed another wild, mountainous landscape bearing a resemblance to his own lost *pays*. He appreciated it, but it is perhaps a measure of how far he had come, in every sense, from his rural childhood, that he saw it not with the eyes of a peasant who might have to scrape a living from this rocky land, but rather with the eyes of a French tourist. There is the obligatory reference to Walter Scott's *Rob Roy*, and the scenic appearance of a large, elderly, bearded highlander (clearly an authentic Celt) in whose fisherman's hut they sheltered to cook an omelette. They rejected, as likely to be too expensive for lunch, a 'superb hotel', presumably an early example of that Victorian Scottish neo-baronialism that was favoured by the queen herself.

Nadaud does not seem to have been aware of the devastation wrought on Scotland by the highland clearances, which were only then just reaching their wretched end: he might in that case have understood rather better the bedraggled street-dwellers of Glasgow. A pity, for this would have made a fine topic, one feels, for a man concerned with the oppression of the people by the upper classes. In Edinburgh on the last leg of his grand tour, he met a man who might have discussed the clearances with him but apparently did not. This was Hugh Miller, the son of a modest family from the remote north-east of Scotland who had become, like Nadaud, a stone-mason, and from thence a self-taught geologist, poet and authority on Scottish folklore. He was also a passionate partisan of the Free Kirk, which had broken away from the Church of Scotland a decade before, and he edited a radical religious and political paper called *The Witness*.

Ludlow had arranged for the two men to meet each other, which was imaginative of him. On the face of it, Miller's religious viewpoint on life, which included a fervent attempt to reconcile what he learnt from fossils with a faith in the essential truth of the Bible to which he clung, would hardly have made him a natural companion for Nadaud. However, taking a longer perspective, it becomes clear that the passion for justice, fairness, self-improvement and the dignity of the ordinary man, which led Hugh Miller into an extreme form of fundamentalist Protestantism, was essentially the same emotion that led Nadaud into his lifetime's faith of republicanism. Each man found his own expression within the history and culture into which he happened to have been born.

Temperamentally they were not dissimilar either. Nadaud was always an emotional man, *vif et emporté* as his father, one of the same kind, once said of him. (While in Edinburgh, he apparently had an argument with an off-hand building contractor engaged on repairs at Holyrood Palace, and threatened to hit him.) Robust in argument, he was actually thin-skinned; he was prone to fits of anger, despair at times gripped him. He tended to drive himself to the limits of his endurance. All this was true of Hugh Miller also, though with an extra dimension of paranoia, which both fed his combative journalism and was fed by it. Although Miller looked the picture of upstanding highland manhood, especially when wrapped in his plaid, his health, unlike Nadaud's, had been permanently damaged by silicosis, the stone-worker's sickness. Gradually morbid depression overcame him and, two years after his meeting with Nadaud, he shot himself.

12

Dark Places and Another Beginning

It was lucky that Nadaud, for all his insecurities, was a tough, determined person, for he needed to be. His journey round Britain and the contacts he had made had allowed him briefly to re-experience the sense of drive, stimulation and his own importance in the scheme of things that had been his in France. But once it was over he had no alternative but to return to life on the London building sites, where the wartime slump continued. The next year, he would be forty. He found himself, after all his experiences, back in exactly the same position he had been in twenty years before, but now he was essentially alone. Something of this anguish does seep into his Memoirs, though he presents it as having been briefer and more readily resolved than was actually the case. A job was found for him by Bourra, an 'old' *proscrit* who had settled in London in 1834 and had started one of the first Building Societies. (He was a fellow Freemason, a society that Nadaud had joined soon after his arrival in England.) But when that job ended –

'I wandered about for weeks, from one side of the huge town to the other, without finding work . . . I was shrivelling up inside myself; I had no idea at all where it would be best to go . . . In London, there is nowhere like the Grève in Paris where workmen congregate each morning. So you are reduced to going from district to district, street to street, trying to get someone to take you on. For me it was the most awful torment . . . asking over and over again of the foreman, "*Chance for job, master?*" [The last phrase is quoted in English.]

'When a man has spent weeks doing this, without success
. . . it doesn't take much more to break the spirit and the
physical resistance of even the hardiest.'

He adds on an adjoining page, 'At this time, one of those
very few friends to whom I unburdened myself, finally said to
me: "It seems to me that your troubles are getting you down
and that grief is taking hold of you. Do take care of yourself;
you seem very low. You must try to get your courage up and
take a firm resolution to get a grip on yourself and escape
from this situation."'

The speaker evidently perceived that Nadaud was
oppressed by something within himself as well as by his
difficult circumstances. I wonder who the person was? I don't
think it was Louis Blanc or Barrère, since both are mentioned
immediately afterwards as having offered other practical
help. Nor was it Ludlow, who was never an intimate friend;
anyway Nadaud, who was proud of his acquaintanceship
with Ludlow, would have said so. The anonymity makes me
think it was probably a woman.

The idea suggested by Barrère and Louis Blanc was that
Nadaud, with his previous teaching experience, should turn
to giving French lessons. Nadaud, in his demoralised state, at
first refused, saying that his time in Parliament had fooled
them into thinking that he was better educated than he really
was. He did not, he said, know anything about how the
French language was constructed, or the English for that
matter. This would just be one more failure.

However, his advisers persevered. Madame Barrère ('good
and decent . . . kind and beautiful') added her persuasions,
and eventually Nadaud promised that he would let Barrère,
who in easier times had run his own boarding school in
central France, take charge of his further instruction. Barrère
did so, and after two months introduced Nadaud to a
scholastic agency in John Adam Street, by Charing Cross.
Three days later, Nadaud found himself transformed into an
assistant teacher in a school in Brighton.

Such, at least, is the version in the Memoirs. The
impression is that the whole process was complete in a

relatively short time: 'At the beginning of 1855 I abandoned the trade of mason to become a French teacher [*un professeur*].'

Surviving letters give a rather different picture. Louis Blanc, writing to Nadaud in late March 1855, apologised for not having immediately sent him 'the small sum of money for which you asked'. A public 'Day of Humiliation' (Good Friday?) had made this impossible. In a second letter shortly after, he expressed himself relieved that Nadaud, after all, had said he could manage without the loan, and added: 'I haven't the time, today, to indicate to you the various mistakes in your letter; I'll send it back with my next one.' So Louis Blanc, too, was lending a hand in the project of turning Nadaud into a credible giver of lessons.

Cabet, writing to Nadaud in the June of that year – regretting that Nadaud's 'family affairs and other circumstances' had always prevented him from coming to the New World, lamenting his own lack of news from the old one and the general decline of everything – remarked: 'I see from your letter that even though you have travelled a bit, you are leading a rather sad life.' Then, in October that year, comes the draft of a long and revelatory letter from Nadaud to Madame Cabet in Paris.

Nadaud's attachment to Madame Cabet is well documented: it must have derived partly from a sense of guilt and loyalty towards Cabet, and partly from the time in Paris in 1849 when he had escaped from police custody and she had sheltered him. She was not her husband's equal, intellectually, educationally or socially. Her surviving missives to Nadaud show her to have been given to intrigues, mystification, grievances and vociferous self-pity. It has even been unkindly suggested to me that one of Cabet's motifs in setting up his Utopian community on the far side of the world was to get away from her, and that she in turn had no desire to participate in these idealistic struggles, and was only too happy to 'sacrifice herself' by staying on to attend to Cabet's tangled affairs in Paris! However, Nadaud found in her a genuinely sympathetic ear, as she apparently did in him.

'From the depths of my tomb, I send you my love which never alters, in spite of anything you may have heard from the lips of some disrespectful chap [*la bouche impie d'un coquin*] who does not want to hand the money on to you.' (This is a reference to one of Madame Cabet's complex fusses about charitable monies due to her, which may or may not have been withheld.) 'There are moments when a man sees nothing all round him but confusion. Life then is like a road, both ends of which are barred. When I wrote my last letter to you I felt I was on the brink of a precipice; I was turning in continual circles in my small room where not so much as the shadow of a friend ever set foot ... For whole hours at a time, it was as if I was staring at all my faults and short-comings. There, on my own, confronting the three great figures who are always in my baggage and to whom I look to recall me to my duty, I would find that I was not a real republican.' It is not clear who these three models were – presumably photographs – but Cabet must have been one.

He goes on to tell her about his plan to become a teacher: 'But I don't promise to keep a straight face when I tell you all this, because once again this morning I was on the point of laughing at myself, and I laugh alone.' Deprived now of the role to which, in France, he had risen, he feels he might either have tried harder to become a building entrepreneur – 'or else resigned myself to living each day as it comes, the ordinary life of the poor'. He had thought at one moment of buying some scaffolding, at another of opening a shop. At one point he bought himself a grammar book, which he learnt by heart but then forgot again. One sees clearly the distress of a man who is intelligent and sensitive, but who, really for the first time in his life, was faced by a wilderness of choice. The traditional peasant and labouring classes never really had choices.

He has had to learn 'to use a pen like any other tool'. In trying to teach, he has been afraid of exposing himself to mockery, and had the sense of getting this work under false pretences. ('Being a robber baron' is the dramatic phrase he uses.) Then there had occurred a strike in the scholastic agency he had been using to get work giving individual lessons, so he was back on the buildings: '*Là, Madame,*' he wrote in Franglais, '*I am at end wits.*' In spite of the use of the present tense, all this part of the letter appears retrospective. The next paragraph would seem to relate to the late winter of 1855 – perhaps the time when he was asking for a loan from Louis Blanc and then deciding he could manage without.

'At one point I fell into despair – really a terrible despair. I went and hid myself away in Greenwich, reduced to eating dry bread . . . The idea of taking up my tools again was constantly in my head, and in the end I had to do it to quiet my conscience.' He went back to central London and got a job from a well-established Frenchman of his acquaintance demolishing five floors of an external stone staircase. 'It was outside and it was horribly cold, with a freezing wind.' After eight or ten days of this, the scholastic agency contacted him with the offer of a job in Brighton. Nadaud, who was understandably wary of letting one part of his socially fractured existence know about the other part, told his employer he might be going to Brighton 'for personal reasons'. He continued to Madame Cabet: 'You would have suffocated laughing if you had been hidden in a corner, but would also have protested.' The hard demolition work, undertaken after a period away from the building trade, had coarsened and cracked his hands again. Luckily, since he was left-handed, that hand was in a worse state than the right one, with which he would be required to shake hands at the interview. He resorted to bandaging his left hand to conceal it – 'I said I was subject to chilblains, but it was my hammer and the cold wind that had done it.'

He was interviewed by three clergymen, one his prospective employer, and got the job – 'He was pleased to get an assistant master so cheaply.' In his Memoirs, he remarks with a rather different nuance:

'The Rev. Allen, whose service I was about to enter, had such a distinguished manner and was so polite . . . that most of my anxieties and timidity disappeared. Three days later I arrived at 4 Vernon Terrace, Brighton.'

When the Census of 1851 was taken, Vernon Terrace, today well within Brighton, was just beginning to be built on the town's edge. No. 4, in one of the earliest blocks, is a stucco-fronted house on three floors plus a basement, with a pretty iron balcony – that style so often described as 'Regency' but which, out of London, is more usually Victorian. A Brighton friend, who initially went to locate it for me, remarked: 'I would have thought a modest home, hardly large enough for a school.' He also checked the street directories for the period in Brighton Reference Library: the early '50s books are missing but Mr Allen was there in 1856 and for the next ten years. He was not listed under any calling or profession and the house did not appear in any separate listing for schools.

Here already, the makings of certain French illusions about Nadaud's career in England become apparent. Clearly, 4 Vernon Terrace was not a school in the French sense of the word *école*. Mr Allen was just a clergyman without a living, one of a multitude in nineteenth-century England. A widower with five children, he capitalised on his classical education to take in a handful of extra boys as paying guests. In France, such an establishment would have been called a *pension* or *pensionnat*, like the one Nadaud's own daughter was attending. Private education in England was in no way regulated, neither then nor for many decades afterwards. Anyone, suitable, unsuitable or frankly eccentric, could be a teacher in such an establishment; the common English word for an assistant master was an 'usher'. One thinks of the downtrodden ushers of Dickens's *David Copperfield* or *Nicholas Nickleby*. But Nadaud, in his Memoirs, used the standard French word for a secondary school teacher, *professeur*. It is difficult to think of another term he could have applied, but it set in train a whole corpus of false assumptions which have lasted to this present day. Indeed, particularly in the twentieth century, *professeur* in France has

implied a nationally recognised and agreed status of belonging to the *professorat*, as to the law or to medicine, which has
misled even well-informed French commentators. How splendid, one French academic has remarked, that the English
education system opened its ranks to the self-educated
Martin Nadaud. Once again, it is difficult to point out,
without sounding too dismissive, that in the world of
nineteenth-century academies for young gentlemen, Nadaud
was just the usual unqualified foreigner who taught French.
Nadaud's own unofficial comment to Madame Cabet, that
Mr Allen was glad to get someone so cheap, was much nearer
the truth.

In reality, Nadaud's English transformation into a teacher
was an achievement, of a personal and private kind – but not
the sort pompously commemorated today on the shuttered
house at La Martinèche. It was a triumph of fresh endeavour
over defeat and despair; it was also a triumph of pragmatism
– of settling for something bearable that, with effort, he
might even enjoy, rather than for an existence that was
becoming intolerable. He could not, after all, know, as we do
following his trail long afterwards, that his exile was going to
end. Maybe he felt he would be in England for ever. But, as
always in such cases, there was a cost: some compromise,
some loss of identity. Tucked away incognito, first in one
school and then in another, was he really continuing to fight
for the ideals of his youth and prime? Was the real Martin
Nadaud, the republican mason, there at all any more?

It is notable that from Brighton onwards, throughout his
fourteen years' teaching, he called himself 'Monsieur Martin',
by and by adding the first name 'Henri', after the well-known
French historian of that name. As a clandestine manoeuvre
this seems unnecessary, Nadaud the politician being
unknown in England: one may wonder why he bothered. The
answer is, I think, twofold. On one level, perhaps he derived
some satisfaction from the notion of living under an assumed
name to outwit his 'enemies' – the Imperial police who, in
fact, knew where he was all along. And, on a deeper level, it
is possible that he felt that by being someone other than

himself in his teaching role, his 'real' life, that of a persecuted republican patriot, could somehow continue untouched. With a further illogicality, however, when, in another school, the rumour got around that he was an exiled French Member of Parliament, he was not really displeased. 'It smoothed the way for me, especially with the other teachers.'

The evidence of letters, though not of his increasingly evasive Memoirs, would suggest that this confusion in his identity set up a conflict in him which continued to trouble him acutely for several years, and that, later in life, he felt the need to present his teaching career in a grander light than it warranted, in order to justify himself.

His letter to Madame Cabet, apparently written soon after his arrival in Brighton, continues with his first experience there.

'[By the first morning] I can tell you I felt more like running away than going to the schoolroom. All my life I shall never forget the night I spent. I was sleeping on a sort of iron folding bed in a small room as long and narrow as the cells in Mazas, and I still marvel that the bed did not collapse under me, since I tossed and turned on it like someone sick with scarlet fever.' Eight o'clock struck, breakfast was got through; he had to be in class by 9.30. 'Less than two hours after, I found that it really wasn't so difficult, and the following night I slept well.'

His letter ends with an anecdote about the visiting drawing master, who had been chatting to him (in what sounds a slightly salacious, chaps-together way) about the difficulty of giving private lessons to 'the daughter of a Lord, beautiful and good as a little angel'. Nadaud did not teach the girl himself, or, as far as I have been able to discover, any aristocratic child at any time. However, there is a further sheet of letter paper shuffled alongside the sheets to Madame Cabet which may come from a subsequent letter to her also but which I suspect, from its tone, was written to someone quite other, probably male. It runs:

'In England, I have the children of aristocrats. Chance has landed me among the Nobility, and I find them all good sorts [*bons enfants*] and they think I am a proper *gentleman* [in English in the original] and so all is for the best. And the master, who's a rich old thing and who's going to retire in a year, is equally mistaken, and thinks I'm well educated.'

It may be that at this point in his new life in schools, Nadaud genuinely mistook the social status of his pupils, in the same way that visiting foreigners, viewing the grandiose detached villas of London's suburbs, over-estimated the standing of their occupants. But by the time he had been teaching for a number of years, and had become properly acquainted with the gradations of bourgeois life, he must have realised that he was not among 'the Nobility' but the commercial middle classes. Nevertheless, the idea that he had taught the aristocracy of England was one that, in later years, this republican democrat, this man of the people, was happy to have the world believe. This subterfuge is, perhaps, a telling indication of the problem of identity under which he laboured during his years in England. It may also have created an inner tension at the time which made the problem worse.

Looking forward a year or two, a letter Madame Cabet wrote to him when he was teaching in a different school, in Ealing, is instructive. Nadaud was ostensibly happy in this school, made some acquaintances in the local Literary Institute and was particularly proud of having been invited to give a talk there – he chose as his subject a highly anti-clerical résumé of French history. All the same, Madame Cabet's motherly advice to him in June 1857 makes it clear that, among his own kind, he did not seem to be a man at ease with himself:

'I hope you are well, in spite of your troubles and your trying work . . . As I look on you as a son, I must give you a piece of advice, which you must take in that spirit. Recently [I heard] you were at a meeting where you got up to say something concerning what you said to B—, but you got into such a state that you weren't able to go on, and I reproach you for that. If, please God, you aren't to stop for ever in London, you'll no doubt be called on to speak in public again

. . . and my advice to you is to keep cool' – and so forth. The rest of the letter disintegrates into torn paper, but the general message is clear: stay calm and you'll earn more respect. 'I'm sure you'll overcome this little defect.'

As for Brighton, he stayed there for nine months, earning little but improving his English considerably, holding French conversation classes and acquiring some of the skills necessary to teach children. His Memoirs remark:

'Every morning, I went down to walk by the sea, I watched how the swimmers were getting on and joined in their fun. My health, which had diminished a little, became vigorous again and I became much more content.'

Perhaps the energetic Nadaud learnt belatedly to swim, something his early life in landlocked central France would have offered him no opportunity to do. Probably he bathed naked, as this was still the general male habit at that time, which we now like to imagine to have been so shrouded in 'Victorian prudishness'. Louis Blanc, who knew Brighton and had friends there, described the place a few years later in one of the *Lettres sur l'Angleterre* that he contributed regularly to French and Belgian magazines. He commented on the fact that, though the turns of phrase used in polite society were much more circumspect than was the case in French, 'I have seen . . . men bathing completely naked only a few hundred yards from ladies, who evidently did not think it worthwhile moving on for such a trivial reason'.

'Fashionable, luxurious Brighton' was by then well established as a residential area; a railway line had connected it with London as early as 1841. Louis Blanc remarked with surprise on the way some City businessmen actually lived there and travelled 52 miles a day up to town and back – the ultimate way of escaping from 'the smoke', and a brand-new phenomenon then unknown elsewhere in the world. England had also invented the Sunday-by-the-sea. Louis Blanc commented on how much drink the third-class-return day-trippers consumed, and added another detail that is equally recognisable today. He was sitting on the beach at Brighton when the man in charge of the seats came to turn him off at six o'clock, explaining: 'It's time for my tea.'

Nadaud says in his Memoirs that he left Brighton after nine months, in June 1856, because a teaching job in Putney paying much more had been found for him by (once again) the helpful Bourra. I don't think, however, that this is quite what happened. I unearthed among his miscellaneous papers a sheet on which, in his best writing, Nadaud had penned an advertisement offering lessons in French given 'in boarding schools or in private houses'. From the address and the mention that 'Rev. J. Allen' would supply a reference, it is clear that this dates from the Brighton period. Perhaps he was initially seeking work to tide him over the summer holidays?

However, the draft of a letter he wrote to his father on 2 June comes from a temporary address on the Old Dover Road in Blackheath, near to where he had hidden away in Greenwich the previous year, and there is no mention in this letter of a new job. It begins with the usual excuses for not having been in touch for so long: attached though he was to his father he seems to have been an erratic correspondent at this period, often letting months go by without a sign. He promises now to try to write once a month 'since a long silence pains you, greater regularity should make you happier – the only happiness, indeed, that I am able to offer you.

'We would never have thought, ten years ago, that our old house would be so empty, that of our whole family there would be only you left to live there and keep an eye on what one must call its ruinous out-buildings, and on our scraps of field and meadow that cost us so much sweat and money.' (The married sisters were, like Désirée, living away: Léonard had complained in a letter, with some exaggeration, 'I don't have daughters any more.' The land was being worked by a tenant.)

'Human life, as you see, is so much a matter of chance, like the clouds in the sky or storms . . . One can no more avoid its hazards than one can avoid eating or sleeping. Active and ambitious men are more apt to encounter hazards than those who wear away their lives in the village in the bosom of their family, just as the traveller who ranges through other countries is more likely to fall on a stone . . . Fate doesn't care if the child is deprived of the support of its father and mother and whether or not the old have a friendly hand to help their failing strength.'

The letter continues in this stoic but not very encouraging vein, via a pregnant discourse on the inadequacy of progress and rationalism as a general panacea. The doctrine of reason always expresses itself in figures, which in turn are translated into sums of money, which then go to pay the forces of law and order – '[this system] is less humane, and perhaps visits on people as many ills, as much shame and poverty, as the old aristocracy did . . .

'May you keep our door open until my return. Whether I come back in poverty or in modest comfort, so long as I see you again I will complain of nothing. There are moments when my heart is bursting with dreams of the happiness of family life. When these fits come over me in my isolation, and I see myself walking along streets where no hand comes out to shake mine, where not a mouth opens to wish one good day, then I transport myself either to Paris, where I lived for so long, or to La Martinèche, which seems to me the best place of any I have known in my life until now. Once I am in our flax field I can wish for nothing better, and, believe me, I would rather see the outline on the Puy Maria than the handsomest landscapes of this cold and selfish nation, where the most calm, law-abiding man might live for fifty years and still be looked on as a foreigner and, as such, be denigrated or exploited.'

The draft is unfinished. One rather hopes that Nadaud never sent poor Léonard this heart-sick missive, at least not in this form.

By August, Nadaud was in work again – not apparently in Putney but in Ealing. There *was* some sort of Putney connection, for in this same letter there is a mention of his having been in Putney the previous year in the house of a lady whose brother was now running the Ealing school. The time-scale alone would not have allowed for Nadaud to teach at Putney in 1856 for much more than a month before moving to Ealing, and he does mention that the Putney school was on the point of closing down. It had been in existence since the beginning of the century, 'highly regarded by the best families in the locality', and the Rev. Edward Trimmer seems to have taken it over in 1834. The 1851 Census records Trimmer, four assistant masters (including one for French), forty-four resident pupils aged from seven to sixteen, and eleven servants. However, the last year Trimmer appears in the church rate books is 1854.

Nadaud genuinely did live and teach for a significant period in the school run by the Trimmer son-in-law, another clergyman, Dr Nicholas of Ealing. He seems to have been established there by mid-August 1856. (Private school terms did not then run on the pattern accepted as conventional in more recent times, partly no doubt because they were boarding and foster-care establishments as much as teaching ones, and many of the pupils spent the whole year there.) To his father he now wrote: 'If my first impressions haven't blinded me, I shall be happy here, as happy as one can be when one is working for foreigners ... I can tell you, I've never been better lodged or fed or worked less hard. All that is certainly not to be disdained, but what I am really looking for is peace of mind [*tranquillité d'esprit*]. Living isolated as I do, if I had to bear the heartache of being ordered about without politeness or just with a sort of haughty indifference, I wouldn't call that being happy, and regardless of the loss of money or comfort a change would bring I wouldn't weigh the matter up – I'd go.'

It appears that his experience in Brighton had not been totally successful, or else he had suffered a separate ordeal in a job the Memoirs do not even mention. However, Ealing promised better; it was there that he put down sufficient roots to give the lecture at the Village Literary Institute, and he was still there at the end of 1857.

When Madame Cabet wrote to him there, she addressed

the letter to 'Ealing, Dr Nicholas House, near London', which sounds like her usual vagueness about proper forms until one realises that Ealing then, and also Putney and Wimbledon, were still genuinely rural communities separated from London by fields. They were not to be so for much longer. In each case, a newly arrived railway line was gradually but inevitably transforming the place into a suburb. All three villages had been popular eighteenth- and early nineteenth-century locations for school and other boarding establishments such as asylums, since these institutions nested conveniently in the large country houses of earlier centuries. Nadaud was experiencing these districts in their last years as smoke-free havens of bucolic peace, before the handsome old houses were finally pulled down and their grounds accommodated rows of new villa-residences. The writer Bulwer-Lytton, who was a pupil at another school in Ealing in the early nineteenth century, described it as a place of 'green, sequestered meadows, through which the humble Brent crept along its snake-like ways'. By the 1850s the meadows were bisected by the railway line, with uncompromising brick bridges over the lanes, and the station (today's Ealing Broadway on the Underground system) had swallowed part of the old central common. But the coaching inn had not yet been rebuilt as the Railway Hotel, and Nadaud found 'some fine pastures and a field of wheat' to appreciate with his country-boy's eye. There was also a road lined with trees 'twice as high and spreading as those of La Martinèche ... and beautiful gardens all round. Oh, this is well-cultivated land.' He also commented that the antique British habit of passing everything on to the eldest son at least had the merit of keeping land-holdings intact and well cared for.

One evening he met two old harvesters sitting sharpening their blades. They questioned him about his own country and, realising that he knew all about rural ways, sent for some bottled beer. 'We drank it lying down on the hay. Ah, I really thought about our mill pasture, but I couldn't tell them I was the son of a peasant, nor that I had been brought up just like the children I saw playing in the stream.' Probably he did not tell his new employer either that the four milk-cows that were kept by the establishment reminded him nostalgically of his own first charges as a boy of eight, including the cow on whom he had liked to ride.

The school Dr Nicholas ran was another genuinely long-established one, with some distinguished ex-pupils, including Thomas Huxley and Cardinal Newman. Nadaud does not seem to have known, however, that one of his predecessors there as a French master earlier in the century had been none other than the future King Louis-Philippe – he of the white waistcoat and the umbrella whom the Revolution of 1848 had deposed! Perhaps Nadaud would not have considered his occupying Louis-Philippe's shoes to be a fact worth celebrating. But nothing could exemplify more clearly the way in which successive waves of French refugees, of all political colours, had traditionally crossed and re-crossed the English Channel and were to continue to do so. Indeed, when Nadaud himself hurried back to France in 1870, after the fall of the Empire at the Battle of Sedan, he almost literally passed in mid-Channel the Emperor Napoleon III, making once again for Anglo-Saxon shores.

Judging from the evidence of successive Censuses, by the 1850s the Ealing school was declining in numbers and prestige: it had moved into a smaller house. One of Nadaud's pupils said that he taught them more French than the teacher who had preceded him. Another of them helped correct his English for the famous Institute lecture. 'The best way of getting youngsters to trust you is to show you like them. I stayed for eighteen months in Dr Nicholas's house, without experiencing any difficulties.'

Yet through this period the other Nadaud, the one inhabiting his old identity as a political exile and frustrated leader of men, continued obscurely to suffer. Late in 1856 his mentor Cabet had died far away in America, banished by the failure of Utopian ideals even from the community he himself had founded. In 1857 we find Nadaud and Louis Blanc trying to raise a subscription for Madame Cabet. Nadaud

wrote to an architect he knew in Paris, urging him to talk to
others about this:

'If I am presuming too far on our old friendship, my dear
Delbrouck, in imposing this task on you . . . forgive me. My
love for Cabet blinds me and knowledge that his family are in
penury clutches at my heart and makes me want to cry . . .

'Oh, my dear Delbrouck, death has also scythed a great
emptiness around me. And this space grows larger in my
imagination as I perceive my daughter growing up. I tell
myself, she hasn't got her mother any longer, nor her
grandmother and her father is far away and can hardly take
care of himself.

'*Adieu*, Nadaud.'

'Eighteen months' from early August 1856 would take us
roughly to the beginning of 1858. The Memoirs suggest that
Nadaud then moved, on the recommendation of another
compatriot, and with Dr Nicholas's blessing, by a smooth
transition, to the school at Wimbledon where he was to stay
until 1870. But in the real world of the letters we find him
writing to his daughter from the Soho accommodation
address half-way through 1858, 'Your nice little letter! It's by
a sort of miracle that it reached me. I haven't been in Ealing
since the 20th of December last, and as the head of the house
[Dr Nicholas, one must suppose] is dead, no one knew my
address.'

So Nadaud had left Ealing just before Christmas. Where
did he go? There is a letter to his father that has no date or
year on it but which mentions 'December 27th' as a recent
day. It is headed from an obscure street in Lambeth,
sandwiched between a railway viaduct, the archbishop's
garden and the slum of Lower Marsh. Lambeth was then a
working-class district of wharves, warehouses, narrow
streets, a lead-smelting works, a brewery, workmen's houses
and river fogs.

In writing that curls bizarrely down the sides of the page,
Nadaud speaks of his desire to work to make his father

happy and of his sense of helplessness 'from which are born all kinds of chimeras which make me see everything in life darkly; they retreat only to make way for fixed ideas which then obsess me entirely and which, in order to accomplish, I willingly abandoned all correspondence'.

Perhaps fortunately, the writing of this letter was, as he goes on to explain, interrupted at that point by three friends, who had come to carry him off on an expedition to the country 'three leagues from London'. The expedition, which cheered him up, appears to have been to Wimbledon, to introduce him to a new potential employer there, where one of the friends had previously been teaching. He says that he is due to start there in February and will write again then.

But if he really settled into Wimbledon as soon as that, why, the following June, should his address have been unknown to his family in France? And why, in May, was a mutual friend writing stiffly to Louis Blanc to say that no one, including Madame Cabet and her daughter, had heard anything from 'our friend Martin' and that this was inexcusable. The writer was a Dr Hubert-Valleroux, who, with his wife, acted as informal guardian to Désirée. The letter continued: 'That he should feel he needn't reply when I write to him might be understandable, but . . . when the subject is one that touches him so closely as the future of his daughter, it is incomprehensible. Please also tell him that I've heard from the schoolmistress in Guéret that his daughter has recovered from a chest infection [*une fluxion de poitrine* – a phrase to strike fear in that tuberculosis-haunted time] she got when she went to a wedding at La Martinèche.' There follow further peremptory remarks about money now due for payment.

Louis Blanc transmitted this letter to Nadaud, as he was clearly intended to, adding to it a note – 'Do write to me, and believe me, you always have my good wishes.' Nadaud seems not to have been in much contact with his friends in England either.

There is another note in the file from Louis Blanc. It has no date or year on it, but Louis Blanc's own address on it would locate it, too, in or around 1858. It says: 'I have just learnt, to my distress, that you have been dangerously ill, so ill that you are hardly recognisable – and I didn't know about it. Tell me –'

The beginning of another undated letter, from Nadaud to a friend in Paris, from the Lambeth address, has also survived. It runs: 'My dear Boquet [Bouquet?], As you know, just now I have nothing to do in London –' The letter was then abandoned, and notes on the English working classes were scribbled on the back of it.

I think there was a gap of many months between Nadaud's departure from Ealing and his establishment in Wimbledon, though he may have started giving a few lessons there in the evenings earlier. In his letter to Désirée of June 1858 he mentions country walks and finding birds' nests, which would fit with regular treks from Lambeth to Wimbledon. The first letter that definitely seems to place him there is one written to his sister Magdelaine Soumis and her husband, using the Gerrard Street address and dated September 1858. In it, he writes guardedly: 'I am living in a village where I am not unhappy, on many counts.' There had been a dark hole in his life which, in his public account, he covered over. Just where he was and what he was doing for much of 1858 I do not know, and it seems that very few of his contemporaries did either.

Once he settled in Wimbledon, he seems to have turned a corner. The letter to the Soumis is still rather forlorn, but a large part of it is taken up with practical plans. At last, instead of simply lamenting his own absence, he evidently felt able to think more specifically about his daughter Désirée.

He had not seen her since she was between five and six. Now she was rising thirteen. Variegated news of her from family and other contacts, and a handful of exquisitely penned letters to *Mon cher petit papa* that bear all the marks of having been written under her schoolmistress's controlling eye, were all he had to feed his dreams. But what steps he now took to resolve this, and how things turned out, I shall leave for the moment, while we explore Wimbledon, the place that was to be his refuge for more than a decade.

13

Idyll in Wimbledon

The twelve years Nadaud was to spend at Wimbledon School are dealt with in his Memoirs in a very few pages. Nevertheless, they came to represent for him the essence of his long time in England, and his outline description is calculated to present this section of his life in the most positive light. Since it was the period that should, by rights, have been his most active one in office in his native land, you might suppose that this public account would stress his continuing links with republicans in France. However, it ignores them almost entirely.

After the Imperial amnesty of 1859, the *proscrits* were no longer proscribed and had the right to return to live in France if they wished. Nadaud did make a visit there then, and sought out his old companions in the Builders' Association he had helped to found, hoping and expecting to be welcomed and even to be made its head. However, life had moved on; his erstwhile allies were earning fortunes under the Haussmann building boom, and it was indicated to him that his presence as a celebrated 'Forty-eighter' would be an embarrassment. He does mention this in his Memoirs, but deals with it by saying that 'My distress was not that great ... I returned to England and stayed there until the war was declared in 1870' – the implication being that he thus continued to make a principled stand against Louis-Napoleon's Empire and all it represented, by refusing even to breathe the same air.

This was not factually true. The relevant police archives in Guéret, mainly consisting of nervous communications between the Préfet and the Ministry of Internal Affairs in Paris, along with grubby anonymous notes from local Creusois informants ('*le nommé Nadaud* was observed taking Pizet's cart to Pontarion . . .'), testify to a number of visits in the course of the 1860s. However, the fact that Nadaud chose to omit all these from his overall account of the period carries its own message about how he saw himself in those years. His conflict about his identity had evidently resolved itself by his turning himself into a real schoolmaster at a credible English school. The axis of his life had finally shifted, and his Sundays were now mainly devoted to voracious study in the newly opened British Museum Reading Room: partly in order to equip himself further as a teacher, partly from an innate love of learning and partly with a view to writing something himself. (If he encountered Karl Marx there, busy on his own magnum opus in those years, he does not say so.)

Even his arrival in Wimbledon is presented, consciously or otherwise, as the definitive break from the preceding years and the assumption of a more impenetrable and permanent disguise. A cabinet photograph of him taken during the Wimbledon period, which has only recently come to light, shows him in the English-tailored garb of a schoolmaster. His expression, too, is gentlemanly and restrained. No more red-checked waistcoats now and, of course, no plaster-spattered ones. But at first he continued to worry obsessively:

'Three years before, I had worked as a builder in that locality. I was haunted by the fear that the pupils, who belonged to the great aristocratic families of England [*aux grandes familles nobiliaires*], might get to know that they were being taught by an ex-builder . . . If such a misfortune should occur, I thought I would not be able to prevaricate: I should have to flee.'

Since his companions on the site had not been local men and had left the area – 'I dared hope that no one would recognise me, except the large family of the man in whose house I had lodged, one Beadle. I made up my mind to confide in this decent man, and to go and tell him my story.

That was a good idea, for during the fourteen years I was in that school [actually twelve, Nadaud seems to be covering his tracks for the preceding difficult two years] the father and his children were all completely discreet.'

Nadaud seems to have missed something in being unaware that the great Ruskin himself had far more exalted views on the dignity and importance of manual labour. I wonder what he would have thought of Ruskin's recruitment of a team of Oxford undergraduates to repair a road? (They made rather a poor job of it.) Or perhaps Nadaud did know of this but thought, probably rightly, that the families who sent their boys to Wimbledon School might not see matters in such visionary terms.

'I still worried; there might be others who would recognise me . . . I decided that in the daytime hours I would confine myself to the school's large grounds where the boys amused themselves and played their games of cricket and football.'

The Beadle clan appear again, though not in the Memoirs.

Nadaud's tendency to aggrandise, for the record, the establishments in which he taught, remained constant. Wimbledon School was a genuine promotion for him, for it was a proper, thriving boys' school that was soon to have over a hundred pupils. But it was by no means the Eton–Harrow–Winchester rival that Nadaud allowed his French readers to assume. Though called 'Collegiate', the place was owned and run as a business by yet another clergyman, J. M. Brackenbury, seconded by C. J. Wynne, and it was an army crammer. The era when commissions in the army could be purchased, or otherwise acquired by family influence, was drawing to its close, hastened along by the disasters of the Crimean War in the hands of such incompetent aristocrats as Lords Raglan and Cardigan. Under Gladstone's ministry were soon to come the 'Cardwell reforms', which aimed to ensure a modicum of efficiency in officers by making them pass through training colleges and take exams. Brackenbury's was one of many schools which, in the 1860s and '70s, thrived on preparing boys for the new entry requirements for Sandhurst and Woolwich – in Brackenbury's case, mainly Woolwich, the seed-bed not for dashing cavalry officers with private incomes but for artillerymen and engineers in less smart regiments.

Looking up the Wimbledon Census records for 1861 (on which Nadaud appears as 'Henri Geo. Martin') I found that large numbers of Brackenbury's boarders were born in what was then still called the East Indies – that is, in India. These would have been, most of them, the sons of Indian army families; Nadaud does indeed refer, slightly confusedly, to the effects of the Indian mutiny and the dissolution of the East India Company on the new military requirements. At this date, many of the ostensibly British families settled in India had that mixture of Indian blood (politely known as 'the strain of the country') that was the natural result of lifetimes spent in a place far from England, with few genuine English ladies as yet coming out to look for husbands. In any case, even the children of unquestionably Anglo-Saxon families were felt to be undesirably 'Indianized' by a childhood out there, therefore all boys of India-based families were sent to the mother country for their later childhood. There they were to lose their singsong accents, to get used to rain and heavy clothes, to learn Latin rather than Hindustani – in short, to be turned into proper English gentlemen before returning eastwards to resume the white man's burden. It seems to have been largely for such boys that Brackenbury catered, plus a sprinkling of others born in similarly far-flung places. There were also a number of older boys, mainly from rural England, whose previous schools had failed to hoist them up to the necessary standard for Woolwich or the Civil Service exams. Wimbledon School was certainly fulfilling a mid-Victorian need and providing a sound, useful education geared to a specific purpose: as such, it offered evidence before the Schools Enquiry Committee of 1866. But it was not, by any stretch of the imagination, serving 'the great aristocratic families of England'.

What it did do was reinforce, if it needed to, the British colonial ethic of service. Nadaud does not mention this specifically, but the atmosphere of the school can only have strengthened his own growing predilections in that direction. It was also at pains to inculcate the Public School Spirit (that, perhaps, was what the term 'collegiate' was intended to suggest), a gospel which had spread round English schools from Dr Arnold of Rugby. Brackenbury, who had previously taught at Marlborough and had married a sister of the headmaster there, was keen on the prefectorial system of giving older boys authority over younger ones. Boys were allowed to roam out of the school grounds into Wimbledon's countryside, but there were two-hourly roll-calls and nightly lock-ins. A rather wild form of rugby football was played. All this was designed to create an ethos that will be instantly familiar to anyone who has read Thomas Hughes's classic *Tom Brown's Schooldays* (1857) and it may not be coincidental that Hughes himself lived near by. He was a lawyer and Member of Parliament and an associate of J. M. Ludlow in the Christian Socialism movement and the Working Men's College. In fact the two families were so close that for a while they shared one large house in Wimbledon called The Firs.

Nadaud kept in contact with Ludlow and had met Hughes (always written by him 'Hugues', as if some Huguenot association of decent protest knocked in his mind). Many things in the atmosphere and ethos of Hughes's famous book should have appealed to him, bearing in mind the affection he finally developed, during his years in Wimbledon, for English attitudes that he had previously considered 'cold' and 'dour'. But I don't think he can actually have read it, or he would hardly have referred to it (as he does in his book on the English working classes) as a 'socialist novel'! The term is wildly inappropriate to the eclectic mixture of altruistic, progressive principle, Anglicanism, pre-industrial snobbish mystique and knock-about realism that informs this archetypal Story for Boys. *Tom Brown*, in other words, embodies the essence of muscular Christianity, that ideal of *mens sana in corpore sano* that became so familiar to several generations of more or less educated Englishmen. It was this peculiarly Anglo-Saxon essence that Nadaud first encountered in full strength in Wimbledon.

Long ago in Paris, as a belligerent young workman, he had enjoyed wrestling and boxing, but even his equally combative father had disapproved of this, and as he grew into adult responsibility there was no physical sport available to him. In France, in the time of Louis-Philippe, only riding or fencing were socially acceptable forms of exercise; everything else was considered common and low. Now, however, in Brackenbury's would-be Rugby, Nadaud found to his pleasure that he could join his pupils in their games and wrestling matches, and that this was actually considered to be setting a good example – 'It is well known that the English, used as they are to athletics, are great admirers of physical strength . . . One day I even managed a feat which surprised and drew applause from them.' He and some of the biggest boys (strapping young men between eighteen and twenty, still struggling to get into the ex-East India Company College at Addiscombe) were competing to see who could lift the heaviest stone above their head. As a mason, Nadaud of course knew the technique for this, and won, in spite of being more than twice their age. He remarks engagingly: 'After this I became very popular among my pupils, and often acted as referee for their football matches.' He also said that he never told any of them his real name 'in case the handle of a mason's trowel should then become apparent'. However, one gets the impression that in spite of this preoccupation with not being found out, he gained an equivocal pleasure from the display of a trick from his secret other life.

He was also delighted in his simple heart when regularly, at the end of the school year, after the sports days whose programmes he kept as souvenirs among his papers, some of the boys would parade him round on their shoulders with cries of '"Hurrah, hurrah for our good old *chap*!"' – the last word in English in the text. 'These youngsters caused me to spend many happy hours – happy years, I should say.'

It seems that the middle-aged man rediscovered, with these sheltered British adolescents, something of the companionship and solidarity that he had known when he was their age on the building sites of Paris. In contrast, in the traditional

boarding establishment in France, whether Jesuit or Napoleonic, the boarders were seen as potential political insurgents, and heads employed the junior staff as spies and
informers. French teenagers played at dangerous adult games:
several of Nadaud's generation of republicans, including his
fellow *député* Félix Pyat, had been college revolutionaries in
1830. How unlike Dr Arnold's England, where the breathless
hush in the Close was not about whether the army would be
called in to dismantle a barricade of desks but about who
would win the annual cricket match; and where those who
had imbibed this ethos would extend it into their adult lives.

> 'Tis the voice of a schoolboy rallies the ranks:
> 'Play up! play up! and play the game!'

Nadaud himself came to understand and misquote in his
Memoirs Wellington's endlessly repeated remark about the
Battle of Waterloo having been won '*à la grande école
d'Arrow*'.

But although the hearty schoolmasters of Victorian England were so different from the black-robed clerics of Roman
Catholic France, they were of course fervently Christian in
their own way. It was in Wimbledon, too, that Nadaud
gravitated naturally to the high-minded, hard-working decen-
cies of Protestantism. In Putney (or was it actually Ealing?) he
had had to accompany the boys to church on Sundays and
describes this as 'the duty I most disliked ... but I simply
stood up and sat down when everyone else did, and no more
was asked of me'. At Wimbledon, however, he conceived a
strong admiration for Brackenbury, who seems to have been
a dedicated, fair and charismatic figure, and with him
Nadaud apparently felt no discomfort in attending morning
prayers. He had, by now, made the important discovery that
here the traditional oppositions on which his own belief
system had been founded did not hold good – that in England
progressive thinking and organised religion often made
common cause.

To the end, Nadaud remained hostile to the dominant
religion of his own country. 'Not at any price is my body

going to be claimed by the church', he wrote in what was probably his last letter. But he had grown up in an awe-inspiring landscape and, like Wordsworth in the Lake District, he seems to have evolved his own view of some kind of Supreme Being. The copious rough notes, quotations and jotted reflections that date from his British Museum years suggest a continual debate on religion going on in his mind – for example: '*There are as many good reasons for believing in God as there are against*' (Guizot). 'There is nothing in us that we cannot control – love, desire, ambition – all should give way to the man who often repeats this short prayer: I want to behave in such and such a way . . . a man is never overcome except by his own fault.'

It no doubt helped that Brackenbury was (at least in Nadaud's version of events) married to 'a Mlle Delafosse, who was descended from a family of *proscrits* from the [repeal of the] Edict of Nantes'. What is meant here, of course, is a Huguenot family. It is typical of Nadaud's desire to make coherent sense of the kaleidoscope of cultures through which he had passed that he here equates *proscrit* with Protestant, and assimilates both to his own liberal, republican ethic, as if he felt that he and the Brackenburys belonged to the same club. (Naturally, it had turned out, when the question of the amnesty arose in 1859, that Brackenbury had known all along of his assistant master's real name and illustrious former post. After all, he had acquired Nadaud through the French political exiles' net-work.) 'When [Brackenbury] invited me to dinner, he always made mention of our distinguished predecessors who had, by their intelligence and hard work, enriched the country from which they had been banished by the brutality of Catholic kings.'

A diplomatic fellow, Brackenbury, evidently. In reality, it is not at all clear which wife Nadaud is referring to, since Brackenbury was married three times. His first wife died in 1841; the second was the sister of the head of Marlborough and (according to Brackenbury's great-grandson) the mother of 'most of his seventeen children'. She too died, during

Nadaud's time at the school, it would seem, and the third Mrs Brackenbury was a Blanche Gervis (not Delafosse) whom he married only in 1867. She was many years younger than he – in fact younger than his unmarried eldest daughter by his first wife. This girl, Anna-Jane, lived at Wimbledon School throughout Nadaud's stay there.

Both Nadaud's own transformation into a permanent, respectably paid member of staff, and the school's physical transformation into a convincing replica of a venerable institution, date from two or three years after he first began to teach there.

In 1858 the school was still called 'Nelson's House', since it occupied an old property of that name in the centre of Wimbledon village. This Jacobean mansion still exists, today serving as an Islamic Cultural Centre. At first Nadaud seems to have come from central London to Wimbledon only twice a week to give his French classes; not until a year or so later – the time-scale is left vague – were his hours and his pay increased when he began to teach French history too. The first lot of pupils he coached for Addiscombe College did not do well; neither Brackenbury nor Wynne was particularly pleased with Nadaud, and he felt himself to be on trial (I think this is what is meant by the 'crisis' he refers to without details in a letter to his father of 1858). However, the next lot of pupils did rather better, and on the evening that the results came he received a bonus cheque for 5 pounds (125 francs in his terms – i.e. the equivalent of about a month's wages as a plasterer) plus a little note from Brackenbury that he was sufficiently proud to quote in English nearly forty years later:

'Dear Sir,
    I pray you receive a small reward for your trouble.'

He adds: 'As may be imagined, the most important thing for me was that my pupils' success confirmed for me, poor uneducated man that I was, how I should continue in the future. It was no small thing for me to have gained the trust of my pupils and also my superiors.'

He might have added 'confidence in myself', which he needed in order to overcome the problem of teaching history that, as he says, he had never actually been taught. 'I was always afraid of having to answer questions that my boys might ask me. I therefore set myself to serious and detailed study of our history. The reading I had begun in Mazas and Sainte-Pélagie . . . suggested to me the idea of reading Guizot, Henri Martin and Augustin Thierry . . . I began writing for myself a small history course, which I have kept.'

In fact, over the next twelve years, Nadaud's readings in the British Museum and in Ludlow's private library were far more extensive, and as much in English as French. In addition to Michelet and Quinet, the rather chaotic notes he kept indicate the study of Locke and Hume, secularists such as Holyoake, Adam Swift, Swift the satirist, Defoe, Addison, and also Robert Owen, with whom he seems to have felt a particular sympathy. Owen's concept of a Utopian manufac-turing community no doubt recalled Nadaud's old hero Cabet, while between Nadaud's own hard, self-educated road and Owen's there were also distinct similarities. All this was the raw material that, after his return to France in 1870, was to become his book *L'Histoire des Classes Ouvrières en Angleterre*.

Like many self-taught people, Nadaud tended to treat reading matter as evidence to support theories about life and society which he had had to work out unaided. Thus he was particularly interested in the history of the Civil War, as if he felt that these distant events had a direct bearing on the socialist crusades of his own time, and he took pleasure from the fact that one of Ludlow's ancestors had been among the principal opponents of Charles I. Ludlow himself, however, tried to influence him, without much success, to take a less polemic view, and to understand that historical events cannot necessarily be categorised as 'good' or 'bad'.

By the same token, Richardson's faintly lubricious eight-eenth-century epistolary novel, *Clarissa Harlowe*, was firmly annexed by Nadaud to the department marked 'Exploitation of the Working Classes', and became, rather surprisingly, a favourite book of his. It seems to have been the first novel he ever had in his hands, at a time when he hardly knew that fiction existed. He was handed volume one (in French) by a fellow prisoner while in Sainte-Pélagie, who told him he needed a change from Guizot's history and promised him the other volumes in due course. But then the political prisoners were all released and went their separate ways. It wasn't for some time that Nadaud was able to assuage his awakened curiosity for the rest of the story. He mentions this in his History, but some notes of his fill in the picture:

'Eight years after, being lost in a manner of speaking in a narrow, dilapidated and often fireless attic room in the little town of Greenwich . . . I managed to get hold of M. Villemain's educational book on English Literature and with this I whiled away the distress of a long period of forced unemployment.' Delighted to discover that his sympathetic response to the tale of 'this hard-working and virtuous girl of the people . . . beautiful and pure' was shared by an expert, he by and by read the whole saga in English. 'Clarissa Harlowe has been brought up in the principles of reform and Puritanism but not in its narrow and extreme form . . . one sees that the evolution [of English society] . . . has introduced a new concept of morality to the working classes.'

In Nadaud's own notes, and in the quotations he selected to write down, often in a mixture of French and English, there is a sense of a passionate, unending search. He seems perpetually wrestling to fashion one coherent picture out of what he read, what his idealism encouraged him to believe and what his own knowledge of the world told him. It is as if his struggle of the early 1850s about what direction his own life should or could take, and whether hope or despair were more realistic, he had now externalised into an intellectual struggle about the future of mankind. Eventually, encouraged and admonished by both Ludlow and Louis Blanc, he managed to develop a more disciplined style of argument and began to contribute articles on the English working classes to the republican newspapers that were now seeing the light of day in Paris. A degree of material and personal security, the mental space to indulge in a taste for study – these were the modest but much valued blessings that his job in Wimbledon bestowed on him.

After the Imperial amnesty of 1859, he felt secure enough in his post to ask Brackenbury if it could be kept open temporarily for him while he returned to France to test the possibilities for himself there? Brackenbury (who, judging from his evidence to the Schools Enquiry Committee, was secretly rather proud of harbouring Nadaud) replied that he and Wynne were planning a brand-new school building on Wimbledon Ridge. If Nadaud chose to come back to England, there would be a living-in job for him there at a considerably increased salary of 4,000 francs 'all found': roughly £160 a year. It sounds little enough by the upper-class standards of that time and place, but for a single man whose board and lodging in term time were also assured it represented substantial comfort and the chance to 'put by'. To Nadaud, with his family responsibilities in France and his memory of the time when, as a young mason, he had worked out that he and his father could never hope to clear the accumulated burden of debt by work alone, a safe salary on this level must have seemed the realisation of a long-held dream.

('*Whether I come back in poverty or in modest comfort, so long as I see you again I will complain of nothing.*')

His Memoirs claim that even as he arrived at La Martinèche in 1860 for the first time in nine years, his father greeted him by saying how right he had been to refuse to submit to the Imperial rule all these years. Whether or not Léonard, the old admirer of the first Napoleon, really felt that, it is evident that that was how the story was to be. One may assume that the new possibilities of visiting his father, added to the greater financial security he could offer, assuaged the guilt and defensiveness that had been such a feature of Martin Nadaud's letters home in the previous decade. It was probably at this time that he and Léonard began to plan, if not yet to build, the new, four-square house in La Martinèche alongside the old home – the typical house that the returned-mason-made-good raised as an outward sign of a lifetime's successful campaigns.

Meanwhile in Wimbledon, Brackenbury's own dream building, the visible evidence of scholastic and business enterprise triumphantly combined, was going up on the crest of the Ridgway. It still stands and is still a boys' school. Even today, when it has lost much of its grounds to suburban housing, and the valley below is filled with roads and roofs, its elevated site is a grand one. When it first went up, its views across fields and woods to the Surrey hills must have seemed truly splendid. Wimbledon then consisted only of the old village in a dip a mile away, some inns and workmen's terraced cottages (including the Beadle home) scattered along the higher ground, and the new railway line in the valley along which the future would come. Ludlow and Hughes had built their joint house on the slopes of the Ridge because they had been enchanted by its secluded bluebell woods and streams with jays and 'fine air' – the inevitable nineteenth-century preoccupation. As for the Collegiate School, *The Ecclesiologist* was writing in 1860, when the plans and drawings were published:

'This is a very large imposing group designed by Mr Teulon. The plan, which appears to be very judiciously distributed, comprises, we observe, classical and mathematical schoolrooms, with a junior school, school library, headmaster's house and rooms for the ushers. There is also a stately dining hall, a covered playground and an infirmary . . . The material is red brick: the style Pointed. The dining room, which has an embattled parapet, looks somewhat later in style than the rest of the design. The cost amounts to £9000. We miss a chapel, which should be indispensable in an establishment of this magnitude.'

And, the writer might have added, of this pseudo-ecclesias-
tical style. A red gothic castle, blood relation to St Pancras
Station Hotel (built in the same decade) the building itself
embodies fantasies about power, tradition and the perma-
nency of these things. As for a chapel, the boys went twice
every Sunday to a nearby new church (Teulon also), but a
few years later business was so good that the school acquired
a further wing with a chapel of its own.

If ever a building was in the vanguard of its time, it was
Brackenbury's. The 1860s was a decade when, all over the
metropolis and its outlying, soon-to-be-included districts, the
Georgian-scale townscape became dotted by much larger and
flamboyant piles of brick and masonry. An article in *The
Builder* in 1864, evoking the London of twenty years hence
in the triumphalist style usually adopted by such predictions,
wrote: 'The dingy old monotonous brick is, indeed, already
fast disappearing, to be replaced by handsomer structures . . .
buildings of real stone, enriched with inlays of polished
granite, marble or terracotta and decorated with real sculp-
ture of great artistic merit.' Buildings, in other words, that
made a statement about social and cultural values, even as
Brackenbury's new school did. It was designed to appear
venerable.

But much of what was constructed in London in the 1860s
also came under the heading of modern improvements. Those
were the years when the Thames's northern foreshore, which
had previously looked not unlike the Paris Grève, was
embanked. Public gardens with statues and water fountains
occupied segments of reclaimed land along the newly constricted river, large modern sewers ran below. In the 1860s,
too, Holborn Viaduct was built, connecting the twin cities of
London and Westminster over what had always been the
awkward valley of the Fleet. The Fleet itself, by then a filthy
open drain, was finally imprisoned in a pipe and disappeared
from view. The upper reaches of other London rivers too,
such as the Tyburn and the Westbourne, were similarly
buried, as new terraces of houses filled up the remaining open
fields further and further to the north and the west. In

Kensington, where Paxton's Crystal Palace had stood, the huge museums were going up. North of King's Cross Station, where Nadaud had walked to his first job on the Meat Market site, the semi-rural landscape of sheep and brickfields was unrecognisable: the Market was surrounded by houses, and the combined shunting and coaling yards of what were now two great stations side by side occupied a huge swathe of London earth.

Later, Nadaud was to write: 'During the last years I spent in England, I saw the equivalent of six towns built around London.' He was much in favour of the English system of cheap fares for workmen on the suburban trains that serviced this extended metropolis: French trains at that time were beyond the daily means of ordinary working people.

But the development which impressed him most was the Metropolitan railway, the world's first underground. The earliest stretch of line opened in 1863 and ran only from Paddington to King's Cross, underneath the Marylebone-Euston Road. It was powered by steam trains, and there were fears before its opening that passengers might faint from the sulphurous smell of soot in a confined tunnel and from the general excitement of it all. However, it proved a great success, and plans were soon made to extend it and link it with the proliferating suburban railways. Nadaud must have used the Metropolitan often in his journeyings around London: it was one more example of the miraculous transformation brought by scientific progress that his eventful life had seen. Once he was back in Paris for his last two decades in public office, the need for Paris, too, to have an underground railway was a theme to which he frequently returned. After many years of municipal procrastination and argument – Was not the French spirit, unlike the fog-bound British one, too airy to submit to the Stygian gloom of an underground railway? Would not elevated tracks running down the principal avenues in tasteful wrought iron suit the Parisian better? – the Métro finally began to be built in 1898, the year of Nadaud's death.

But no echo of change in the outside world touches the

Wimbledon years of the Memoirs, from which one would gather that Nadaud spent nearly all his time in the College's gothic seclusion, either in class or on the playing field, or in one of Teulon's specially built attic rooms for ushers. Here he sometimes coached his slower boys 'until eleven at night', so determined was he that they should not let him down in their exams. He was also determined not to have an assistant to take some of the load from him: partly, he says, in order to earn all the available salary himself, and partly because he was nervous that someone else might notice his weak points or his lack of a proper educational grounding.

'My time was occupied in the following way: I taught the first class from 7 to 8 in the morning. Breakfast was next; then from 9 to 1 four other classes came to me in turn. Two others appeared from 3 to 5, and finally there was another period between 7.30 and 9 in the evening. After that, once we had locked the boys into their rooms, we would find our last meal laid ready for us. This supper for the staff always consisted of cold meat, good cheese and all the beer we wanted.'

However, there were other dimensions to his life of which he does not speak. Apart from anything else, you would never guess from this account that his daughter was actually in London from the autumn of 1858 and remained there some years.

· 14 ·

Désirée and Other Female Company

I had picked up traces of Désirée in the boxes of unsorted papers. In particular, there was an extremely neat letter without a date, in which she reproached Nadaud gently for writing to her so seldom: 'Do you not know, dearest father, that your letters are an encouragement for me and that the good advice they include does not fall among thorns or on stony ground but on good earth? I read and re-read them many times, and I try to put the advice you give me into practice, always hoping to gain the approval of my Mistress.'

Madame Baillet had allowed her grand-daughter and Désirée to have their own little gardens:

'We planted roses, violets, primroses and pansies [*pensées –* the same as the word for thoughts] and each time I pick one of these I say to myself that it stands for all those thoughts I send *mon père cheri*. If you only knew how often I think of you and talk to you; I feel I can see you and kiss you, but unfortunately these are only vain illusions which fade to give way to the sad reality. I often pray to God and His Holy Mother that they should send my father back to me. When I see other little girls embracing their own fathers, my heart is so heavy that big tears fall from my eyes. I am very glad to have found a second mother in Madame Baillet; please thank her for all the care she takes of me and for the trouble she takes in correcting my faults. But I am afraid you will think I am running on too long, dearest father, so I take my leave.'

Readers will not be surprised to hear that this missive from a Model Little Girl has a note on the bottom in Madame

Baillet's own hand sending Nadaud her good wishes. One may wonder if Nadaud was really delighted to hear that his daughter was offering regular prayers to the Holy Family. (Madame Baillet ran one of the rare non-religious training courses for female teachers that then existed, but evidently a touch of religion in a young girl was *de bon ton* even there.) One can only pity the child writing to a fantasy father she can hardly have remembered, and the father receiving such a communication from a daughter who was a perfect stranger in every sense. The one or two letters from him to her that survive from this period dwell nostalgically on recollections of his own childhood at La Martinèche – the one possible point of contact for the father who had almost no shared memories of hers.

At one point – it was in 1854 after his return from his travels around Britain – he wrote to Madame Baillet: 'Is it really true that she who used to be so boisterous has become so docile? You, who have so much experience in bringing up children, must tell me if in your judgement she will make an intelligent woman . . . Do you think her health is good, is she pretty? It seems to me she is rather too dark in complexion, and her eyes and mouth lack something to be desired, I can't exactly say what.' The tone chills one, in a father. It seems too detached. But life, indeed, had detached him. 'Soon she will be nine, and I have never spent one entire week with her. Her bearing seems to me, from my vantage point of age, quite lively and easy, but I can't tell what she may turn into. If she grows up physically like her mother that would be a very good thing. Her mother was a delightful country girl [*une charmante campagnarde*] as pretty as she was good-hearted.'

A slight corrective to the image of Model Little Girl is supplied by one of Madame Cabet's effusions (from June 1857), which mentions in passing some trouble from that quarter. Madame Cabet, like her friends Dr and Madame Hubert-Valleroux, kept an eye on Désirée.

'I told them that if we were sure she was being ill-treated I'd go down there and get her out myself, they reassured me, they said it was just a little assistant-teacher who slapped her once or twice and the others too but that it wouldn't happen again. The Mistress is coming to Paris soon, Monsieur Hubert will take the opportunity to have her bring our little girl so that she can spend her holidays here, we would like to have her with us for as many days as possible, that would be a real joy for us, we would talk to her about you, my poor dear friend, for we want her to love you . . .'

'Us' is Madame Cabet and her widowed daughter. Poor dears, they did their best, but evidently Nadaud's deeper emotions were engaged in some place inaccessible to them. It was the following year that Dr Hubert was writing stiffly to Louis Blanc, telling him that Nadaud had not treated the Cabet ladies as he should.

In my mind I had Désirée permanently fixed in Guéret, in a stone house among the narrow, steep streets which still form the heart of the town. Madame Baillet lived across the way from the inn where Nadaud had stopped for a meal on his first-ever journey away from home: the family who had made a fuss then of the tired fourteen-year-old now kept a sympathetic eye on his daughter. Désirée had La Martinèche and her grandfather and other country relatives for her holidays. There are references in letters to her coming and going in the cart belonging to Pizet, whose own inn in Pontarion had been shut down in 1851, and whose daughter, Julie, became Désirée's best friend. Occasionally Léonard Nadaud would put on his Sunday suit and come to Guéret – for a genteel prize-giving in the school, or for the more robust town carnival. Désirée had insisted on him coming too, he wrote to Nadaud in July 1856: they had dined with the innkeeper's family and Désirée had impressed him by her 'nice behaviour and reasonable manner'. On another occasion there was the wedding, of Roby's daughter Amélie, at which Désirée allegedly contracted *une fluxion de poitrine* from dancing too energetically.

And yet, however timeless this essentially rural world may seem to have been, Désirée was growing up and what was all her education for if not to fit her for other things? When I came upon the cache of papers that the French police had kept on Nadaud during his English years, a quite different picture emerged. The Ministry of Security in Paris, ruffled by Nadaud's visit to France after the amnesty, early in 1860, and convinced this dangerous Red had come to stir up trouble, contacted the Préfecture in Guéret. Since his name was spelt wrong, Guéret first stoutly replied that they'd never heard of him. But, having finally identified 'this person' about whom cloak-and-dagger notices were being circulated, they informed Paris: 'His presence in the area has not, in any case, provoked any noticeable effect. He has let it be known he has a good job in England, where he has left his daughter, and is counting on returning there at the end of the month.'

Was this, however, true or were the police misinformed? I was lucky to obtain copies of other family letters which carried the fugitive story of Désirée a little further.

Nadaud's grief at not having a proper hand in his daughter's upbringing was expressed in various ways over the years; it was also fed by the intimations that occasionally reached him that all was not well. In 1856, at the end of the same summer in which Léonard Nadaud had been happy with Désirée's behaviour at the carnival, we find him mentioning in a letter to his son (dictated to Soumis and mainly devoted to the harvest and to the further misdeeds of the other son-in-law, Bouteille): 'Désirée can read letters just like you do, without any difficulty, but she has an awkward nature [*un petit caractère dangereux*].'

He does not elaborate further but almost on the same date Désirée herself, who had presumably just returned to Guéret, wrote her father a docile little letter, assuring him as usual that she was doing her best to behave soberly (*me corriger de toutes mes fantaisies*). To this, Madame Baillet added a less anodyne message of her own:

'I have left your little Désirée to write from her innocent heart, *cher monsieur* . . . I can tell you that her health leaves nothing to be desired, that she is growing taller and is beginning to develop, although she is still quite fat [*bien grasse*], that her intelligence and her spirit are well above average, and her heart is good. But the liveliness of her character often leads her into small faults, a fact she recognises and regrets. This makes her rather difficult to control, since she has a pronounced tendency to dominate.' In short, she was leading the other little girls astray, arguing and causing trouble.

Where have we heard of such a turbulent and well-built child before? It does not sound as if Désirée took after her 'tall, graceful' and apparently quiet mother, but after her stocky, pugnacious father. '*Bien grasse*' may just be an allusion to puppy fat that had not yet resolved itself into the bosom and hips (with a neat waist in between, confined by stays) that were then considered desirable in a young lady. But it may also indicate a physique more naturally suited to taxing farm labour than to the almost entirely sedentary existence of a *jeune fille bien élevée*. If she was her father's daughter in any way, or, come to that, Léonard Nadaud's grand-daughter, a daily life bounded by lessons, embroidery, prayers to the Virgin, the contemplation of one's own faults and a little light gardening would hardly absorb her restless energies.

She was in any case, poor child, living between two worlds, if not three. In Guéret, her companions would have been the daughters of the rural bourgeoisie, including some of Nadaud's political opponents. But in the holidays she was returned to a peasant society where little-madame ways were not appreciated. Meanwhile, there was the mysteriously glamorous and/or disgraced father over the water, and the intermittent promise from that direction that there a quite different life again waited her. As soon as he felt established in Wimbledon in the summer of 1858, Nadaud wrote:

'My daughter, towards the end of this year I shall be in a position to have you here to learn English.' He recommended reading matter to her of a highly conventional kind: *Paul et Virginie* and the Fables of La Fontaine. He told her that he had used to read them with her mother just after their marriage. 'Tell me, do you feel strong again? [This was after the *fluxion de poitrine*.] Have you a good appetite, do you enjoy getting up in the morning, getting ready for the day? Tidiness, cleanliness – all that, *ma bonne amie*, is good for the health. I should be so unhappy if you were with me and I thought you were not strong.' He had had that experience once in his life already.

Over the next few months, the plans were laid. Léonard Nadaud (now over seventy and feeling his age) wrote that Désirée only wanted to stay in England for two or three months – 'but I suggest that you keep her there until she is seventeen or eighteen.' And would Nadaud please send some details of how he would like his daughter clothed for her momentous journey? She had a good new dress from Amélie's wedding, and a silk one that had been her mother's and he couldn't say what else besides ... In Léonard Nadaud's day young women had only one decent dress, to last them for the rest of their lives.

A building entrepreneur of Nadaud's acquaintance happened to be travelling with his family from the area of La Martinèche to Paris: Désirée would accompany them that far and someone else would escort her to London from there. Nadaud wrote in September to the Soumis asking them to make sure she visited her mother's family at La Chaux and that she saw all the neighbours to say goodbye – 'I would really like her to be more sedate [*moins turbulante*] ... We have to try to see that children close to us have a good reputation. Often outsiders will pick out, and even invite, faults which are only there on the surface.'

Désirée might be on the point of leaving, perhaps for ever, this rural world where everyone gossiped about everyone else, but her father still carried its standards ingrained within himself.

By October, Désirée was in London. Her father placed her in an English boarding establishment which appears on one letter-heading as 'Walham House'. I guessed this to be in Fulham, since the junction of the Fulham Road and North End Road, which today forms Fulham Broadway, then bore the name Walham Green. Fulham, situated on the road between London and Wimbledon, was in itself still countrified. As in Putney and Ealing, there were good-sized old houses there set in their own grounds.

Sure enough, the Census of 1861 lists Walham House, North End Road. In residence was a Clara Burbidge, the middle-aged spinster headmistress of a school, a place which sounds like an English version of Madame Baillet's. There were seven girl pupils aged six to fifteen, one assistant-teacher, and one seventeen-year-old 'governess-pupil' (pupil-teacher), as well as three servants.

During Nadaud's first return to France, in January 1860, the Imperial Police had the idea that his daughter was 'employed in a teaching establishment in England'. It is just possible that she was the predecessor to the governess-pupil who was there a year later, but it seems unlikely, since, in October 1858 when she arrived, she had only just turned thirteen. In any case I found receipted bills, made out to 'Monsieur Martin', for board, tuition, exercise books, galoshes and so forth, submitted by a Miss Burbidge, tucked away among Nadaud's mass of miscellaneous papers, and Nadaud was to complain to his own father in the summer of 1859, 'She costs me about 750 francs per annum. She'll have to leave at the end of the year.'

Thirteen or fourteen was hardly old enough, by educated standards, for a young girl to be in paid employment, though of course it was by the standards of the peasant world of La Martinèche. Which scale was being applied? Here, no doubt, is one of several hidden sources for the tension that had by then come to a head between Nadaud and his child. It is as if, though all those years of paying for her to be turned into a young lady by Madame Baillet, Nadaud had not really made up his mind what sort of life he expected a daughter of his to lead. The identity problem that was central to his own life (was he still a workman disguised as a gentleman? Or was he, rather, a leader of men disguised as an assistant-master?) was now visited on the luckless Désirée. By the summer of '59 the honeymoon dream of loving father at last reunited with his adoring daughter was over.

'Having lived in the same house with Désirée for three weeks [presumably in temporary rented accommodation] it has become easy for me to study her character. She is a spoilt child, passably lazy and extremely obstinate and mutinous. The way I pull her up each time that she does a wrong thing seems entirely new to her. Each morning at six she has to get up, make her bed, sweep her room and get dressed. Then she begins her English lessons, and after that there's her embroidery and mending our clothes and getting our meals. However, she is finally beginning to understand that it is no good sulking with me.'

Désirée was not the only one to be obstinate.

'At least she has the merit of not arguing back at me, and she learns her lessons well.'

A sad letter from Désirée in mid-August, the only one from the Walham House period to survive, suggests that their holiday together had ended in a quarrel. She begs for a letter from him – 'I know I've been quite wrong, I see it myself, but words come from my heart. At first, when you were so angry with me, I didn't send you a letter though I wanted to. I've gone over and over my behaviour as I've never done before in my life –'

I assume that Nadaud left Désirée at Walham House during his trip to France early in 1860, and perhaps for longer. It is not entirely clear, however, what he did with her afterwards. The few other letters from her that survive seem to date from at least a couple of years later, by which time she was sixteen or seventeen. The tone has changed, she is more adult and self-possessed. The handwriting has also changed considerably: it is now the dashing, hard-to-read hand of an energetic, ambitious and probably rather self-centred adult. The tension between her and her father does not appear to have been entirely resolved. Once again the phrase 'you were so angry' appears, but the affection seems to have continued also from 'a daughter who, in spite of everything, loves her old father with all her heart'.

One letter is headed from St Peter Street in Islington, which I know to have been the home of the Chevassus family,

French gold- and silver-thread importers who were in London for the same reasons as Nadaud. Hélène Chevassus is mentioned in another letter, as having given Désirée a lace collar and cuffs for her '*birth-day*' (in English in the original). Evidently Désirée now had her own little London world. Other French friends are mentioned, including the Barrères, and also 'Madame Ludlow', John Malcolm's mother. One letter complains that she had no news to tell her father 'as I never go anywhere' but the same sheet continues with a description of a gathering with the Chevassus family and others, where someone had brought a violin and 'everyone sang and danced'.

Apart from her time in Islington, Désirée was apparently living at 24 Percy Street, described as being 'off Bedford Square' although in fact that more select locality was on the other side of the Tottenham Court Road. Percy Street, lined with late eighteenth-century mansarded brick houses, was and is the sort of Georgian architecture which appeared less desirable in the 1860s than it does to us today. But, like Gerrard Street and Newman Street, which were not far off, it was perfectly respectable; the fashionable Victorian poet Coventry Patmore lived there in the same decade. What exactly Désirée's role was at No. 24 is less clear. In a letter her grandfather wrote her in January 1862, he remarked, apropos of his own recent poor harvests, 'I am so glad you are in a good place' (*une bonne maison*), implying 'at least you are earning your keep', but then Léonard Nadaud retained his peasant outlook, including the fear that absolute want might always be round the corner. The Imperial Police, in one of their obsessional internal communications, seem to have thought that Désirée was 'apprenticed to an artificial flower maker'.

At first sight, this seemed to me implausible. Surely Nadaud's daughter, brought up expensively to be a lady, should not have been consigned to an occupation so working-class and (in England) barely even respectable? However, in the census of 1861, 24 Percy Street was occupied by a Marie Mardin, unmarried, born in Paris – who was indeed listed as 'artificial flower maker'. She was eighty-five, if the census-taker was not mistaken; so she was presumably retired. She seems to have occupied the entire house with one living-in servant, which suggests a middle-class way of life. Désirée's name does not appear: if she was already living there, she must have been away the April weekend when the Census was taken. It seems unlikely that her role there was anything more than that of paying guest with a respectable and very elderly compatriot.

However, I did eventually turn up, among other papers, a stamped receipt made out to Nadaud for £9 sterling but written in French, 'for part of the apprenticeship of his daughter'. The name on the bottom is male and not Mardin, but clearly Désirée had been set to learn some skilled occupation. Maybe, in the French community, the confection of silk flowers for bonnets was considered not sweated labour but an art? Or maybe Désirée was put in to learn the trade with a view to later book-keeping and management – there is a reference in a letter of hers to Julie Pizet, years later, to having been 'in business' (*dans les affaires*). Another reference suggests that she was a skilled dressmaker. At all events, it looks as if her father's work-ethic had prevailed over any more ladylike conception of Désirée's place in the scheme of things.

Nadaud made another visit to central France in July and August 1862 (more eager surveillance and local tale-telling to the Préfecture) and took Désirée home with him. Six weeks before, she wrote joyfully to her grandfather, 'I'll write to you again to tell you the day we will arrive, and I would like it if you came to meet us in Bourganeuf with Julie and another of my friends.' To Julie Pizet, she wrote, 'I'll tell you all about London', but she seemed to be looking forward more to 'our fun and games together' (*nos farces*). 'It's been four years since I've seen my own country.'

One other letter to Julie suggests she may have returned to England for a further period, but after that are only two or three that she wrote later, as a married woman. For, on 14 October 1865, three days after her twentieth birthday, she was married in Paris to Victor Bouquet, a building entrepreneur. Given Nadaud's vagueness about the spelling of proper names, the groom may have been one of the same family who had brought Désirée from the Creuse to Paris when she was thirteen. Another builder, Nadaud's old boss Delavallade, was among the witnesses. In spite of Nadaud's continuing sojourn in England, a suitable union between Creusois neighbours with common interests had been arranged and successfully brought off. Nadaud's principal task as a father had been accomplished.

Désirée had three children within five years, two girls and a boy. She and her husband lived in Paris, where his highly modern speciality was building bakeries. The construction boom continued, even with Haussmann gone, and they seem to have prospered. But in the summer of 1879, in the new family house at La Martinèche that had superseded the old one, Victor Bouquet died. He was thirty-nine.

Less than two years later, in the same house, Désirée herself died, at thirty-five. The children were fourteen, eleven and nine, and it fell to Martin Nadaud to provide for them, materially and in terms of their upbringing, to educate and admonish and love them and marry them off suitably. History had, tragically, repeated itself.

Just how exact the repetition was, I do not know. French death registers, while providing a wealth of incidental evidence on networks of family and friendship, do not offer any cause of death. The newspaper *L'Echo de la Creuse*, which supported Martin Nadaud on his return as newly nominated Préfet in 1870 and continued to do so once he was the Member of Parliament again, published an obituary of Victor Bouquet: 'Indefatigable worker, conscientious, devoted republican citizen, Monsieur Bouquet had in prospect, if not spectacular wealth, at least a comfortable sufficiency, the fruits of years dedicated to hard labours, and the chance to give his children a good start in life, at the moment when death has struck him down.' The passage also mentions '*une longue et douloureuse maladie*', a long and painful illness, almost the same phrase Martin Nadaud had used about Julie's death thirty years before. I assumed from this that tuberculosis, that late nineteenth-century scourge, is once again what is indicated. One may conjecture that the fatal strain was lying in wait in the Bouquet family as in the Aupetit one, that of Désirée's mother. It might, classically, have been activated by the demanding, materialistic life the young couple led in Paris: there is some evidence from family letters that they were 'too busy' to pay much attention there to their humbler relatives, such as the Bouteille family.

But in the case of Désirée the tuberculosis theory can only be speculative. Apart from her *fluxion de poitrine* when she was twelve, there is no sign that she was considered delicate. In a note she wrote five months after her husband's death to her little son Louis (who was a weekly boarder elsewhere in the Paris region) she mentions being 'ill', but this does not seem necessarily significant. What does make one wonder is that two different dates in March, fourteen days apart, are given for her death in different copies of the registers, and that the entry in the register kept in the archives in Guéret appears to have been remade the following September. Her father does not seem to have been present in the Creuse when she died, whichever the true date. It is not even clear that he attended her funeral. It is also odd, you may feel, that there had been no mention of her in her husband's obituary notice two years earlier, although sympathies were offered to Martin Nadaud. Her own death seems to have gone unmentioned by any of the local papers. At the very least, this would suggest that Désirée had had little contact with the Creuse in recent years. It may just possibly suggest something sadder – some shame or horror associated with her ending.

I see Désirée in her permanent widow's black, moving about in the silent house that was furnished in high bourgeois style, quite alone except for an old maid-servant of her father's and perhaps an 'outside man' for the vegetable garden and the horse. The road beyond the neat, solid front door is a track where few but farm carts and cows pass, adding their sludge to the thick country mud. The old house, where Désirée spent the most carefree and affectionate days of her early life, has been discarded; the family fields are farmed by strangers. The grandfather who was the guardian of her childhood memories here is a dozen years dead; her own children are far away in Paris; so is Julie Pizet. What is there for Désirée here, or anywhere, she who shuttled between different worlds in her formative years, in thrall to the needs and dreams of others? Is it possible that the mortal weakness that will finish her life is located not so much in her physical health as in her morale, her perception of her own worth, her faith in the clouded future? She has no coherent religious faith: her father has seen to that. I have the indistinct but persistent impression that her last years were darkened by something both greater and less mentionable than either tuberculosis or widowhood.

For what is also striking is that, once dead, Désirée seems to have dropped out of the family history. Unlike that of her mother, Julie Aupetit, her name does not crop up, even fleetingly, in family letters. Martin Nadaud, in his assiduous correspondence with his orphaned grandchildren, never mentions their mother to them. When, many years later, grandson Louis' wife had a miscarriage, the aged Martin Nadaud wrote to sympathise with her, saying that long ago a similar 'accident' had occurred to his own wife. But on the life and death of Louis' mother a profound silence seems to have settled. Only once, in a letter written in the last year of Nadaud's own life, does her name even occur, and that in connection with Louis' birth, 'one of the days most deeply imprinted on my memory and my life'.

As we know, Désirée does not exist in Nadaud's Memoirs either. It may be that this sensitive man, who once admitted that he could barely bring himself to write his dead wife's name, simply found it impossible to refer to his dead daughter at all. Or, if there is a darker story surrounding her end, then time and family constraint on the subject have done their work: the details are now irrecoverable.

*

If a man manages to write his only child out of his otherwise detailed Memoirs, then one wonders what other significant elements in his life have been omitted? At the very least, there seem to have been long-lasting social contacts that have gone undocumented.

On an intellectual level, Nadaud was interested in the whole workers' self-improvement movement fostered by Ludlow and Hughes. He was particularly charmed by the way the bourgeoisie of places such as Ealing and Wimbledon interested themselves in local Mechanics' Institutes – winter lectures on Dickens and Scott, concerts given 'by ladies and their daughters . . . in these village get-togethers, which are the more agreeable because everyone knows each other, conversation before and after is always animated, even if less relaxed and expansive than it would be in France'.

These were just the kind of initiatives that he would like to have seen take off more successfully in his own country. But he had, I think, a more personal investment also in the strata of very English upper-working-class life for which the Institutes catered.

The name of the Beadle family of Wimbledon crops up just once in all his writings, in reference to their having known him as a builder in his early days in London. However, other scattered descriptions seem to lead back to them also, and it is indicated in his Memoirs that he was in touch with them for many years. I decided to do a little work on them.

The Trades Directory published for the Wimbledon area in 1860 revealed a Robert Beadle, 'carpenter and rent collector', living in South Place, which was a row of pleasant brick cottages just off the Ridgway. The Census for 1861 shows Robert Beadle at No. 27, aged fifty, with his wife Elizabeth and three unmarried sons in their twenties: John, a carpenter like his father, and Samuel and Frederick who were bricklayers. Also living in the house was a grand-daughter of fifteen with a different surname (Rapley) and a Beadle grandson of two. Just along the way, at No. 13, lived another son, Thomas, already married at nineteen with a month-old son. Ten years earlier, he had figured, along with Samuel, as a

'scholar' – that is, attending school, a sign of respectability –
when most of the large family were still at home and living in
more humble tenement accommodation near by.

There were more Beadle relatives living elsewhere in
Wimbledon; they were an extensive clan who had been in the
area long before it began to be colonised as a suburb. When
Nadaud came to write his *History of the Working Classes in
England*, it is clear from internal evidence that they provided
significant material for him. After giving a sample weekly
budget to a total of 40 francs 80 centimes (something over 30
shillings), in which the largest items after the rent are bread
and meat, then shoes for all, he continues:

'I should add that very often the house makes it possible to
accommodate one or two lodgers, which helps to pay the
rent. At thirteen or fourteen, the eldest child will earn 6 or 7
francs a week. Once they have got to this point the family has
won through, and the number of children they have will no
longer be a problem.

'For a long time I was a lodger in the house of a carpenter
who had nine children, five boys, four girls.' This would have
been almost unthinkable in Paris, and very rare in rural
France also: the large British families of the nineteenth
century, in which child death was no longer a constant fact,
were an index of England's relative prosperity. This prosperity, and the social attitudes that accompanied it, was one of
the fundamental differences between France and England at
the period that Nadaud's book set out to explore.

'The eldest son, who was twenty-one and in the same trade
as his father, earned, like him, 40 francs 80 centimes a week.
The next son earned 21 francs and the two younger ones 9
francs each. Each week there came into that household,
where nothing was wanting, between 100 and 120 francs.'

At that time 100 francs was about £4 a week, an income
indeed on a comfortable lower-middle-class level. This would
have gone a long way, since people like the Beadles did not
try to 'keep up appearances' or employ a servant as a clerk's
family would have done. Indeed the four daughters were
probably *in* service by then in more affluent Wimbledon

homes. 'So, on Sundays, when we were all seated round the dinner table, the family seemed more like that of a prosperous tradesman than a workman.'

Sitting at such a table, Nadaud must have felt temporarily back among the relaxed, simple, convivial habits of the master builders of Paris or the innkeepers and tradesmen of Guéret and Pontarion, who were his most natural companions. The upper-middle-class households of people like the Blancs, the Barrères or John Malcolm Ludlow, however hospitable, could not provide this for him.

Other glimpses of the Beadle family idyll flit through his work and his notes. Having explained that English workmen, unlike French, had won the right to be paid promptly on Saturday at midday and have the rest of that day and the whole of Sunday free, he remarked that respectable men turned the whole wage packet over to their wives:

'They come back home for dinner, their wages with them. Afterwards they wash themselves at the tap, since water is piped, unrestricted, into humble houses just as into the grandest ones. Once they are quite clean, they put on fresh clothes and go into their gardens or take up a book. After tea, they take their children for a walk, while the mother goes to the shops to buy the food for Sunday. Then, at nine in the evening, they meet up in a public house, have a pint of beer, or a glass of brandy-and-water or gin. There, they discuss politics or matters concerning their own trade. However, I should add that these pub meetings are less general than they were, since Literary Clubs and other amusements are replacing them.'

This may have been true of the upwardly mobile Beadles but one doubts if, in general, pubs were falling out of favour with the working classes. Very large numbers of erstwhile country pubs were rebuilt in the 1850s and '60s in a more opulent, stucco-fronted style, and new ones were added all the time as London expanded.

'Sunday is spent still more peacefully. The workman rarely gets up that day before 7 or 8 in the morning. After breakfast [Nadaud calls this *déjeuner* so one assumes it was a fairly substantial meal] comes the time for Morning Service; however, a very large number of working men (about three quarters) do not attend this. Instead, they devote themselves to a tranquil reading of their weekly newspapers. Then, after dinner, they have a nap and read again.

'Truth to tell, Sunday is rather monotonous, since games and sports are not practised on that day. However, in summer, people go for many walks.'

His conclusion is that, all in all, the English Sunday was preferable to the day-in-day-out working habits of the French, and that he had been wrong to oppose in Parliament the concept of an obligatory day of rest.

The iconic importance in English life of tea and newspapers, which still strikes the visiting foreigner today, is a recurrent theme in Nadaud's descriptions. The working man he had been, who had read aloud to his fellows twenty years earlier, was impressed by the sheer number and range of newspapers published in England and by the almost universal literacy he found there; he quoted Michelet's 'a Protestant country is a country where everyone reads'. As ever, he does not seem to have penetrated the lowest social circles where reading was certainly not yet a habit.

'Most building workers read a lot in England, and not only on Saturday afternoon and Sunday; at breakfast and dinner many have a newspaper to hand. They are very civil to each other, and most of them are sober men. Almost all go to work without having a drink first, and do not spend much during meal-breaks. Many bring their dinner with them from home in a small box, and have another container for tea.

'These workmen make good use of the classes for draftsmen and the *Workmen College* [in English in the original]. I have known certain ones who were very skilled and extremely intelligent and well-educated.'

I rather think that the Beadles themselves were 'Temperance', that badge of social aspiration which became increasingly significant as Victorian England prospered and the gap widened between the respectable working classes and the unrespectable. They seem to crop up again in one of

Nadaud's rough notes recalling the days when he was 'lost in the suburbs of London, speaking little English' and two carpenters were kinder and more polite to him than any of the other men on site. One day, one of them sent to the foot of the scaffold where Nadaud was working his 'tall and handsome' son, who said to Nadaud in careful French, '*Il fait chaud aujourd'hui.*' Nadaud was touched and cheered by this little overture, and was subsequently invited to Sunday dinner. He found he was the only one to drink beer, and was instructed for the first time in his life in the existence of the 'TT' movement, which he initially misheard as 'teat'.

His comment on this shows how much heavy drinking was part of French urban existence. He remarked jovially to the assembled company that in England when people fell out and came to blows it must be that much more serious, since there would not be to hand the ready morning-after excuse available to those who had been drinking? One does see that a dinner followed by a family evening at a Temperance meeting (also described), where tracts were handed out, would seem rather a sedate form of celebration by French standards, whether urban or rural. The same could be said of a summer fête he attended, where 'gaiety and happiness were clear on every face ... but no one laughed or sang'. Elsewhere, Nadaud remarked of the Temperance Movement that 'without adhering to a rule of life which is in some ways eccentric, one is forced to admire the moral and material results'. The days were gone when he had railed in a letter to his father about the cold, glum English families, each living isolated in their own little domain and not teaching their children any history. Instead, he was full of admiration for the way in which the Building Societies and Friendly Societies were enabling people like the Beadles to buy their own homes, complete with little vegetable gardens – the classless suburban dream: 'While the Parisians have seen their town transformed by those in power, we in London have seen it transformed by liberty, at no cost to the ratepayer.' There is the brochure of one of the Mutual Benefit Societies among his papers: '*A House for Every Man on paying its Rent for ten years by Advancing Two Hundred Pounds . . .*'

Rather oddly, there is also young Samuel Beadle's membership certificate of a Friendly Society. Why did Nadaud have it in his possession? It does seem as if his close, informal relations with the Beadles continued through the years. Since they had first known him as a builder like themselves, presumably they did not feel the usual constraint at entertaining someone of better education. His French accent, too, would have been classless to the English ear – something that would have worked in his favour when visiting wealthy households also. By such means, his tendency to lead parallel lives, which scarcely intersected with one another, must have been fostered.

In fact, the Beadles too had their hidden side. They were not quite the entirely model, mid-Victorian family, tediously above reproach, that they might seem. The grand-daughter, Sarah Rapley, was not simply visiting in 1851, for she was there again, aged fifteen, ten years later: it would appear that Robert and Elizabeth Beadle brought her up. When the family were living in the old tenement a Rapley family had lived next door, but none of them seemed to me of appropriate age to be a Beadle son-in-law. Various other explanations suggested themselves, none entirely convincing. Curiosity led me to obtain a copy of Sarah's birth certificate.

The only female Rapley in the records for the right period was an unnamed baby girl born to a Margaret Rapley in Queen Charlotte's, then a charity lying-in hospital in Marylebone, offering 'asylum to indigent females . . . and to facilitate the repentance of suffering and contrite sinners'. There is no father on the birth certificate.

This is the point at which the close web of factual research, which, like a spider's handiwork, can be spun wider and wider and finer and finer with the material of lost lives, begins to give way under the pressure of imagined possibilities. You could devote a whole other study to the Beadles and their world, evoking their slightly mysterious French friend from their point of view.

*

I admit that, when I first discovered the existence of the largely unsorted boxes of papers in the archive library, I hoped to find some packet of letters in English that might have been overlooked, and which would point to a coherent, encapsulated personal relationship that had left no other trace. But I have also to admit, on reflection, that given Nadaud's secretiveness about the different parts of his life, and also his long-standing reluctance to sustain regular correspondence even with close family, it is more likely that any really intimate relationship he had during his English years was conducted without much communication on paper.

The very few letters in English that have survived seem to derive from his later years. For example, there is an undated note from a retired maths teacher, who has picked up a reference to Nadaud and to Wimbledon College in the English weekly abstract of *Le Figaro* – 'If you are the dear old colleague of those days, you will perhaps call to mind my leaving there in a state of illness – gastric fever – and not returning to my post? in fact it was Monsieur Martin who carried me in a fainting condition from the Master's room alongside of the French room to my bedroom, and knowing that Monsieur Martin was an assumed name . . .' Etc.

Among the Wimbledon College mark lists and exam papers that Nadaud also kept as souvenirs is a letter in French that gave me pause for thought. Dated July 1866, it appears to be from a youngish female compatriot. It is not legibly signed, as if the writer knew her identity would be immediately apparent. It begins *Cher Monsieur*, a mode of address slightly more intimate in French than it may appear to English eyes, and informs Nadaud that she has been in Brighton but is now going to take up a job as a governess with a family in Hampshire, the winters to be spent in London. The letter is elaborately casual: she gives him her new address in Hampshire in full, tells him how busy she's been, and that she is coming to London on the 23rd for an interview 'but only for a few hours. I shall therefore have to abandon the hope of seeing you before your departure.'

(Nadaud, indeed, visited France again that month, which is when Désirée had her first child.) 'I have nothing special for you to say or give to my family ... I just wanted you to be able to give fresh news of me to my mother, and I was really eager to come to London. It's also a great disappointment for me not to be able to make the journey to France this year ... but I could not afford to turn down this new job.' She ends by excusing herself for 'this hurried letter'. In fact, it appears rather heavily contrived.

All one can note is that, on his final removal to France and through the thirty-odd years that remained to him, Nadaud thought it worth keeping. It would have been unlikely that this attractive and emotionally vulnerable widower had not been the target, during his years in England, of such hopeful, veiled overtures from single female members of the Anglo-French community.

Nadaud's relations with the extensive Brackenbury family, too, provide material for speculation. We know that the Reverend J. M. Brackenbury married a third, much younger wife during Nadaud's time at Wimbledon College. Nadaud says nothing of this, nor gives any details of the children, though he must have met the oldest, Anna-Jane, on those occasions he was invited to dinner. Born *circa* 1840, she was a year or two older than her second stepmother, which cannot have been easy for her. Like her half-sister Ellen, she lived out a long life in and around Wimbledon and Norwood, and died, unmarried, in the 1920s. She seems to have been one of those many maiden aunts that were, paradoxically, produced by the lavishly fertile families of Victorian England. These superfluous women were victims of a social evolution that had removed a whole stratum of female society from straightforward labour, agricultural or domestic, and had also abandoned the system of arranged marriages that still held society together in France. Without a real occupation or significant means, their lives strike a note of bleakness all the more poignant for being usually mute.

J. M. Brackenbury's children were all 'as poor as church mice', according to a descendant, which shut many doors to them. Their later years were spent as nursery governesses or as paid companions to elderly ladies richer than themselves. Yet when she was a young woman in her father's house, Anna-Jane might reasonably have hoped to attract one of the six assistant masters who were, except for 'Monsieur Martin', all quite young too. As her thirtieth birthday edged perilously near, I wonder what she thought of 'Monsieur Martin', the French teacher who was whispered to be far more important than he seemed, and what he thought of her? Did they, on occasions, walk round the cricket field together while a match was in progress, self-consciously discussing the school's chances against Whitgift, their private minds elsewhere? Or might they have had real exchanges of views about ideas and national differences, which illuminated Anna-Jane's constricted life through the years with an interest in that looking-glass world across the Channel? One would like to think so. One would like to believe that, in middle age, she and her half-sister even managed a once-in-a-lifetime excursion to Paris, Baedeker's Guide in cotton-gloved hands, eyes everywhere . . .

There is, unfortunately, no evidence among Nadaud's papers that he 'kept up' with any of the Brackenburys after his helter-skelter return to France in triumph. Probably, in spite of his warm feelings towards the family, there was no more contact. At any rate he does not seem to have known what happened afterwards.

The reason that Anna-Jane and the others ended up poor was that Brackenbury's fine school, which very nearly succeeded in becoming a fixture in the English educational scene, was effectively bankrupt some dozen years after Nadaud left it. The official story is that it thrived until Brackenbury himself retired in 1882, and C. J. Wynne was unable to attract pupils in the same way. Certainly, eighteen months after he took over, the school roll was reduced to 40, far below what the establishment must have needed simply to break even. But already, when Brackenbury left, taking with him a three-fifths share of the profits, the numbers were down to 91 from the 150 there had been a few years earlier. The demand for such education was not limitless, and many other army crammers had joined in the competition. An old boy from those years, who went on to be a First World War general, always maintained that the food was 'quite insufficient'. In any case, earlier profits must, said Brackenbury's descendant, have been largely swallowed up in paying off a large mortgage still outstanding from the great rebuilding of 1860. The grandiose 'Collegiate' school, intended to be an advertisement for British Imperial supremacy, was, in reality, a façade covering a high Victorian speculative adventure that could not sustain itself.

The mock-gothic pile stood empty for years until it was bought in 1892 by the Jesuits, who turned it into a successful Roman Catholic grammar school. I hope that Nadaud, with his entrenched views on the priesthood and with his happy memories, never knew this. Today it is still a Catholic boys' school, but is within the state system. The retired deputy head, who showed me round, gazed down with me into the playground where Nadaud's pupils once disported themselves and where black-blazered boys were ambling, chatting, wrestling, lounging, chasing each other round in circles and having mock fights perched on each other's shoulders. No one was throwing sand down from the roof, as the Creusois boys had done long ago, no doubt simply because they could not get there. The deputy head said: 'Boys' games never really change.'

In Which We Leave Nadaud to History

In the end, Martin Nadaud's long retreat in another place, being a different person under a different name, ended with dramatic suddenness. During the last three years of the Second Empire he made several visits to France – the cross-Channel steamers now plied, with railway connections on both sides. The longer sea-journeys beginning or ending up the River Thames were becoming, like much else in Nadaud's variegated life, a thing of the antique past. The Empire was dying slowly on its feet; its opponents were becoming bolder. There were repeated suggestions that Nadaud might return to stand again as a republican candidate. He chose not to, but immediately after the Imperial collapse at the Battle of Sedan, at the beginning of September 1870, it is clear that he was in France. His Memoirs are confusing as to dates, but he was in contact with Léon Gambetta, whom he had met in Paris the previous Easter, and who became the new Minister of the Interior. Gambetta despatched him without delay to the Creuse, nominating him as its new Préfet.

This triumphant re-reversal of fortune, this stunning, Cinderella-like transformation from obscurity to total visibility, was his final identity-change and the most extraordinary of all. Within weeks at the most, he had exchanged the modest attic bedroom and the bread-and-cheese suppers with other ushers in Wimbledon for an entire Renaissance town-castle – the Hôtel des Moneyroux in the centre of Guéret. This was the official residence of the Préfet, next door to the huge Napoleonic Préfecture itself. The man who had had to go cap in hand, begging jobs on strange London building sites, cold-shouldered as a foreigner, who had known black despair and loneliness and who later derived such sorely needed comfort from 'his' boys' successes in exams and football matches, now wielded power over 275,000 fellow citizens. In effect, he was Commissioner of War for the Creuse, for the Prussians had invaded northern France and were soon to besiege Paris. Gambetta escaped by balloon to Tours – the famous exploit in which his school history-book image is forever fixed. Cut off from the rest of the government, he became the virtual dictator over much of France for several months. He took the absolutist line that no compromise with the enemy was possible, a view that came naturally to Nadaud as well: his years at the military academy had imbued Nadaud with the British perception that the French were weak and the Prussians dauntingly strong. His role, as he conceived it, was to stir local patriotism and to raise and equip troops to go and fight off this terrible threat. With no experience at all of administration, power-structures or delegation, with a largely outdated 'Forty-eighter's' concept of republican values and with even his French oratory gone rusty and odd after years of addressing classes in English, he nevertheless threw himself into the job heart and soul.

There was a ludicrous delay on Châteauroux station on the journey down when, because he was jotting in a note-book, he was mistaken for a Prussian spy. He did not reach Guéret till late at night, when the suspicious concierge at the Préfecture refused him entry. According to his own account, *Six Mois de Préfecture*, he chivalrously allowed the outgoing Imperial Préfet and his lady to stay on three more nights, thereby giving that gentleman the chance, in the time-honoured fashion, to burn compromising papers. Within two days more (according to the nineteen-year-old Camille Barrère who had eagerly come to join him as his secretary) he had infuriated the staff of the Hôtel des Moneyroux by giving notice to most of them, declaring that, as a plain man, he did not need such a retinue. His meals he arranged to have sent in from the nearby inn, constant after forty years to those who had been good to him in youth and good to his family. A week later, he was distractedly ordering himself a silk frock-coat and white flannel waistcoats from the principal Guéret tailor, who was a relative of the innkeeper, while trying also to get under way the more massive task of providing hundreds of not particularly willing recruits with military cloaks and muskets. To this rabble of local lads drilling on the main square or leaving on special trains at the railway station, he made fiery speeches, and tried his utmost to inspire the whole local population with his patriotic vision. Perhaps the ladies, he appealed, could form working parties to make the equally necessary flannel underwear? The high-minded ladies and their daughters of the Wimbledon Literary Institute were still invisibly with him.

And this, essentially, is where we shall leave him. In the event, for reasons beyond his control and to some extent, one feels, beyond his comprehension, his days of nerve-racking power and glory lasted less than half a year. But in relinquishing his post he kept his integrity and dignity. Gambetta resigned in February 1871, over the peace with the Prussians that had been ignominiously if necessarily cobbled together, and Nadaud followed his example. The first days of the Paris uprising in mid-March, when the People for the last time in French history rose up against their government and pro-claimed a new order, found him back at home at La Martinèche. He was setting to work to repair with his own hands a barn 'to which a well-disposed neighbour had set fire'. In his Memoirs, written much later, he says more charitably that the arsonist was up to his ears in debt. However, there is no doubt that with his enthusiasm for conscription and belt-tightening, and his general incorrupti-ble intransigence, Nadaud had made fresh enemies in the district.

In both his Memoirs and in *Six Mois de Préfecture*, he

claims to have set off that very night for the nearest railway station, but the vehicle (Pizet's again, I rather think) ended up in a ditch in the dark. His shoulder was dislocated – probably the shoulder he had damaged in the same way long ago in his second building accident. He says he had to stay in bed for several days in the village of Janaillat – 'where I had every care from a kind and delightful person, Madame Lunaud'. A diplomatic injury, in someone who was wary of what events in Paris might portend? At all events, although he did eventually reach there, thus demonstrating his allegiance with the Parisian people rather than with the governmental troops now ranged against them at Versailles, he took no active part in either the innocent or the murderous days of the Commune. That *temps de cerises* was something for which, as a man of fifty-five, he had little taste. He had done too much, seen too much, in other uprisings long before.

During the increasingly desperate days of the Commune, at the end of April, Désirée's third child was born, with great suddenness and in his grandfather's presence. He was named Louis, an apparently royalist name that was in reality a tribute to Louis Blanc, who became an honorary godfather. A few days later (Nadaud was to write to his grandson in old age) the fighting on the southern edges of the city where the Bouquet family lived was so intense that he took the baby in his arms and carried him 'across fields' to a friend in another suburb.

Later, when the dust of the Commune had settled, the blood of 147 summarily executed Communards had been washed from the wall of Père Lachaise cemetery, and many others (including young Barrère) were in exile again in England, Nadaud returned to public life again as a Paris municipal councillor. In 1876 he was re-elected to represent in Parliament his old constituency of Bourganeuf, and remained in that seat for thirteen years. He was ousted in 1889 by a more right-wing candidate, who claimed to represent country interests better than this old Parisian mason.

It is because those chaotic, stressful, valiant and ultimately unsucessful months in the Préfecture were, in their way, Nadaud's finest hour that I shall pursue his story no longer. All that came after – the devoted, busy life in office, the welfare causes espoused, the flying years, the ephemeral triumphs and set-backs of a man in public life growing older, the long-drawn-out Creusois row about where exactly the branch line to Bourganeuf was to run, the final opening of the station in 1883 with fireworks, a brass band and a speech from Nadaud on top form – all this is implicit already in what has gone before. There is no need to follow the Memoirs for this last quarter-century; they are in any case reduced, with many omissions and blurred patches, to an outline. There is no mention, except in a dedicatory preface, of the grandchildren who cost him so much further effort to launch into life, nor yet of his sisters' lives and endings, nor yet of *their* progeny. By this stage, the transformation of the vibrant memories of 'Léonard', the boy-mason, into the doughy Memoirs of a Public Figure, is total.

The real Léonard Nadaud did not, sadly, live to see his adored son as the administrative leader of the Creuse. He had died two years before, in May 1868, after falling down when he went to see how the cutting was getting on in a hay-field. Martin Nadaud was teaching in Wimbledon when he received the news – I imagine by the telegram service which, during his years in England, had become well established. Chevassus, the father of the Islington family, who had by then returned to their home in Lyon, wrote to him that Léonard Nadaud had 'forged a life's career such as few other men attain. The fact that he succumbed so quickly that you did not have time to get to him and receive his last goodbye you should look on as a blessing.'

Léonard Nadaud was in his eighty-second year when he died. His son was to live to eighty-three, his own last few years shadowed by that failing sight that is particularly dreaded by those who have used their eyes a great deal. One of his late letters to Louis speaks of receiving a magnifying glass as a present, and of being able to read and write only in the mornings when the light was good. The evenings, he said, were sad times for him – *bien tristes*. I wonder if the word raised echoes for him of Charlotte Deedy and the efforts she had once made to alleviate sad evenings for him? Another letter, in a shaky hand, tells of a glut of cherries. A last photograph shows the bearded, patriarchal figure sitting beached in his garden beneath a tree in a comfortable old dressing gown, a cord knotted round his much-expanded waistline. The legs that had carried him so far were now so swollen and weak he could hardly walk. Like his father before him, he had finally returned to the simple comforts of life at La Martinèche, attended by one devoted female servant.

When death claimed him, in the last days of 1898, he was expecting it, but there were some things for which he was ready to fight to the last. 'If the end comes [*Si la débâcle arrive*],' he wrote to his grandson, 'try to be here to stop our priest from coming into the house.' Among the letters of condolence that Louis, as chief mourner, received after the large (secular) funeral in Soubrebost, was one from Camille Barrère. He had known Martin Nadaud from his earliest childhood and throughout the London years, he had been Nadaud's closest companion in the months in Guéret, and he had now reached the summit of his own career as the French ambassador to Rome. On account of his upbringing, Camille Barrère was bilingual and bicultural. He wrote now, without pretension or rhetorical flourish: 'He was my oldest friend.'

In 1942, when the Occupation forces scrapped the statue of Nadaud which had stood in the centre of Bourganeuf for the previous forty years, they may not have had only the value of the metal in mind. Might not the likeness of this People's leader be an inspiration and a rallying point for local Resistance activity? The Creusois had a long tradition of subversive behaviour and lack of respect for those in power.

Not that Nadaud's was the only statue to disappear under

the German Reich. From 1875 on, the Third Republic, as part of its drive to weld France finally into one nation, had been enthusiastic about populating city streets with life-size effigies of national figures, and these secular saints of the reformed school system provided a rich crop. Various Parisian statues of Nadaud's one-time colleagues, some of which he himself had unveiled, went after 1940. Among them, on the left bank place Monge, was one of Louis Blanc, who had died in 1882: its named pedestal alone survived the war and was there for another generation. But that, too, has now gone.

Nadaud's own Métro station, near the leafy heights of Père Lachaise in the old working-class heartland of Belleville, survived till the 1970s. Then alterations and extensions to the system led to the small station, with its original iron canopy and lamp-stands, being amalgamated with the much larger Gambetta station along the boulevard and re-baptised as a subsiduary entrance to it. There were those who said that, in the lifetime of both men, the younger and more flamboyant Gambetta had too much influence over Nadaud: it seems an ironic detail that, long after they are both dead, Gambetta should have swallowed him all over again. However, even as I write, there are plans afoot in the Mairie of the Twentieth Arrondissement, Nadaud's one-time power-base, to get the enlarged station renamed jointly with both names.

In Bourganeuf the railway line inaugurated with such dispute and triumph in 1883 has not survived either. Nor does Bourganeuf even have any more the modest industries (small coal-mine, porcelain factory, carpet works) that it enjoyed in Nadaud's heyday. However, it does have a tower in which a Turkish prince was once incarcerated, in luxurious prison-quarters, gazing out forlornly over the alien greenness of central France. It also has a newly enlarged museum, and an energetic mayor.

Pontarion, similarly endowed, is one of the few Creusois villages whose population has actually increased in recent years. It has a small exhibition centre overlooking the Taurion, in whose waters Nadaud used to catch chub and trout by hand. In the summer of 1998, a lovingly constructed display on the life of Martin Nadaud circulated between Bourganeuf, Pontarion and other local centres. In the same period a second exhibition, which I would hesitate to describe as a 'rival' one, graced another local mairie. As the centenary of Nadaud's death approached, one had the feeling that interest in Nadaud, and in the world from which he came, was swelling and consolidating, and that tensions were being stirred at the same time. Books relevant to the subject, ranging from the scholarly to the derivative and populist, were rushed into print by a local desk-top publisher. A new edition of his Memoirs from the same source appeared in the local bookshops.

Tensions certainly exist. The Creuse has never been an entirely easy place. In researching this book I have met with outstanding kindness and welcome from some Creusois citizens. I have also become aware of reticences and resentments in other quarters against which I have stumbled inadvertently, since these feelings do not seem to relate to me personally so much as to the whole subject of the masons and what they represent. The traditional French rivalries and enmities of Nadaud's own time – between right and left, bourgeois and peasant, Paris and the Creuse – are replayed today in essentially the same form attached to newer issues, some profound, some disconcertingly trivial.

One chilly night in the late autumn of 1997, I attended a meeting in the mustard-yellow-and-chocolate-brown décor of a small village *mairie*. A large gathering of people, some with local power, some with nothing but their vocal enthusiasm or their unspoken anxieties, had gathered to discuss how to celebrate Martin Nadaud's life. Chairing this delicate encounter was one of those dynamic citizens the Creuse has always bred, trying his best to unite the disparate, covert factions in the hall in mutual co-operation for a worthy cause. It might have been a gathering of disaffected republican exiles in the 1850s – or yet the row about the siting of the Bourganeuf railways line all over again. ('It is evident from the absurd route favoured by *monsieur le député* Nadaud that his main wish is to see a future prolongation of the line pass near his own property at La Martinèche –')

But there were mysteries in the vested interests, or supposed vested interests, involved in the present-day tensions, that remained to me unfathomable. Shortly after that meeting, when I had returned to London, I received several telephone calls from a convincing person who announced herself as an elderly lady living in Bourganeuf, and who said she was in possession of some letters written by Martin Nadaud to her mason grandfather. She could not allow the letters out of her hands but thought I would like to see them. Then again, she was due shortly to go into an old people's home in another Creusois town, but she had a niece in yet another who would be glad to help: her niece's telephone number was such-and-such . . .

It was all entirely plausible, as were the local surnames proffered. But when I and others tried to follow up this overture, it became apparent that no such person of that name lived in or near Bourganeuf and, moreover, that the telephone codes supplied did not fit the districts to which they supposedly related. Further enquiries of my own with British Telecom indicated that the calls had come not from the Creuse at all but from the Paris region.

For some people who live in central France, or for Parisians whose families originated there, the whole subject of the Creusois masons is freighted with ambivalence and constraint. Today, they are invited to celebrate their forebears' lives with pride and gaiety: the one-time hardships and struggles are transformed into picturesque fêtes and tales of derring-do. But at the same time there is an uncomfortable awareness that the road travelled by these long-ago migrant labourers is very similar to the one travelled in more recent generations by Italian and Portuguese workmen, and then by those from North Africa. They too, driven by economic need, have arrived in Paris in male groups without their families, speaking their own tongues, lodging communally in the poorest quarters, suffering pangs of homesickness for the distant *pays*. Martin Nadaud, as more than one commentator has observed, is in many respects the first notable example of an immigrant labourer making it in an alien culture. Many present-day inhabitants of Bourganeuf, Guéret or Paris do not want to see their great-grandfather's silhouette in the little-regarded Arab workman on the nearby construction site. Some would rather glorify the past; others, closing the shutters over the windows of their neat modern villas, deny it entirely.

I have stayed in Guéret, lying awake a couple of hundred yards from where Nadaud the Préfet lay alone in his huge Hôtel des Moneyroux, hearing the bells chime that he heard. Occasional late footsteps came and went on the same narrow, cobbled streets that he knew, streets that have now once again become pedestrian ways. Wind blew on old slates and tiles, timeless rain fell. In the night the place felt hostile to me, though in the day the geography of the town seemed friendly enough with the familiar names of men who were Nadaud's associates and companions in exile: rues Victor Hugo, Lamartine, Gambetta, Alfred Assolant, Favolle, Pierre Leroux . . . Not to mention the Martin Nadaud comprehensive school down beyond the station. In the café below my room stocky, dark-haired youngsters in leather jackets smoked and drank rather sombrely; there is too little employment today in and around Guéret to support even its modest population. Guéret has some grandiose late nineteenth-century public buildings on the main square, and modern versions of the same round the bleak ring-road that was constructed in the 1970s, but it is still today basically what it always was: a tough little mountain town turned in upon itself. In spite of its continuing status as a Préfecture, it has none of the sense of mild urban sophistication that characterises country towns elsewhere in France. There is not even a good hotel in the centre; the one that used to stand on the main square was the headquarters of the local Gauleiter during the Nazi Occupation, and was comprehensively fired by the Resistance during the long-drawn-out and bloody liberation of the area in the summer of 1944. The fact that all this, now, was more than fifty years ago seems to make little difference. Memories are long in such rural societies, as they were in Nadaud's lifetime, when the republican of 1848 and even 1870 was treated as if he were the *sans-culotte* of 1791. Bitter, internecine warfare in the Creuse in the 1940s, between resistant and collaborator, Communist and non-Communist, fire-brands and peaceable citizens, is not forgotten yet.

In the remote and tiny village of Vidaillat, some miles east of Pontarion and Soubrebost, where Nadaud and his friends danced the night away in their second-hand Parisian clothes and Nadaud's fashionable trousers split from his exertions, a schoolhouse stands. It dates from long after his dancing days but was certainly built within his lifetime, one of the many rural schools that, under the Third Republic and Jules Ferry, at last brought homogenous French culture even into these remote parts. On either side of its main door a wall-plaque has been placed. One reads:

> *Enfant,*
> *Souviens-toi*
> *que Grâce*
> *au sacrifice*
> *de tes aînés*
> *tu peux revenir*
> *étudier*
> *librement*
> *dans cette*
> *école.*

(Child, remember that it is thanks to the sacrifice of your elders you are able to come back to study freely in this school.)

The other reads:

Ce   (This school was set on
groupe scolaire   fire as a revenge attack
a été incendié   on 16 July 1944 by
par   the Nazi hordes.)
représailles
le 16 juillet
1944
par les
hordes nazies.

It seems right that such traumatic events should be signalled and made meaningful to subsequent generations. An extra layer of unwanted meaning, however, is added by the fact that the building is a school no longer. There are few children living near by today and those that are there are bussed to a larger centre. The population of the Creuse, which was approaching 300,000 near the end of the nineteenth century, is currently under 130,000 and is continuing to fall by about a thousand each year, faster than that of any other of France's beleaguered rural *départements*. Its manufacturing base was always small and has shrunk further, its terrain is too precipitous and stony for large-scale agricultural methods, its chestnut groves stand abandoned. Its hills and valleys and strange rocks are indisputably beautiful, its streams run clear and its air is pure, but its climate is uncertain and its winters are too severe to attract a substantial tourist trade. Forestry and cattle-farming are currently the vulnerable pillars on which community life is sustained.

The labour and enthusiasm of a few key individuals count, as ever, for very much. The hamlet of La Martinèche is now semi-abandoned. In Nadaud's shuttered houses the spider weaves and the mouse trots; flowering creeper grows unchecked over the older home, pushing its tiny, destructive tentacles under the eaves. The walled garden at the back, once planted with orchard trees and rows of vegetables, is returning to the wild. But there are signs across the lane that a handsome derelict old farmhouse is being restored, and a newer house has been built further up. In contrast, in the hamlet of Lachaud (La Chaux) where the Aupetits dwelt, the two substantial houses, one of which must have been theirs, are lived in and cherished with a profusion of flowering plants in pots.

In Paris, Martin Nadaud's art deco Métro station waits for its name to be restored. The façade of the Mairie by the Panthéon now proclaims itself as belonging to the Fifth Arrondissement (V) but the extra space once occupied by the Roman numerals XII that Nadaud put there is apparent. Most of the buildings he ever built still stand. The truncated remains of the rue de la Mortellerie are safe from further assault, cleaned up, preserved and pedestrianised. The 'hovel' in the adjacent rue de Barrès by Saint-Gervais Church, where he lived briefly with Roby, has vanished under a small public garden and crèche. Would he, who did not approve of crèches, regard this as an unqualified improvement? An ancient house on the same street called Le Grenier sur l'Eau (the Seine once lapped at its footings) still hangs over the roadway at a perilous angle. It has become a smart restaurant. In this vestigial corner of Old Paris, great oak beams and fine stones, which were long covered in layers of rendering and ramshackle additions, are once again proudly exposed. Old, huge doorways have been restored. A cornerstone with 'Mortellerie' engraved on it is on view also. In what is perhaps a more significant memorial of the past, the street still shelters the headquarters of one of the semi-secret trade guilds that have come down from pre-Revolutionary times – Les Compagnons du Devoir de la Tour de France. The last time I went to have a look round, a young mason was at work laying fine, large cobbles over the redone roadway, selecting them skilfully for size and shape in a manner Nadaud would have approved.

In a London terrace house not far from the Caledonian Road, a house that was well established already when Nadaud passed that way, a French regional television team come to interview me about Nadaud's London years. They also want to know what sites to film. They had hoped for a shot of the present-day shipping on the Thames where Nadaud arrived in 1852, and are disappointed to hear that the traffic has gone downriver and that the tides now lap the old wharves at Wapping largely undisturbed. However, by an extraordinary chance, the hotel in which they are booked to stay turns out to be one of the original public houses built at the four corners of the Meat Market, and thus one of Nadaud's own buildings. We all marvel at this apparently fated coincidence, and the surviving railings of the Market provide some elegaic shots.

Focusing on a page of my scribbled notes for an atmospheric shot, the camera-man remarks that they seem to be in a confused mixture of French and English. So were Nadaud's, I reply – something that has only now struck me. I think humbly of the incredulous pleasure Nadaud would surely have felt, in his loneliest days in London, if he could have perceived the long posthumous existence time had in store for him.

In the depths of winter, and the depths of France, I complete this account, in a house in the Indre near the old masons' route from Guéret to Issoudun. As I do so, there happen to be masons working on our roof. A man in his forties, black-eyed and heavily moustached, with a Creusois name, from time to time sings a snatch of a nostalgic air, always the same one. At work on the guttering, he slings tiles up to a younger man. This one is poised on the roof-tree, placing the tiles with light, balletic movements in his heavy boots.

The third member of the team passing the tiles up is a teenager. Between whiles he mixes cement, which he brings up to the middle-aged man as it is needed. He fills a small wooden trough, balances it on his shoulder, and then is up the ladder one-handed with the same delicate, precarious bearing that the boy-masons have adopted for generations. *Lorsque le bâtiment va –*

Acknowledgements

In researching the material of this book, I have been aware of how much I owe to a small number of other people, some known personally to me and some not, who from a French vantage point have already explored aspects of Nadaud's life and world. Without the work of Professor Maurice Agulhon, the principal modern editor of the Memoirs, of Professor Alain Corbin and of Pierre Urien, among others, who have undertaken meticulous research into the lives and habits of the Creusois masons, my task would have been far harder and longer. But I was particularly fortunate also in meeting, in separate circumstances, two people both of whom were generous with their time and interest well beyond anything I might have dared to hope. Each of them was instrumental in helping me to gain access to collections of unpublished papers and letters without which my book would have been a shadow of its present self. To Jeanne Wirrmann then, and above all to Daniel Dayen, my deep and heartfelt gratitude.

My warmest thanks, too, to Amédée Carriat, to Daniel Bernard and to Professor John L. Halstead, who all gave me important help at the start; also to Professor Nicholas Deakin and Professor Roger Morgan, each of whom brought their expertise to bear on the final text. I am also indebted variously for help, encouragement, suggestions, information, for the loan of books and for fact-finding expeditions carried out on my behalf in scattered places, to Victor Laks, Gérard Coulon, Professor Pierre Coustillas, Professor Douglas Johnson, Michael de la Noy, Tom Nelson, Roland Thorne,

Geoffrey Woollen, Sharon Cowan, Roland and Renée Nicoux, Dorian Gerhold, John Richardson, the late Professor Donald J. Olsen and my husband, Richard Lansdown. Also to Colin Thubron, to my supportive editor, Roger Cazalet, and to Douglas Matthews for his exemplary index.

I also owe a wider debt to many French citizens who, while not in a position to offer me specific help, have collectively enriched my understanding of central France and its modern history. They are so numerous that to single out names would be invidious, but they include the mayors of several Communes; also two separate television teams, who made their way to London to explore with me Nadaud's years in England.

My grateful thanks also, for their professional help and understanding, to the French Institute of London, its erstwhile director Olivier Poivre d'Avor and its library staff, in particular Chantal Morel. Also to the London Library staff (who turned out to have a first edition of Nadaud's book on the working classes on their shelves, and who, in their accustomed admirable way, allowed me to transfer it to my own shelves for some time). Grateful appreciation also to the Bibliothèque Nationale and its staff in Paris, to the Bibliothèque Municipale in Guéret, Creuse, and especially to its librarian, Mme Parenton; also to the Archives Départementales of the Creuse and their director, Mme Morin-Joffre; also to the Public Record Office in London. I am indebted for kind incidental help to the librarian of the Freemason's Hall in London, the County Library of Lancashire, the local history libraries of the London Boroughs of Merton, Ealing and Wandsworth and particularly to Anthony Shaw of Wandsworth. Also to the headmaster and staff of Wimbledon College, and especially to the recently retired archivist, Anthony Poole, who, as well as showing me round the building, passed on to me letters received by his predecessor from J. M. Brackenbury's great-grandson, the late C. F. Shaw-Hamilton.

I should also like to offer my specific and heartfelt thanks to the Trustees of the interests of Mme Tournyol, Martin

Nadaud's great-great-grand-daughter, and to Philippe Bouquet-Nadaud, his great-great-grandson, for their permission to consult and quote from hitherto unpublished family letters and papers.

I am indebted to the Associations du Plateau des Combes and des Maçons de la Creuse for access to illustrations 2c, 3a, 3b and 4b, and especially to Roland Nicoux and to Pierre Urien, to whose picture research I owe much; to Daniel Dayen for 1 and 8a; to Philippe Bouquet-Nadaud for 8c; and to the Trustees of the interests of Mme Tournyol for permission to reproduce 7a and 7b; also to Télé Millevaches for supplying me with copies of these last.

Bibliography

Writings of Martin Nadaud

L'Histoire des Classes Ouvrières en Angleterre, Paris, 1872

Discours de Martin Nadaud à l'Assemblée Legislative (1849–1851). Questions ouvrières en Angleterre et en France, Paris, 1884

Discours et Conférences de Martin Nadaud (1870–1878). Six Mois de Préfecture et comment j'ai connu Gambetta. Cinq ans au Conseil municipal de Paris, Guéret, 1889

Les Mémoires de Léonard, un Garçon Maçon, first published Bourganeuf, 1895; extracts with a biographical preface by H. Germouty, Paris, 1912; extracts with a preface by Jean Follain and a biographical section by George Duveau published Paris, Egloff, 1948; published in full with a preface by J.-P. Rioux, Paris, Maspéro, 1976; published in full edited and annotated by Maurice Agulhon, Paris, Hachette, 1976, re-issued by Lucien Souny, 1998

While it is impossible for me to list every work that has added something to my understanding of the world in which Nadaud lived, the following I know have contributed to the present book.

Agulhon, Maurice, *1848, ou l'apprentissage de la République 1848–1852*, Paris, Editions du Seuil, 1973 and 1992

——*Les Quarante-Huitards*, Paris, Gallimard, 1975 and 1992

Balzac, Honoré de, *La Cousine Bette*, Paris, 1846

Bandy de Nalèche, Louis, *Les Maçons de la Creuse*, 1859

Blanc, Louis, *Lettres sur Angleterre*, Paris, 1866

Bord, M., *Biographie de Martin Nadaud, Ancien Réprésentant du Peuple, Ancien Député de la Creuse*, Bourganeuf, 1902

Boudard, René, *Bourganeuf au fil des ages*, Guéret, Imprimerie Lecante, c. 1980

Braudel, Fernand, *L'Identité de la France, Vol. I, Espace et Histoire*, Paris, Arthaud-Flammarion, 1986

Bruhat, Jean, *Histoire du Mouvement Ouvrier Français*, Paris, published by La Confédération Génerale du Travail, 1952

Carver, Terrell, *Friedrich Engels, his Life and Thought*, London, Macmillan, 1989

Chatelain, Abel, *Les Migrants temporains en France de 1800 à 1914*, University of Lille Press, 1976

Chevalier, Louis, *Classes Laborieuses et Classes Dangereuses à Paris pendant la première moitié du XIX siècle*, Paris, Plon, 1958

Corbin, Alain, *Archaisme et Modernité en Limousin au XIXième siècle*, Paris, Rivière, 1975

——*Le Temps, le Désir, l'Horreur*, Paris, Aubier, 1991; Flammarion, 1998

——*L'Agriculture et la Population*, Paris, 1865

des Cars, Jean, et Pinon, Pierre, *Paris-Haussmann*, Paris, Pavillon de l'Arsenal, 1991

Dickens, Charles, *Hard Times*, London, 1854

——*Nicholas Nickleby*, London, 1839

Dickinson, Lowes G., *Revolution and Reaction in Modern France*, London, Allen & Unwin, 1892 and 1927

Duveau, Georges, *La Vie Ouvrière en France sous la Second Empire*, Paris, 1946

Flaubert, Gustave, *L'Education sentimentale*, Paris, 1869

Gerhold, Dorian, *Putney and Roehampton Past*, London, Historical Publications, 1994

Gibson, Robert, *The Best of Enemies: Anglo-French Relations since the Norman Conquest*, London, Sinclair-Stevenson, 1995

Girouard, Mark, *Cities and People*, New Haven & London, Yale, 1985

de Goncourt, Jules et Edmond, *Germinie Lacerteux*, Paris, 1864

Guillaumin, Emile, *La Vie d'un Simple*, Paris, 1904

Guinot, Robert, *La Creuse autrefois*, Lyon, Editions Horvath, 1995

Halévy, Daniel, *Visites au Paysans du Centre 1907–1934*, Paris, Grasset, 1935

Hawtin, Gillian, *Wimbledon*, privately published, 1994

Hillairet, Jacques, *Connaissance de Vieux Paris*, Paris, Payant et Rivages, 1951 and 1993.

Hounsell, Peter, *Ealing and Hamwell Past*, London, Historical Publications, 1991

Hugo, Victor, *Les Misérables*, Paris, 1862

Joanne, Adolphe, *Géographie du Département de la Creuse*, Paris, Hachette, 1882

Johnson, Douglas, *Guizot: Aspects of French History 1787–1874*, London, Routledge & Kegan Paul, 1963

de Lavergne, M. Léonce, *L'Economie Rurale de la France*, Paris, 1857

Lecouturier, Henri, *Paris, incompatible avec la République: plan d'un nouveau Paris où les Revolutions seront impossibles*, Paris, 1848

Loyer, François, *Paris XIXième siècle: l'immeuble et la rue*, Paris, Editions Hazan, c. 1986

Ludlow, John Malcolm, *The Autobiography of a Christian Socialist*, London, 1901; ed. by A. D. Murray, Frank Cass, 1981

Mack, Edward C., and Armytage, W. H. G., *Thomas Hughes, the Life of the Author of 'Tom Brown's Schooldays'*, London, Ernest Benn, 1952

Maneglier, Hervé, *Paris-Impérial: la Vie Quotidienne sous le Second Empire*, Paris, Editions Armand Colin, 1990

Masterman, N. C., *John Malcolm Ludlow, the Builder of Christian Socialism*, Cambridge University Press, 1963

Maupassant, Guy de, *Mont-Oriol*, Paris, 1887

Mayhew, Henry, *London Labour and the London Poor*, London, 1851–62

Mazerolles, Pierre, *La Misère de Paris, les mauvais gîtes*, Paris, 1875

Metcalf, Priscilla, *Victorian London*, London, Cassell, 1972

Mercier, *Paris Delineated* (adapted English edition), 2 vols, London, 1802

Miller, Hugh, *My Schools and Schoolmasters, or the Story of my Education*, Edinburgh, 1854

Olsen, Donald J., *The Growth of Victorian London*, London, Batsford, 1976

——*The City as a Work of Art: London, Paris, Vienna*, New Haven & London, Yale, 1986

Poole, Anthony, *The History of Wimbledon College*, privately published, 1992

Postgate, R. W., *The Builders' History*, published by the National Federation of Building Trade Operatives, 1923

Rivet, Robert, *Les chemins de fer en Creuse*, Editions Copia, 1984

Sand, George, *Le Compagnon du Tour de France*, Paris, 1840

——*Journal d'un voyageur pendant la guerre*, Paris, 1871

Seaman, L. C. B., *From Vienna to Versailles*, London, Methuen, 1955

——*Life in Victorian London*, London, Batsford, 1973

Simond, Louis, *Voyage en Angleterre 1812*, Paris, 1816

Sue, Eugène, *Les Mystères de Paris*, c. 1854

Taine, Hippolyte, *Notes sur l'Angleterre*, Paris, 1872

Tombs, Robert, *France 1814–1914*, London, Longman, 1996

Trollope, Fanny, *Paris and the Parisians*, London, 1835

Vidalenc, Jean, *La Société Française de 1815 à 1848: le peuple des campagnes*, Paris, Rivière, 1969

Vinçart, Pierre, *Les Ouvriers de Paris*, c. 1850

Weber, Eugen, *Peasants into Frenchmen: the Modernisation of Rural France, 1870–1914*, London, Chatto & Windus, 1977

Articles in journals

Bernard, Daniel, 'La Circulation des Ambulants et Itinérants dans l'Indre au XIXe siècle', *Société des Sciences Naturelles et Archéologiques de la Creuse*, 1955

Corbin, Alain, 'Migrations Temporaires et Société Rurale au XIX siècle: le cas des Limousins', *Revue Historique*, No. 500, October–December 1971

——'Les Paysans de Paris: Histoire des Limousins du Bâtiment au XIXe siècle', *Ethnologie Française*, X, 1980

Dayen, Daniel, 'La Vie Politique Creusoise à la fin de la Monarchie de Juillet', *Société des Sciences Naturelles et Archéologiques de la Creuse*, XLIII, 1987

——'Un "Vieux Républicain Creusois", le Docteur Moreau', *Société des Sciences Naturelles et Archéologiques de la Creuse*, XLIV, 1990

——'1889: l'Echec de Martin Nadaud', *Société des Sciences Naturelles et Archéologiques de la Creuse*, XLIV, 1991

——'La Vie tumultueuse d'Emile Cornudet, Député de la Creuse', *Société des Sciences Naturelles et Archéologiques de la Creuse*, XLV, 1993

——'Les Victimes Creusoises du Coup d'Etat et la Loi de Réparation de 1881', *Société des Sciences Naturelles et Archéologiques de la Creuse*, XLV, 1995

D'Hollander, Paul, 'L'Emigration Temporaire dans l'arrondissement de Bellac dans la première moitié du XIXe siècle', *Société des Sciences Naturelles et Archéologiques de la Creuse*, May 1995

Goldman, Philippe, 'Contestations et Révoltes lycéenne à Bourges au XIX siècle', *Berry Magazine*, Nos 36 and 37, December 1995 and March 1996

Kneyts, Louis, 'Martin Nadaud: Comment un ouvrier maçon devient un bourgeois franc-maçon', *Espace-Temps*, No. 8, 1978

Mathias, Marie-Claude, 'Les Maçons Marchois', *Ethnologia*, No. 5, 1978

Moulin, Marie-Annie, 'Les Maçons de la Haute-Marche au XVIIIe siècle', *A.S.P.H.A.R.E.S.D.*, bulletin No. 5, 1989

Urien, Pierre, 'Les Maçons Migrants de la Creuse du 19ième siècle', *Cahiers Laïques*, Cercle Parisien de la Ligue Française de l'Enseignement, No. 214, 1988

I have also made use of a series of pamphlets and reports published in Guéret by Dr Ferdinand Villard 1881–93, now bound together and available in the Bibliothèque Nationale, especially of *L'Emigration des Ouvriers Creusois consideré au point de vue hygiènique et sanitaire.*

I have also consulted the *Dictionnaire Biographique du Mouvement Ouvrier Français*, published in Paris by Les Editions Ouvriers, 1966; the *Dictionnaire de Biographie Française* published by Librairie Letouzey,

1948–94; and the *Dictionnaire Bio-bibliographique des Auteurs du Pays Creusois*, published in Guéret, Lecante, 1968, especially the entry for Martin Nadaud, by Amédée Carriat. Also the *Almanach pittoresque & historique de la Creuse pour 1998*, Lecante, 1997.

I have also consulted the archives of the newspaper *L'Echo de la Creuse*, particularly for the years 1870–1, 1879 and 1881; also *The Builder*, for 1851–2, 1864 and 1868–9.

I have also made use of two unpublished theses: Daniel Coudert, *Martin Nadaud et la Politique Française et Creusoise*, University of Limoges, 1983; Jean-Louis Jorrand, *Martin Nadaud, ses rapports avec Cabet et Louis Blanc*, Clermond-Ferrand, 1958.

I am indebted to the Association du Plateau des Combes (Felletin) and especially to the catalogue produced under its auspices by Roland Nicoux and Pierre Urien to accompany an exhibition in 1987. Also to the related association Les Maçons de la Creuse (Felletin) to whose 1998 exhibition I was privileged to contribute.

Daniel Dayan's book *Martin Nadaud, ouvrier maçon et député 1815–1898*, published by Lucien Souny, 1998, appeared only when my own book was substantially complete, but it will be an invaluable, authoritative reference book for any future explorer of Nadaud's long, variable and complex life.

Index